Reflections

BOOKS BY THOMAS HAUSER

GENERAL NON-FICTION

Missing
The Trial of Patrolman Thomas Shea
For Our Children (with Frank Macchiarola)
The Family Legal Companion
Final Warning: The Legacy of Chernobyl (with Dr. Robert Gale)
Arnold Palmer: A Personal Journey
Confronting America's Moral Crisis (with Frank Macchiarola)
Healing: A Journal of Tolerance and Understanding
With This Ring (with Frank Macchiarola)
Thomas Hauser on Sports
Reflections

BOXING NON-FICTION

The Black Lights: Inside the World of Professional Boxing
Muhammad Ali: His Life and Times
Muhammad Ali: Memories
Muhammad Ali: In Perspective
Muhammad Ali & Company
A Beautiful Sickness
A Year At The Fights
Brutal Artistry
The View From Ringside
Chaos, Corruption, Courage, and Glory
The Lost Legacy of Muhammad Ali
I Don't Believe It, But It's True
Knockout (with Vikki LaMotta)
The Greatest Sport of All
The Boxing Scene
An Unforgiving Sport
Boxing Is . . .
Box: The Face of Boxing
The Legend of Muhammad Ali (with Bart Barry)
Winks and Daggers
And the New . . .
Straight Writes and Jabs

FICTION

Ashworth & Palmer
Agatha's Friends
The Beethoven Conspiracy
Hanneman's War
The Fantasy
Dear Hannah
The Hawthorne Group
Mark Twain Remembers
Finding The Princess
Waiting For Carver Boyd

FOR CHILDREN

Martin Bear & Friends

Reflections

Conversations, Essays, and Other Writings

Thomas Hauser

The University of Arkansas Press
Fayetteville
2014

Copyright © 2014 by Thomas Hauser

All rights reserved
Manufactured in the United States of America

ISBN-10: 1-55728-650-7
ISBN-13: 978-1-55728-650-5
e-ISBN: 978-1-61075-535-1

18   17   16   15   14   5   4   3   2   1

⊗ The paper used in this publication meets the minimum requirements of the
American National Standard for Permanence of Paper for Printed Library Materials
Z39.48-1984.

Library of Congress Control Number: 2013956217

In September 1963, I enrolled as a freshman at Columbia College in the City of New York. I spent seven years at Columbia; four as an undergraduate and three more at the Columbia School of Law.

The years I spent at Columbia shaped my thinking and contributed enormously to the person I am today. I learned in and out of the classroom and had a wonderful time during those years.

This book is dedicated with gratitude to Columbia and to the many good people I met there.

CENTRAL ARKANSAS LIBRARY SYSTEM
LITTLE ROCK PUBLIC LIBRARY
100 ROCK STREET
LITTLE ROCK, ARKANSAS 72201

Contents

Personal Notes

A God to Hope For

The End of the Year

Author's Note

The first writing I did for publication after leaving the practice of law to become an author was for *New York Magazine*. It was entitled "The Crank-Call Caper" and recounted the frustrations inherent in having an anonymous nuisance telephone caller. Since then, I've written my share of novels and full-length non-fiction books. But essays and other articles have remained part of my literary output.

Most of the articles I've written over the years have been about boxing. They're available in fifteen books (eight of which have been published by the University of Arkansas Press). UAP has also published a ninth collection of articles under the title *Thomas Hauser on Sports*.

Reflections covers different terrain. It contains virtually all of the essays and articles that I've written over the years on subjects other than sports. Some deal with public matters; others are intensely personal. Some are interpretative and analytical. Others are reportorial or whimsical. They're a journey through life.

Thomas Hauser
New York, NY
2014

Reflections on the
Beatles in America

Writing this essay in 2013 involved revisiting touchstones of my young adulthood.

Reflections on the Beatles in America

Strawberry Fields is a 2.5-acre memorial to John Lennon located just inside the West 72nd Street entrance to Central Park in New York. Its focal point is a circular black-and-white mosaic with the word "Imagine" embedded in a winding asphalt walk. The walk widens at the mosaic and is rimmed by benches. Then it narrows again and leads past a large rock outcropping with a bronze plaque listing more than one hundred countries that contributed shrubs and trees to the site.

For the last seven years of his life, Lennon lived in the Dakota at the edge of Central Park. When he died there at the hands of an assassin in 1980, the end of the Beatles as a corporeal entity became irrevocable. Because of its proximity to the Dakota, Strawberry Fields has the feel of a cemetery. That's unfortunate.

The Beatles, who captivated America a half-century ago, were about happiness and joy. They sang with incredible energy and sent a thrill through an entire generation. Their music was their own. They wrote it themselves, performed it in their own unique way, and evolved under the brightest spotlight that ever shone on performing artists. They were four remarkably gifted young men who blended their talents into something extraordinary that changed music and the world. They were a celebration of life.

If it seems like a long time ago, that's because it was.

I

John Lennon, Paul McCartney, George Harrison, and Richard Starkey (better known as Ringo Starr) were born in the port city of Liverpool during World War II. The city was subjected to heavy bombardment as the Royal Air Force struggled valiantly to defend England against the German Air Force during the most sustained aerial assault in history.

Lennon was born on October 9, 1940. His father was a merchant sea-man who abandoned the family when John was five. Thereafter, his mother chose to "live in sin" with another man who had no interest in raising "someone else's son." John was sent to live with his aunt and uncle, who were childless.

"There were five women that were my family," Lennon later recalled. "Five strong, intelligent, beautiful women, five sisters. One happened to be my mother. She just couldn't deal with life. She was the youngest and she had a husband who ran away to sea and the war was on and she couldn't cope with me, and I ended up living with her elder sister."

Julia Lennon visited her son regularly. In 1956, she bought him his first guitar and taught him to play it. He then joined an amateur skiffle group called the Quarrymen and was performing at a church picnic on July 6, 1957, when he met fifteen-year-old Paul McCartney.

Paul's father was a salesman and former jazz band musician who'd taught his son to play piano and trumpet. When Paul was fourteen, his father had given him a trumpet, which Paul traded in for a guitar.

John invited Paul to join the Quarrymen. Years later, Paul told Barry Miles (author of a superb biography entitled *Paul McCartney: Many Years from Now*), "John and I were two of the luckiest people in the twentieth century to have found each other."

Similarly, Bob Spitz (author of the equally outstanding *The Beatles: A Biography*) would observe, "A rhythm developed between John and Paul that got stronger and tighter. No doubt about it; they were tuned to the same groove."

On the surface, Paul was easygoing. John was sarcastic and sometimes belligerent but had a wonderful smile that masked his anger and pain.

"Where John was impatient and careless," Spitz writes, "Paul was a perfectionist. Where John was moody and aloof, Paul was blithe and out-going, gregarious, and irrepressibly cheerful. While John was straightfor-ward if brutally frank, Paul practiced diplomacy to manipulate a situation."

Both John and Paul wrote music. They became even closer when Lennon's mother was killed by a speeding motorist while crossing the street on July 15, 1958. Paul's mother had died of cancer two years before.

"Now we were both in this; both losing our mothers," Paul later recalled. "This was a bond for us, something of ours, a special thing."

"I lost her twice," John said about his mother. "Once as a five-year-old when I moved in with my auntie. And once again at seventeen when she actually physically died. That was a really hard time for me. It absolutely made me very very bitter."

In the late 1950s, a new kind of guitar-oriented music was coming into vogue.

"When I was sixteen, Elvis [Presley] was what was happening," John later reminisced. "A guy with long greasy hair, wiggling his ass and singing *Hound Dog* and *That's All Right, Mamma* and those early Sun records. Nothing really affected me until I heard Elvis. If there hadn't been an Elvis, there wouldn't have been the Beatles. Before Elvis there was nothing."

Paul had a similar epiphany: "It was Elvis who really got me hooked on beat music. When I heard *Heartbreak Hotel*, I thought, this is it. That's the guru we've been waiting for. The Messiah has arrived."

And there were other role models.

"There were lots of people coming up then," Paul noted. "One of them was Buddy Holly. We loved his vocal sound and we loved his guitar playing. But most of all was the fact that he actually wrote the stuff himself. That's what turned us on."

In late 1957, Paul persuaded John to let George Harrison join the group. The new member, fourteen years old, was the most accomplished guitarist of the three.

"I think George quite liked the way we had about us," Paul later said. "I don't think he was that convinced about our musical ability."

But Harrison was impressed by John's persona. "He had a lot of power," George noted years later. "Sometimes they pick somebody to march behind on the way to war. He was certainly out front."

Paul concurred, saying, "I definitely did look up to John. We all looked up to John. He was older and he was very much the leader. He was the quickest wit and the smartest and all that kind of thing."

The band evolved from there. In 1960, a friend of Lennon's named Stu Sutcliffe joined the group as a bass guitarist and Pete Best replaced drummer Tommy Moore. The name of the band changed to Silver Beatles and, soon after that, to the Beatles. Then Sutcliffe left, Paul switched to bass guitar, and the Beatles became a four-piece band instead of five with George and John on lead and rhythm guitar respectively.

They played gigs when and where they could find them; four young men barely removed from adolescence, sleeping four in a dingy room or in the back of clubs on the road.

"It was pre-fame," Paul noted decades later. "Rock and roll was a great golden vision for us. Just the idea of maybe going to do this as a living instead of getting what we thought was going to be a boring job was exciting."

And they loved what they were doing.

"Before we made it, money was partly the goal," John said. "But it wasn't 'let's go get some money.' That wasn't it."

On February 21, 1961, the Beatles made the first of what would be several hundred appearances at the Cavern in Liverpool. Later that year, they were spotted by Brian Epstein.

Epstein's family owned a series of music stores in northern England. Brian was charged with managing the record departments. He was twenty-seven years old and gay at a time when the stigma attached to homosexuality was overwhelming.

"Brian was besotted the minute he saw the Beatles," Bob Spitz writes. "From the outset, he had been attracted to rough trade; tough rugged young men of a lower class than his who were a threat to degrade and inflict harm on him. He'd seen guys like this all his life around the docks, fancied them from afar. Clad in cheap skintight leather suits, ruggedly built, marginally educated, foul-mouthed, completely disrespectful, and bashing away at their instruments, the Beatles revved his engine like nothing he'd experienced. John especially. Lennon was catnip. No young man could have filled Brian's sexual fantasies more perfectly. Like other encounters Epstein had responded to, John was young, studly, foul-mouthed, dangerous, alternately caring and cruel. And off limits."

"We'd heard that Brian was queer, as we would have called him," Paul told Barry Miles. "Nobody used the word 'gay' then. But we didn't hold that against him."

On January 24, 1962, the Beatles signed a management contract with Epstein. He cleaned up their act, replacing black leather jackets and tight jeans with matching gray suits. Greased hair gave way to mop-top haircuts. At Epstein's suggestion, the Beatles also adopted the practice of bowing to their audience after each song.

"We'd gladly switch to suits if it would get us some more money and some more gigs," George said.

Thereafter, record label after record label rejected Epstein's entreaties to sign the Beatles. Finally, on May 9, 1962, producer George Martin offered them a contract with Parlophone Records. But it was contingent on their performing well at a June 6 recording session. After that session, Martin told Epstein that the band needed a new drummer. On August 16, 1962, Pete Best was asked to leave the group and was replaced by Ringo Starr.

"It was a strictly professional decision," Paul said afterward. "If Pete wasn't up to the mark, then there was no other choice."

Ringo, age twenty-two, was the oldest of the Beatles. His parents had divorced when he was three years old and he lived with his mother, who had since remarried. At the time the Beatles approached him, he was the drummer for a Liverpool band called Rory Storm and the Hurricanes.

"I joined the Beatles because they were the best band in Liverpool," Ringo said years later. "I always wanted to play with good players. We didn't really know each other. But if we looked at each other's record collection, the four of us had virtually the same records."

"When we got Ringo into the band, it really jelled." Paul said of the Beatles' new addition.

On September 11, 1962, the newly reconstituted Beatles recorded two songs for Parlophone. One of them—"Love Me Do"—had been written by John and Paul four years earlier. The other was "P.S. I Love You." The songs were released on October 5 as the "A" and "B" sides of a record that climbed to #17 on sales charts in England.

Four months later, "Please Please Me" (with "Ask Me Why" on the "B" side) was released and rose to the top of the charts. That was followed by "With Love from Me to You" (backed by "Thank You Girl"), which met with similar success.

The aftermath of World War II had lasted far longer in England than in the United States. Bombs had fallen on British soil. A generation of English men had been decimated by the war. The nation had still not fully emerged from a protracted period of economic austerity and gloom.

And now, here were the Beatles, full of personality and brimming with life. They were the cute boys who every teenage girl loved. Playful like overgrown children with expressive faces, funny hair falling over their foreheads, a twinkle in their eye as though they didn't take themselves too seriously, and music that was different from anything that had come before.

The Beatles sounded like nobody else in the way their voices melded together and the way they played their guitars. Somehow, Paul's sweet sound and John's raw delivery fit together just right when blended with George.

"We'd never heard of anything in rock and roll lasting more than a couple of years," Paul said decades later. "So we thought we were about the same."

They weren't.

In February 1963, as "Please Please Me" moved toward the top of the charts, girls began screaming at Beatles performances. Pictures of the "Fab Four" went up on bedroom walls. Then "She Loves You" was released and swept England, selling more copies on Shakespeare's sceptered isle than any recorded single in history up until that time.

The screaming was contagious, By mid-year, the Beatles had to be shielded from their fans. Police protection was necessary at their concerts. Sobbing and fainting girls were also part of the show.

"We do like the fans and we enjoy reading the publicity," George acknowledged. "From time to time, you don't realize that it's actually about yourself. You see pictures and read articles about George Harrison and Ringo Starr and Paul and John, and you don't actually think, 'That's me.' It's as though it's a different person."

In October 1963, the *Daily Mirror* coined the phrase "Beatlemania."

Then the establishment gave the Beatles its blessing. On November 4, 1963, with the Queen Mother and Princess Margaret in attendance, the band performed at the Royal Variety Show.

They played three songs: "With Love from Me to You," "Till There Was You," and "Twist and Shout." Prior to the final offering, John told the audience, "For our last number, I'd like to ask your help. The people in your cheaper seats, clap your hands. And the rest of you; if you just rattle your jewelry."

It was jolly good fun. Those in attendance didn't know that John had planned to say "rattle your fucking jewelry" and resisted efforts to sanitize the quip until the final hour.

"We were the first working-class singers that stayed working class and pronounced it," Lennon said years later.

The Beatles, with their working-class roots, were England's new royal family.

II

As Beatlemania spread throughout England, Americans were largely oblivious to the phenomenon.

American rock and roll had traction in England. But popular music (and particularly rock and roll) was exported from the United States to the United Kingdom, not the other way around. What few British rock and rollers there were had no impact in the colonies. Their repertoire was largely limited to cover versions of American songs.

Indeed, prior to the Beatles, only two Brits had recorded songs that made their way onto "Top 40" charts in the United States. One was a fourteen-year-old boy named Laurie London who, in 1958, recorded a song entitled "He's Got the Whole World in his Hands." The other was Scotsman Lonnie Donagen, whose novelty ditty "Does Your Chewing Gum Lose It's Flavour on the Bedpost Overnight" cracked the charts in 1961.

Meanwhile, pop music in the United States was stagnating. Americans were watching *Sing Along with Mitch* on television. "Top 40" hits had become a collection of formulaic compositions. In 1962 and 1963, recordings like "The Locomotion," "Mashed Potato Time," "Roses Are Red," "Johnny Angel," "Sugar Shack," and "Hey Paula" were listed among the year's ten best-selling songs.

The first Beatles record released in the United States—"Please Please Me" (with "Ask Me Why" on the "B" side)—was issued by Vee Jay on February 25, 1963. That was followed by "From Me To You" (paired with "Thank You Girl") on May 27 and a Vee Jay album entitled *Introducing the Beatles* that went on sale on July 22. On September 16, 1963, Swan records issued "She Loves You" (backed by "I'll Get You").

Each of those songs did poorly in the US market. Then George Martin persuaded Capitol records to release the Beatles' fourth American single, "I Want to Hold Your Hand" (with "I Saw Her Standing There" on the flip side). And more significantly, Capitol agreed to put forty thousand dollars into promoting the record.

There was no instant culture in the United States in the 1960s; no YouTube videos that could go viral in a matter of days. The radio stations, television networks, and print media were gate-keepers for the culture, and barriers to entry were high. Now the Beatles had money behind them.

"I Want to Hold Your Hand" was released in the United States on December 26, 1963, and sold 250,000 copies in three days. By January 10, 1964, it had passed the one-million mark and was the best-selling record in America.

That was followed on January 20 by the American release of a Capitol album entitled *Meet the Beatles*. Its Vee Jay predecessor had done so poorly in the United States that, beneath the title, the album sleeve for *Meet The Beatles* bore the words, "The First Album by England's Phenomenal Pop Combo."

All of the songs on *Meet the Beatles* were written by John Lennon and Paul McCartney with the exception of "Don't Bother Me" (George Harrison) and "Till There Was You" (a popular ballad from the Broadway musical, *The Music Man*, written by Meredith Wilson).

That set the stage for the Beatles' first trip to America. Four thousand fans saw them off at Heathrow Airport in London. Prior to their departure, a reporter asked Lennon, "British pop stars have not had a tremendous impact in the United States. How do you think you're going to fare?

"Well, I can't really say, can I?" John answered. "Is it up to me? No. I just hope we go all right."

"It was like flying into the unknown," Paul said years later. "We didn't know what to expect."

The youth of America welcomed the Beatles with open arms. Three thousand fans, most of them screaming teenage girls, greeted them at the airport when their plane landed in New York. A well-oiled publicity machine had arranged for an airport press conference. Two hundred reporters attended; a remarkable turnout for that era.

Unlike Elvis Presley, who had groped for words in media sessions, the Beatles had quick answers for everything. They had an advantage, of course, in that there were four of them. Questions were generally put to the group rather than to one individual, so any of the four could answer.

John was particularly quick-witted.

"How do you feel about teenagers imitating you with Beatles wigs?"

Lennon: "They're not imitating us, because we don't wear Beatles wigs."

"Some people say your haircuts are un-American."

Lennon: "That's very observant of them because we aren't American, actually."

"The French have not made up their minds about the Beatles. What do you think of them?"

Lennon: "Oh, we like the Beatles."

"Will you sing something for us?"

Lennon: "We need money first."

After the press conference, the Beatles were taken by limousine to the Plaza Hotel in Manhattan.

"I remember a great moment, going into the limo," Paul later reminisced. "The music we loved had come from America, so just to be there was exciting. We got in the limo, and there we were on American radio."

When the group arrived at the Plaza, another mob of screaming fans surrounded their car. That prompted Lennon to wonder aloud, "How are we going to get in there?" Later that day, John observed, "They're all wild. It seems like they're all out of their minds."

The Beatles had a ten-room suite on the twelfth floor of the Plaza. The hotel was surrounded by police barricades and under virtual siege throughout their stay.

"It was a surprise," George said later. "We thought we'd have to work a little bit for this notoriety."

There had been four transformative icons of popular music in the United States before the Beatles: Rudy Vallée, Bing Crosby, Frank Sinatra, and Elvis Presley. Unlike their predecessors, the Beatles were a group.

"We reckoned we could make it because there were four of us," John said later. "None at us would have made it alone because Paul wasn't quite strong enough, I didn't have enough girl-appeal, George was too quiet, and Ringo was the drummer. But we thought that everyone would be able to dig at least one of us, and that's how it turned out."

The Beatles had charisma. They were identifiable on a first-name basis. Despite their uniform look, each member of the band had his own unique personality that was clearly and distinctly different from the others.

Paul was the cute Beatle, a showman at heart. John was witty and acerbic. George was steady, the quiet Beatle (if there was such as thing). Ringo (like his name) was perceived as being a bit odd.

They complemented each other well. Paul softened John's harsh edges with his personality and voice. George seemed to derive his purest satisfaction from playing the guitar. Ringo loved playing drums.

They were good-looking. At least, three of them were. The fact that they came from England was an engaging novelty. They spoke differently, sang differently, dressed differently, and styled their hair differently. On the surface, they were uncomplicated, innocent, and so much fun.

There was an exuberance about them. They seemed like boys who hadn't grown up—Peter Pan, perhaps—overgrown kids having a good time. One could easily imagine John or Paul transformed into Cupid.

The Beatles were a happy show. And Americans—young people in particular—needed something to boost their spirits. Eleven weeks earlier, John F. Kennedy had been assassinated in Dallas. A pall had settled over the nation as the tragic events of November 1963 unfolded on television.

On February 9, 1964, Americans had their second shared national viewing experience within the span of seven weeks. But this one came with a smile. The Beatles were introduced to the country on *The Ed Sullivan Show*.

Virtually everyone in America knew that the Beatles would be on *Ed Sullivan*. No one had a VHS player or DVR. The experience of watching and listening to the band perform live was shared simultaneously by 73 million people. In 45 percent of all homes with a television set, the TV was turned on and people were watching the Beatles.

Eight years earlier, Sullivan had hosted Elvis Presley (idolized by the boys who would become Beatles) as Elvis was ascending to stardom. This was bigger. The Beatles attracted the largest television audience in history for anything that had aired up until that time.

Inside the theater, the atmosphere was electric. CBS had received fifty thousand requests from people with favors to trade who wanted tickets to the show. There were seats for seven hundred.

In living rooms, in college dormitories, in cocktail lounges, tens of millions of Americans gathered around small black-and-white television sets. They had listened to Beatles records and seen photographs of the group. This was the first opportunity to witness them as live performers.

Sullivan wasted no time, introducing the Beatles at the top of the show. They were wearing their trademark matching suits and ties. Their hair, a bit long for that era, crept down over each man's forehead and the top of his ears. John, Paul, and George were standing in the foreground. Ringo was in the background with his drums.

The music began . . .

"Close your eyes and I'll kiss you. Tomorrow I'll miss you."

Suddenly, the Beatles were more than voices on scratchy pre-stereo vinyl records. They weren't just black-and-white photos in a teen magazine. They were real. They were flesh and blood. They were alive.

The group performed five songs that night. After "All My Loving," they turned one-hundred-eighty degrees and Paul sang "Till There Was You." It was the reinvention of a popular American standard carried by an angelic voice with soft guitar accompaniment and a trace of drums. Now an older generation knew that the Beatles could sing.

Then came "She Loves You." One year earlier, repeating "she loves you, yeah, yeah, yeah" three times at the start of a song would not have seemed a logical roadmap for success. But the Beatles had moved beyond logic.

Bob Spitz later wrote, "What the Beatles built into the song provided for them a perfect lasting image. The yeah-yeah-yeahs and the falsetto ooooos (when performing this, they shook their heads in unison, setting off rapturous shrieks from the fans) became iconic symbols. No matter how their music evolved, no matter how they experimented with complex musical textures and electronics, it is hard to think of the Beatles today without visualizing them as four grinding mop tops positioned in that classic pose."

They looked like they were having so much fun. In some respects, they resembled live bobble-head dolls. Their lyrics were innocent, bubbly, and ebullient. There was excitement in their high harmonies. Like Sinatra and Elvis, they transmitted sexual energy, but it was of a less threatening kind.

At the end of the telecast, the Beatles sang two more songs: "I Saw Her Standing There" and "I Want to Hold Your Hand." Images of the group and their music blended with the sight and sound of frenzied girls screaming in the theater.

That night, the Beatles exploded into American culture and entered the consciousness of a nation. Young people, in particular, now had a magic carpet that they could ride on away from the sadness of the Kennedy assassination and into the storm that would follow as the 1960s unfolded.

The day after the Beatles appeared on *Ed Sullivan*, virtually everyone in America knew of their existence. That said, the establishment reviews were not kind.

The *New York Times* branded the Beatles "a fad." The *New York Herald Tribune* called them "seventy-five percent publicity, twenty percent haircut, and five percent lilting lament." To the *Washington Post*, they were "asexual and homely."

Newsweek devoted a cover story to the group and proclaimed, "Visually, they are a nightmare: tight, dandified, Edwardian/Beatnik suits and great pudding bowls of hair. Musically, they are a near-disaster: guitars and drums slamming out a merciless beat that does away with secondary rhythms, harmony, and melody. Their lyrics (punctuated by nutty shouts of 'yeah, yeah, yeah!') are a catastrophe, a preposterous farrago of Valentine-card romantic sentiments. The odds are they will fade away, as most adults confidently predict."

But young Americans were talking about the Beatles. Boys were showing up in school with hair combed over their forehead. Something powerful was happening.

On February 11, 1964, the Beatles traveled by train to Washington, DC. Three thousand screaming fans were there when the train arrived at Union Station. There was a reception in the Beatles' honor at the British embassy and a sold-out concert at the eighteen-thousand-seat Washington Coliseum (the largest venue they'd performed in up until that time). Introducing "Please Please Me" at the Coliseum, Paul told the audience, "This song was released in America, and it didn't do anything. Then it was released again, and now it's doing something."

Next, the Beatles returned to New York for two performances at Carnegie Hall (the first rock-and-roll shows ever at that site).

After that, they flew to Florida, where *The Ed Sullivan Show* had relocated to the Deauville Hotel for one night. Sullivan introduced the Beatles as "four of the nicest youngsters we've ever had on our stage."

As they'd done a week earlier, the band performed two sets. They began with "She Loves You" and "This Boy." Then Paul spoke to the hotel audience and to America beyond.

"Thank you. Thank you very much, everybody. And good evening. How are you? All right. This song we just done was called "This Boy." And it was off the album we made for Capitol. We'd like to sing another one. It's off the same LP. It's called *All My Loving*.

The second set consisted of "I Saw Her Standing There," "With Love from Me to You," and "I Want to Hold Your Hand."

Heavyweight champion Sonny Liston was in the audience. Publicist Harold Conrad had brought him to the Deauville to be introduced during the telecast as a way of garnering publicity for Liston's February 24 title defense at the Miami Beach Convention Center against seven-to-one underdog Cassius Clay.

"A couple of minutes after the Beatles started singing," Conrad later recalled, "Sonny sticks an elbow in my ribs and says, 'Are these motherfuckers what all the people are screaming about? My dog plays drums better than that kid with the big nose.'"

Two day later, on February 18, Conrad arranged for the Beatles to meet Cassius Clay.

"He didn't know who they were," Harold reminisced. "He had some idea they were rock stars from England, but that's all."

The meeting took place at the 5th Street Gym in Miami Beach, where Clay was training for the upcoming fight. Robert Lipsyte, then a young sports reporter for the *New York Times*, was climbing the stairs to the second-floor gym when he became aware of a commotion behind him. He turned and saw four similarly dressed young men about his age climbing the stairs in his wake. It was the Beatles.

At the entrance to the gym, the Beatles were told that Clay hadn't arrived yet.

"Let's get the fuck out of here," John said.

Two security guards herded the group into a dressing room and barred the door behind them. Lipsyte was pushed in with them and recounts what happened next.

"The Beatles were in a foul mood. The dressing room was small and smelly, and they didn't want to be there. I introduced myself with great self-importance as a reporter for the *New York Times*. John shook my hand and told me he was Ringo; Paul said that he was John; and so on. Then the door to the dressing room opened and there was a collective gasp."

The Beatles had charisma. Clay had CHARISMA.

"Hello there, Beatles," Clay said.

Then the Beatles and Clay went to the ring and cavorted around, posing for photos, the most famous of which shows the young men from Liverpool lined up and Cassius hitting George with a jab, after which all four Beatles fell down like dominoes.

"I didn't know it at the time," Lipsyte says. "None of us could have. But The Sixties were blooming right there in front of me."

As was often the case, John had the last word.

"They were all up in the ring together, talking about how much money they made," Harold Conrad later recalled. "Cassius pulled out a line he used all the time. He looked at them and said, 'You guys ain't as dumb as you look.' Lennon looked him right in the eye and told him, 'No, but you are.'"

On February 22, 1964, the Beatles returned to London. Arriving home, Paul was asked at Heathrow Airport about the fans in America.

"We expected them to be very different," Paul answered. "But they weren't at all. The accent was the only thing."

The following night, a pre-taped third performance aired on *Ed Sullivan*. This time, the Beatles sang three songs: "Twist and Shout," "Please Please Me," and "I Want to Hold Your Hand."

"All of us on the show are so darn sorry that this is the third and thus our last current show with the Beatles," Sullivan told America. "These youngsters from Liverpool, England, and their conduct over here, not only as fine professional singers but as a group of fine youngsters, will leave an imprint with everyone over here who has met them."

The Beatles had conquered America.

Two nights later, Cassius Clay knocked out Sonny Liston to claim the heavyweight championship of the world.

"The Sixties" had begun.

III

The tumultuous reception that the Beatles received in America in February 1964 elevated their standing at home. When they arrived at Heathrow Airport after their visit to the United States, ten thousand fans greeted them as if they had conquered the world.

A "British invasion" of the colonies followed. Popular music in the United States needed fresh voices. Elvis was making bad movies in Hollywood. Sinatra had become passé. The Dave Clark Five, Gerry and the Pacemakers, Billy J. Kramer, Peter and Gordon, the Hollies, the Animals, the Searchers, the Kinks, and, most notably, the Rolling Stones all made their way to America.

There was resistance some quarters. Sinatra called the Beatles "unfit to sing in public." Billy Graham spoke for religious conservatives, saying, "The Beatles are a passing phase. They are the symptoms of the uncertainties of the times."

William F. Buckley, an icon of the political right, declared, "The Beatles are not merely awful. They are so unbelievably horrible, so appallingly unmusical, so dogmatically insensitive to the magic of the art, that they qualify as crowned heads of anti-music."

But Leonard Bernstein (who wrote the music for Broadway shows like *West Side Story* and was the most celebrated American classical conductor of his time) voiced the view that the best of the Beatles' music was "more adventurous than anything else written in serious music today."

The Beatles were different from any group that had preceded them, in their music and their appearance. Everything they did seemed fresh and new.

On April 4, 1964, "Can't Buy Me Love" became the first record ever to reach #1 on the American and British charts simultaneously. That week, the Beatles occupied the top five slots on *Billboard's* "Top 40" singles list in the United States with "Twist and Shout," #2; "She Loves You," #3; "I Want to Hold Your Hand #4; and "Please Please Me," #5. During the course of the year, six Beatles singles would hold down the #1 slot at various times, and three Beatles albums spent a combined thirty weeks at #1 on the album listings.

On April 10, 1964, the second Beatles album released by Capitol in the United States went on sale. Anchored by "She Loves You" and entitled simply *The Beatles' Second Album*, it had five Lennon-McCartney compositions. Earlier recorded Beatles cover versions of songs like "Roll Over Beethoven," "Long Tall Sally," and "Please Mr. Postman," were included. The album clearly demonstrated that the Beatles could cover rock and roll by black recording artists.

Then, on June 26, the Beatles released their third album in America; this one from the soundtrack of their forthcoming United Artists film, *A Hard Day's Night*. Eight vocals and four instrumentals were included. All of the music was written by Lennon and McCartney; the first time that a Beatles album consisted entirely of original compositions.

That was followed twenty-four days later by the release of *Something New* (the Beatles third Capitol Album). *Something New* had a lot that wasn't. Five of its eleven song were taken from the soundtrack of *A Hard Day's Night*, reflecting a turf war between United Artists and Capitol. There were only three "new" Lennon-McCartney compositions. The album's primary innovation was that, for the first time, Ringo got to sing. He had the lead on "Matchbox," a song written by Carl Perkins.

Meanwhile, the film version of *A Hard Day's Night* was causing a sensation. The movie, shot in black-and-white, was an impressionistic look at what it was like to be a Beatle (minus the drinking and sex) and to experience Beatlemania from the center of the storm.

Princess Margaret attended the world premiere in London on July 6. Then the Beatles journeyed north for the "northern England premiere" in Liverpool, where two hundred thousand fans lined the parade route to greet them. One month later, the film was released in the United States.

The Beatles had become the most famous entertainers in the world. They were constantly under a microscope. The frenzied crowds that greeted them went beyond anything that other performing artists had known.

John reacted to their fame with bemusement. Paul rode it for all it was worth. George tolerated and suffered through it. Ringo handled it with good cheer.

Whatever else was going on, each Beatle could trust that the other three weren't hanging around him for the big money and bright lights.

"It all changed out there," Ringo said years later. "You were never really secure with who your friends were unless you had them before. The bigger we got, the closer we became. The days that we spent as Beatles; we understood it. No one else will ever understand that."

"There are only four people who knew what the Beatles were about," Paul confirmed. "We were each other's intimates. We knew things about each other that most other people didn't know. For all of us, it was a family."

The Beatles lived for their art. They wanted to write, sing, and play music. Musically, they brought out the best in each other. There were times when John and Paul seemed capable of writing music the way Picasso tossed off a sketch.

"We just work well together," Paul said. "That's a very special thing. When you find someone you can talk to, it's a special thing. When you find someone you can play music with, it's something."

"John had his thing, and Paul had his," musician Billy Preston (who contributed to several later Beatles albums) observed. "They were two different things all together, but they fit."

Lennon and McCartney wrote myriad songs. If one of them wrote something alone, the other's name went on it.

"A body of work was produced that I don't believe he alone could have produced or I alone could have produced," Paul said after John's death. "It was me that sat in those hotel rooms, in his house in the attic. It wasn't Yoko; it wasn't Sean or Julian [Lennon's sons]; it wasn't George; it wasn't Mimi [John's aunt]; it wasn't Ringo. It was me that sat in those rooms, seeing him in all his moods and all his little things, seeing him not being able to write a song and having me help; seeing me not able to write a song and him help me."

George worked alone as a songwriter, and it took a while for him to come into his own. But he was the most gifted guitarist of the three.

Some guitarists try to dazzle with a lot of notes. George sought out the few unique right ones. The opening chord of "A Hard Day's Night" is instantly recognizable. One chord. George's genius. The same is true of the closing notes in "And I Love Her" and George's work on later songs like "Something."

"I believe I love my guitar more than the others love theirs," George said. "For John and Paul, songwriting is pretty important and guitar playing is a means to an end. While they're making up new tunes, I can thoroughly enjoy myself just doodling around with a guitar for a whole evening. I'm fascinated by new sounds I can get from different instruments I try out. Just call me a guitar fanatic, and I'll be satisfied."

Ringo played what the music called for.

"First and foremost, I'm a drummer," Ringo offered. "But I didn't play drums to make money. I played drums because I loved them. My soul

is that of a drummer. It came to where I had to make a decision: everything else goes now; I play drums. It was a conscious moment in my life
when I said the rest of the things were getting in the way. I didn't do it to
become rich and famous. I did it because it was the love of my life."

When *A Hard Day's Night* was released, the Beatles weren't far
removed from adolescence. Ringo (the oldest member of the group) was
twenty-three. But the band gave each of its members a framework within
which to operate. They grounded each other.

"We were always a little nervous before each step we went up the
ladder," George later confessed. "We always had that conversation. That
was the good thing about being four together. I always felt sorry for Elvis
because he was on his own. He had his guys with him, but there was only
one Elvis. Nobody else knew what he felt like. For us, we all shared the
experience."

"In the Beatles, if any one didn't agree with the plan, it was vetoed,"
Paul said.

Meanwhile, reflecting back on his feelings in 1964, Ringo recalled,
"Even though we felt, yes, we're established and we've conquered all these
countries and we've sold a lot of records and they all love us, it was not a
thought, 'It's going to end tomorrow' or 'It's going to go on forever.' I
never had that sort of thought. It was just happening now. I wasn't making
plans for the future. We were on this roll and we were all in our early
twenties and we were just going with it."

In August 1964, the Beatles returned to America for a concert tour
that saw them perform thirty-two shows in twenty-four cities over the
course of thirty-four days. By year's end, they had visited locales as far
away as Hong Kong and Australia. The pace of their activity was extraordinary.

"If you look at our itinerary," George said, reflecting on that time,
"some of those years where we did a tour of England, a tour of Europe, a
tour of America, two albums, and made a movie all in the same year, you
think, 'Oh Jesus, how did we do that?'"

In December 1964, *Beatles '65* was released in the United States. That
was followed by *The Early Beatles* in March 1965 and *Beatles VI* in June.
Actually, *Beatles VI* was *Beatles VII* if one counted *A Hard Day's Night*
(which Capitol didn't).

These albums were a mix of new material and tying up old loose ends. Four of the eleven songs on *Beatles '65* were non-Beatles compositions. *The Early Beatles* included previously recorded songs that had been released as singles and appeared on earlier albums in England; most notably "Love Me Do," "Please Please Me," "PS I Love You," and "Do You Want to Know a Secret" (all written by Lennon and McCartney). *Beatles VI* included "You Like Me Too Much" (George's most popular songwriting effort up until that time).

In August 1965, *Help* was released as an album and film in the United Sates. All of the songs were written by Lennon and McCartney except "I Need You" (written by George). The movie was silly and farcical with virtually no intelligent dialogue. It made *A Hard Day's Night* look like *Citizen Kane*. But like everything else the Beatles touched, it turned to gold. The revenue from their records, live concerts, and films was astronomical.

On August 13, the Beatles arrived in New York for the start of a North American concert tour. This time, they stayed at the Warwick Hotel with one hundred policemen on guard. The following night, they appeared again on *The Ed Sullivan Show*. They still wore matching suits. But their hair was longer than before, flowing down the back of their necks and covering more of their ears.

On April 15, to open the tour, the Beatles performed at the first open-air major-stadium concert ever. 55,600 fans jammed Shea Stadium to witness the event.

Bob Spitz writes, "As the Beatles charged from the dugout to the stage situated over second base, mass hysteria broke out. More than fifty thousand kids jumped to their feet and screamed, wept, thrashed, and contorted themselves in a tableau that personified pure bedlam."

A *New York Times* account of the evening picks up the narrative: "Their lungs produced a sound so staggering, so massive, so shrill and sustained that it quickly crossed the line from enthusiasm into hysteria and was soon in the area of the classic Greek meaning of the word 'pandemonium'—the region of all demons."

The crowd screamed through the entire show. Special amplifiers had been installed, but the screams drowned out the music. Security broke down. Girls ran through police barricades onto the field.

"It was ridiculous," John said afterward. "We couldn't hear ourselves sing. You can see it in the film. George and I aren't even bothering playing half the chords."

"If you look at the footage of that show," Ringo agreed, "it's very strange. It was scary.

Worse than strange. It was scary.

The world was closing in on the Beatles. They were no longer free. In transit, at shows, wherever they went, they were mobbed. Getting them in and out of hotels and concert venues was like a paramilitary operation. The crowds were becoming increasingly aggressive and more difficult to control.

"It felt dangerous," George later recalled. "Everybody was out of hand. Even the cops were out of line. They were all just caught up in the mania. It was like they were in this big movie. It was like we were the ones trapped in the middle of it while everyone else was going mad. We were the sanest people in the whole thing. Even when we got away from the screaming fans, there were all the screaming policemen and the lord mayors and their wives, the hotel manager and his entourage. We were just in the middle of a car or a hotel room. We couldn't do much. We couldn't go out. We couldn't do anything. The only place we ever got any peace was when we were in the suite."

John, Paul, George, and Ringo loved being musicians. Being a Beatle was a more complicated matter. It gave them unimaginable wealth and the freedom to create the music they wanted to create. But their art was being overwhelmed by their status as Beatles.

"We were getting a little crazy with it," Paul acknowledged.

But 1965 also brought reminders of the benefits that came with being a Beatle.

Recalling his adolescence, John Lennon once declared, "Nothing really affected me until Elvis. "Heartbreak Hotel" was the most exciting thing I ever heard. It was the spark, and then the whole world opened."

Paul had similar recollections. "I remember being in school," he said. "Somebody had a picture of Elvis. It was an advert for "Heartbreak Hotel." I looked at it and thought, 'He's so good-looking.' He looked perfect. We tried many times to meet Elvis. Colonel Tom Parker [Presley's manager] would just show up with a few souvenirs and that would have to do us for a while. We didn't feel brushed off. We felt we deserved to be brushed off. After all, he was Elvis, and who were we to dare to want to meet him?"

In late August 1965, when the Beatles concert tour reached California, they were invited to meet Presley at a house in Bel Air where the American rock icon was staying. Elvis hadn't begun the precipitous decline that would characterize his later years. But this was the post-Army Elvis.

A string of fabricated quotes was released to the press after the get-together.

"There's only one person in the United States we ever wanted to meet," John was quoted as saying. "And we met him last night. We can't tell you how we felt. We just idolized him so much. You can't imagine what a thrill that was last night."

In private, John confided his disappointment. "It was like meeting Englebert Humperdinck," he said.

Ringo noted simply, "I felt I was more thrilled to meet him than he was to meet me."

A decade later, George met Presley again at Madison Square Garden.

"It was a couple of years before the end," Harrison said of the occasion. "I went backstage to meet him in one those big dressing rooms. I was sitting there, talking with the guys, and he was nowhere to be seen. Then finally, he came around the corner. I was like a hippie and I had long hair. He had that big white outfit with gold things and a big belt-buckle. His hair was black and he was all tanned and stuff. I thought I was meeting Vishnu or Krishna or somebody like that. It was like WOW. And I felt like this smutty grubby little, 'Hello, Elvis; how are you?" But it was sad, really. He had all those squawking girl singers and trumpet players and [imitating] 'Ewwww; I did it my way.' All that stuff. I wanted to say to him, 'Why don't you just do "That's All Right, Mama?" Get your jeans on and get your guitar and booger all that other crap. But he was great when he was great."

1965 also saw another encomium. On October 26 at Buckingham Palace, the Beatles were honored by Queen Elizabeth as members of the Order of the British Empire.

"Have you ever met the Queen before?" they were asked afterward.

"No," John answered. "But she seemed pleasant enough."

Still, Beatlemania had begun to weigh heavily on its subjects. The crushing demands and intrusions of fame had imprisoned them together.

"It's great in the beginning," Ringo said. "You're recognized. You get a great seat in the restaurant. Things are bigger. All that is great. You fight to get it. And then you really want that to end."

"The nicest thing is to open the newspapers and not to find yourself in them," George noted.

There was no let-up the following year. In 1966, the crowds grew larger and the demands greater. In July, the Beatles caused a diplomatic stir by refusing to make a courtesy call on Philippines president Ferdinand Marcos and his wife in conjunction with a concert in Manila. The situation turned ugly and dangerous.

"The world used us as an excuse to go mad," George said.

Meanwhile, the Beatles' music was getting harder to replicate on stage. And the joy in performing "live" was gone.

"Does it bother you that you can't hear what you sing during concerts?" John was asked.

"No," Lennon answered. "We don't mind. We've got the records at home."

But it did bother them. The Beatles loved making music. And their public performances had long since ceased being about the music. Later, each of them would reflect on that time:

John: "It was just sort of a freak show. The Beatles were the show, and the music had nothing to do with it. We might have been wax works for all the good we did. Nobody heard anything. For us, it was a drag because it was like a riot, not a show."

George: "We were just tired. It had been four years for us of screaming in this mania. You could never hear anything. The Beatlemania took its toll. It was becoming too difficult on the nervous system. It wasn't fun anymore."

Ringo: "I never felt that people came to hear our show. I felt they came to see us because, from the counting on the first number, the screams just drowned everything out. That was okay at the beginning. But worse than that was, we were playing so bad. I don't think anyone didn't want to stop touring."

Paul: "How much of a good thing can you have? We were getting a bit fed up. This wasn't fun anymore. I think that's the main point. You've got to keep some fun in it for yourself in anything you do."

On August 29, 1966, the Beatles gave their last scheduled concert performance at Candlestick Park in San Francisco. As George left the stage, he said to himself, "This is going to be such a relief, not to have to go through this madness anymore."

IV

If the Beatles hadn't grown musically past their first eight American albums ending with *Help*, they would merit significant mention in the history of popular music. But they were eager to build on their earlier work and evolve into something more.

The band wasn't afraid to change an already successful formula. "We wanted every single record to have a different sound," Paul said. And they were fortunate in that they had the power to control their creative destiny.

The Beatles experimented from album to album. They saw what worked and didn't work. In the beginning, they were a rock band. Then they became studio musicians and their music became more complex.

Rubber Soul was recorded in October and November 1965 and released in the United States on December 6. It marked a conscious turn away from the juvenile appeal of the Beatles' earlier music toward personal and artistic maturity, self-exploration, vulnerability, and confession.

"The direction was changing away from the early stuff," Paul noted later. "There came a point where we said, 'We've done enough of that. We can branch out a bit.'"

"*Rubber Soul* really was a matter of having grown musically, but mainly having experienced the studio and knowing the possibilities," John added.

"We were starting to find ourselves in the studio, where what we could do was beyond just the four of us playing our instruments and the vocals," Ringo said. "This was the departure record."

No single was released from *Rubber Soul;* a first for a Beatles album. All of the songs were written by Lennon and McCartney except "Think for Yourself " (written by George).

During the filming of *Help*, Harrison had become interested in Indian music. Then he'd met Ravi Shankar and bought a sitar.

"When we were working on "Norwegian Wood" (one of the songs on *Rubber Soul*)," George recounted, "it just needed something. It was quite spontaneous. I just picked the sitar up and kind of found the notes and played it."

Rubber Soul was an enchanting mix of songs like "Norwegian Wood," "I've Just Seen a Face" (a touch of country), "Michelle" (sweet Paul with soft harmony in the background from John and George), "You Won't See Me" (a bit of the old Beatles), and "In My Life" (lyrics reflecting the perspective and wisdom of an older man).

In June 1966, *Yesterday and Today* was released. Most of the material on the album preceded *Rubber Soul*. Its most notable entry—"Yesterday"—was recorded with a classical string quartet. Paul wrote and sang "Yesterday" by himself. It marked the first time that a musician other than one of the Beatles was heard on a Beatles record.

Seven weeks after that, *Revolver* went on sale in the United States.

"I don't see much difference between *Rubber Soul* and *Revolver*," George said. "To me, they could be Volume One and Volume Two."

Meanwhile, the tumultuous turbulent exciting time known as "The Sixties" was flowering.

It's hard to explain the spirit that wafted through America to someone who didn't live through that era.

The Sixties were idealistic. John F. Kennedy's inaugural declaration—"Ask not what your country can do for you. Ask what you can do for your country"—was followed by Lyndon Johnson's effort to build a Great Society.

The Sixties were hedonistic in the expansion of sexual freedom and the proliferation of recreational drugs.

Black America rose to assert itself in a largely non-violent civil right movement, while riots exploded in the nation's inner cities.

The war in Vietnam tore America apart and gave birth to an anti-war movement that raged on college campuses, fueled in large part by students' fears of being drafted.

Freedom of expression was becoming a reality rather than just an ideal in ways that hadn't been contemplated before.

Countless individual rebellions formed a cultural revolution. There has never been a time in American history when the youth culture was more central to the nation as a whole. Young people provided the impetus for much of the civil rights and anti-war movements, the sexual revolution, the recreational drug culture, and more.

Music was the primary lifeline of the youth culture in the 1960s. It was a communal experience. Hit songs were pervasive in a very public way. They weren't listened to through a tiny earpiece. When there was a big hit, people heard it everywhere.

As a form of communication among the young, music was the Internet of the 1960s. The Beatles provided the soundtrack. Their songs (along with those of Bob Dylan and other seminal artists) were the language of The Sixties.

"The Beatles weren't the leaders of the generation but the spokesmen," Paul later posited.

The Beatles always seemed to know where the culture was going. Much of what they did was in vogue several months after they did it. They inspired a separate fashion market for teenagers and young adults. As their hair grew longer, long hair became the style.

Young Americans looked at them, listened to them, and said, "Yes; that's the way I feel."

"We didn't try to make an image," George said afterward. "It just happened as we were. To keep it up, we just remained ourselves."

The Beatles had been marketed as good boys. Unlike Elvis Presley and the Rolling Stones, they weren't overtly sexual. Their longish hair was an oddity, not the symbol of revolution that long hair would later become.

But the cultural revolution was anathema to many.

In February 1966, after Muhammad Ali uttered the polarizing words, "I ain't got no quarrel with them Vietcong," sportswriter Jimmy Cannon fulminated, "Clay is part of the Beatle movement. He fits in with the famous singers no one can hear and the punks riding motorcycles with iron crosses pinned to their leather jackets and the boys with their long dirty hair and the girls with the unwashed look and the college kids dancing naked at secret proms held in apartments and the painters who copy the labels off soup cans and the whole pampered style-making cult of the bored young."

That was followed by condemnation from different quarters.

In March 1966, John had given an interview to a writer named Maureen Cleave for an article that appeared in the *London Evening Standard*. Among other things, he'd said, "Christianity will go. It will vanish and shrink. I needn't argue about that. I'm right and I'll be proved right. We're more popular than Jesus now. I don't know which will go first, rock and roll or Christianity. Jesus was all right, but his disciples were thick and ordinary. It's them twisting it that ruins it for me."

In late July, the interview was repackaged and published in the United States. That led some radio stations in the Bible Belt to ban the playing of Beatles records. Then record burnings were organized (although as John pointed out, in order to burn Beatles records, people first had to buy them).

Hoping to calm the waters, Brian Epstein issued a "clarification" of Lennon's remarks. It did no good. Finally, on August 11 in Chicago, John addressed the issue with the American press.

"If I had said television is more popular than Jesus, I might have got away with it," John said. "But I just happened to be talking to a friend and I used the word 'Beatles.' Not as what I think [of] as Beatles; [but] as those other Beatles, like other people see us. I just said 'they' are having more influence on kids and things than anything else, including Jesus. But I said it in the wrong way."

"Some teenagers have repeated your statement—'I like the Beatles more than Jesus Christ,'" a reporter pressed. "What do you think about that?"

"Well, originally, I pointed out that fact in reference to England. That we meant more to kids than Jesus did or religion at that time. I wasn't knocking it or putting it down. I was just saying it as a fact, and it's true more for England than here. I'm not saying that we're better or greater or comparing us with Jesus Christ as a person or God as a thing or whatever it is. I just said what I said and it was wrong. Or it was taken wrong. And now it's all this."

"But are you prepared to apologize?"

"I wasn't saying whatever they're saying I was saying. I'm sorry I said it, really. I never meant it to be a lousy anti-religious thing. I'll apologize if that will make you happy. I still don't know quite what I've done. I've tried to tell you what I did do. But if you want me to apologize, if that will make you happy, then okay, I'm sorry."

Meanwhile, the Beatles continued to both reflect and shape The Sixties. That was evident in the link between the band's music and recreational drugs.

By the mid-1960s, a new drug culture was taking hold among young people in England and the United States. Each of the Beatles chain-smoked cigarettes. That would become one of their lesser vices.

John, Paul, and George had experimented with marijuana while performing in Hamburg before they became famous. But none of them had gotten high. Then, in late summer 1964, they met with Bob Dylan in their suite at the Delmonico Hotel in New York after the first of two shows at the Forest Hills Tennis Stadium. That night, in a back room of their suite, Dylan introduced them to marijuana. The order in which they tried it that evening was Ringo-John-Paul-George.

Paul later recalled, "This was beginning to get into that period when people were giving up the drink and getting into the herbal jazz cigarettes. It was changing things a bit. Things were getting a little more imaginative."

By the time the Beatles started filming *Help* in February 1965, they were stoned almost every day.

"We were smoking marijuana for breakfast," George later recalled. "We were well into marijuana, and nobody could communicate with us because it was just four pairs of glazed eyes giggling all the time."

"I think that was one of the reasons for not following the script," Paul confirmed. "We showed up a bit stoned and smiled a lot and hoped we'd get through it."

"Our whole attitude was changing," Ringo added. "I think grass was influential in a lot of our changes, especially with the writers. And because they were writing different stuff, we were playing differently, expanding. [But] whenever we overdid our intake, the music we did was absolutely shit. It didn't work."

Then the drugs got more potent.

John and George were first given LSD without their knowledge when their host put sugar cubes laced with LSD in their coffee at a dinner party in 1965. Paul was the last of the Beatles to experiment.

"I was really frightened of that kind of stuff," Paul said later. "It's what you're taught when you're young. Watch out for those devil drugs. When acid came around, we'd heard, 'You're never the same. It alters your life, and you're never the same again.' I think John was rather excited by that prospect. I delayed. Just what I need; some little thing where I never get back home again. I was seen to stall a little bit within the group. There was a lot of peer pressure. Talk about peer pressure. The Beatles."

Finally, in late-1966, Paul took LSD with a friend named Tara Browne.

"I was never that in love with it," he said years later. "But it was a thing you did. It was quite freaky, but I guess it was something I wouldn't have wanted to have missed. I had mixed feelings about it, certainly."

Mixed feelings or not, nothing the Beatles did happened in a vacuum. The release of each new album was an event received as the next cultural message by millions of young people around the world.

The Beatles' music had broken the mold with their emergence in 1963. In late 1965, *Rubber Soul* changed the narrative. They were allowed to try new things and push the boundaries because they were the Beatles. They broke the mold again with *Sergeant Pepper's Lonely Hearts Club Band*.

"We're now mid-sixties," Paul later recalled. "We were fed up with being the Beatles. We really hated that fucking four little mop-top boys approach, all that screaming. We didn't want anymore. We'd stopped touring. And we'd sort of lost our spiritual direction; not that we ever had one. We were experimenting in anything. Then I got this idea. Let's not be ourselves. I'd written a song, the title song. I put it to the guys. I said, 'We need to get away from ourselves. How about if we just become sort of an alter ego band?' We can make a record now under another persona. We'll be this other band, and it will free us. The idea was, we can bring anything we wanted."

In their early years, the Beatles hadn't paid much attention to studio production. "There wasn't time," producer George Martin noted. "They would dash into the studio, put down their tracks, and leave all the work to us. They were incredibly busy."

That had changed with *Rubber Soul*. From then on, the group would take a song into the studio and mold it into something different from what it had been before.

The Beatles spent five months in the studio making *Sergeant Pepper*. Most of the songs on the album were designed as studio production numbers. They didn't sound the same (or as good) when sung live. Years later, Paul recalled, "I remember saying at the time, now our performance is that record."

On March 21, 1967, during a recording session for *Sergeant Pepper*, John mistakenly popped an LSD tablet instead of an "upper" and became ill. The session was cut short and Paul brought him home.

"I thought, maybe this is the moment I should take a trip with him," Paul later told Barry Miles. "It's been coming for a long time. It's often the best way, without thinking about it too much, just slip into it. John's on it already, so I'll sort of catch up. We stayed up all night, sat around and hallucinated a lot. We looked into each other's eyes, which is fairly mind-boggling. You dissolve into each other. And it was amazing. You're looking in each other's eyes and you would want to look away. But you wouldn't and you could see yourself in the other person. It was a very freaky experience and I was totally blown away. There's something disturbing about it. You ask yourself, 'How do you come back from it? How do you lead a normal life after that?' And the answer is, you don't."

The most praised song on *Sergeant Pepper* is "A Day in the Life," which was written primarily by John.

"The moment I remember best," Paul said years later, "was when we got to a moment that he didn't have [in the lyrics] and we sort of sang 'I'd love to turn you on.' We looked at each other and said, 'We know what we're doing here, don't we? We're actually saying for the first time ever words like turn you on,' which was in the culture but no one had actually said it on a record yet. And there was a little look of recognition between us like, 'Do it! Do it! Get it down.'"

Sergeant Pepper's Lonely Hearts Club Band was released in the United States on June 2, 1967, with an iconic sleeve that depicted the Beatles in psychedelic band uniforms surrounded by scores of famous people from all walks of life. Three years earlier, the costumes would have been ridiculed. Now they were in keeping with the tenor of the times.

In the past, Beatles albums had been released around the world with different content from album to album. For example, "Nowhere Man" was on the British version of *Rubber Soul* but appeared on *Yesterday and Today* in the United States. *Sergeant Pepper* was identical from country to country, as would be the case with most of the Beatles' future albums. Within three months, it sold 2,500,000 copies worldwide.

With the release of *Sergeant Pepper*, a barrier of conformity was shattered. It was unlike anything that had come before. The screaming of

Beatles fans gave way to awe. The first time they listened to the album—and many of them had been forewarned to listen when stoned—there was a sense of anticipation and "Omigod! What comes next?" with each song.

The Beatles had created an alternative universe.

The album opens with a blast of energy and three remarkable songs: "Sergeant Pepper's Lonely Hearts Club Band," "With a Little Help from My Friends," and "Lucy in the Sky with Diamonds."

"With a Little Help from My Friends" was the first notable Beatles song on which Ringo sang lead. "It was written specifically for me," he later recalled. "But they had one line that I wouldn't sing. It was 'What would you do if I sang out of tune? Would you stand up and throw tomatoes at me?' I said, 'There's not a chance in hell am I going to sing this line.' Because we still had lots of really deep memories of the kids throwing jelly beans on stage. And I thought that, if we ever did get out there again, I was not going to be bombarded with tomatoes."

There was some underbrush on *Sergeant Pepper* like "Good Morning, Good Morning." "Within You Without You" (the only song not written by Lennon and McCartney) was a George Harrison experiment keyed to the sitar. Not all experiments work. But they were the Beatles. They could do with they wanted to do with their albums. And while they might not be able to make people like Eastern music, their power was such that they could make people aware of it.

"It wasn't that spectacular when you look back on it," John said of *Sergeant Pepper*. "It's called the first concept album, but it really doesn't go anywhere. It starts out with *Sergeant Pepper* and introducing Billy Shears. And that's the end apart from the so-called reprise. Otherwise, every other song could have been on any other album. It was great then. But people have this dream about Pepper."

They dreamt because of songs like "I'm Fixing a Hole," "For the Benefit of Mr. Kite," "When I'm Sixty-Four." And the finale: "A Day in the Life."

"Found my way upstairs and had a smoke . . . I'd love to turn you on."

Clearly, the Beatles were no longer the clean-cut kids who cheerfully sang "I Want to Hold Your Hand." As Paul later acknowledged, "In songs like "Lucy in the Sky with Diamonds," when we were talking about 'cellophane flowers' and 'kaleidoscope eyes' and 'grow so incredibly high,' we were talking about drug experiences. No doubt about it."

And let's not forget Ringo singing the lyric, "I get high with a little help from my friends."

On June 19, 1967, Paul was interviewed outside his home by two reporters from ITN News and asked the inevitable question: "How often have you taken LSD?"

Years later, he would recall saying to himself at that moment, "I'm either going to bluff this or I'm going to tell the truth."

"About four times," Paul answered.

His response was televised one day later, provoking a firestorm of tabloid coverage and condemnation.

"Do you think that you have now encouraged your fans to take drugs?" he was asked during a follow-up interview.

"I don't think it will make any difference," Paul answered. "I don't think my fans will take drugs just because I did. That's not the point, anyway. I was asked whether I had or not. And from then on, the whole bit about how far it's going to go and how many people it will encourage is up to the newspapers and you on television. You're spreading this now at the moment. This is going into all the homes in Britain. I'd rather it didn't, but you're asking me the question. You want me to be honest, and I'll be honest."

Sergeant Pepper's Lonely Hearts Club Band was followed six months later by the release of *Magical Mystery Tour*. The album was notable for "Strawberry Fields" and "Penny Lane" (which preceded *Sergeant Pepper* as opposite sides of a single) in addition to "Fool on the Hill," "Your Mother Should Know," "I Am the Walrus," and "All You Need Is Love." All of the songs on *Magical Mystery Tour* were written by Lennon and McCartney except "Blue Jay Way" (penned by George).

Then the Beatles stumbled. On December 26, 1967, the BBC televised an unscripted film version of *Magical Mystery Tour* that had been made after the album was released. The film itself was less than an hour long and looked like a bad home movie. It was savaged by the media. Beatles fans didn't like it much either.

"*Magical Mystery Tour* was the equivalent of a drug trip, and we made the film based on that," Paul said afterward. "At the time, it was all right.

It wasn't the greatest thing we'd ever done. I defend it on the lines that nowhere else do you see a performance of "I Am the Walrus." That's the only performance ever."

Sergeant Pepper's Lonely Hearts Club Band and *Magical Mystery Tour* marked the apex of the Beatles as spokespeople for recreational drugs. By the time the latter album was released, the band was already searching for something more.

George had taken the lead in this new quest. In 1966, as his interest in Indian music grew, he'd traveled to Bombay, where he studied sitar and the fundamentals of Indian mysticism.

"By having money, we found that money wasn't the answer," Harrison said later. "We had lots of material things that people spend their whole life to get. We managed to get them at quite an early age. And it was good, really, because we learned that wasn't it. We still lacked something."

After George returned to England, the Beatles recorded *Sergeant Pepper*. "For me, it was a bit boring," he confessed. "I had a few moments in there that I enjoyed. But generally, I didn't like the album much. My heart was still in India. That was the big thing for me. After that, everything else seemed like hard work. It was a job, like doing something I didn't want to do. I was losing interest in being fab."

In August 1967, George visited Haight-Ashbury, an area in San Francisco then known as the center of the "hippie" movement.

"I went to Haight-Ashbury expecting it to be this brilliant place," he later reminisced. "I thought it was all these really groovy people having a spiritual awakening and being artistic. But instead, it turned out to be just a lot of bums; many of them just young kids who'd come from all over America to drop acid at this mecca of LSD. It certainly showed me what was really happening in the drug culture. It was like The Bowery. It was like alcoholism. It was like any addiction. At that point, I stopped taking it, the dreaded lysergic [LSD]. I couldn't put that in my brain anymore. That's when I really went for the meditation. It's a big change within your life when you start making the journey inward."

On August 24, 1967 (shortly after his trip to Haight-Ashbury), George went with John and Paul to hear the Maharishi Mahesh Yogi speak in London. Then, with Ringo, they traveled to Wales to hear the Maharishi speak again.

While the Beatles were in Wales, Brian Epstein died. He was thirty-two years old. The most likely cause of death was an accidental overdose of prescription drugs. But Epstein had never fully come to terms with his homosexuality and, over the years, had repeatedly subjected himself to dangerous sexual encounters that led to beatings and robberies. In September 1966, he'd attempted suicide by taking an overdose of pills.

Epstein's commercial judgment had been flawed in many respects. Despite his genius in recognizing the Beatles' talent and repackaging them, he often negotiated poorly on his clients' behalf. Even after the group became famous, he unwittingly put them into a series of songwriting and recording deals that gave them less than full value for their services. But he'd overseen the Beatles' business empire and coordinated of all the lawyers and accountants.

"We were suddenly like chickens without heads," Ringo later recalled.

In February 1968, all four Beatles went to the Maharishi Mahesh Yogi's ashram in India. They were looking for a framework for their lives that was more meaningful than their fame.

"We'd been into drugs," Paul said of the decision to go to the ashram. "The next step then is, you've got to find a meaning."

The Maharishi preached spiritual regeneration within the framework of Indian teachings. To some, he was like a character in a Monty Python skit. The Beatles saw him as a passageway to Eastern philosophy. While at the ashram, they were alcohol and drug free. But the trip fell short of their expectations.

Ringo left after a few weeks. Paul was the next to go, a month and a half ahead of schedule. John and George stayed longer, but had a falling out with the maharishi (whose integrity they had come to doubt).

"Looking back," Paul said years later, "I feel that the maharishi experience was worthwhile. I'd been doing a bunch of drugs. I wasn't in love with anyone. I hadn't settled down. I think maybe I was looking for something to fill some sort of hole. I remember at the time feeling a little bit empty."

After the Beatles returned from India, the next Beatles venture to capture the public imagination was the theatrical release of a full-length cartoon.

Yellow Submarine was a visual interpretation of the Beatles' personae and music with psychedelic graphics and a pedestrian storyline set in a faraway place called Pepperland. The band had little direct involvement with the movie. Not only didn't they write it; they even didn't do the voiceovers for their respective characters. They did make a cameo appearance at the end of the film and write four songs that were added to a dozen compositions from previously released albums.

The critical and public reaction to *Yellow Submarine* was enthusiastic. An album coupling the four new songs with instrumental tracks from the movie was released.

The Beatles were continuing to reflect and shape the 1960s. Unfortunately, The Sixties were turning ugly.

1968 had begun with the Tet Offensive in Vietnam; a series of surprise attacks that undermined American assumptions regarding the war effort. Then Martin Luther King Jr and Robert Kennedy—two icons of hope— were assassinated. In late August, anti-war dissidents were crushed by the political establishment and police at the Democratic National Convention in Chicago. On November 5, 1968, Richard Nixon was elected president of the United States.

The old culture was reasserting itself.

And the Beatles were on the verge of disintegrating.

V

John Lennon married Cynthia Powell, who was pregnant at the time, in a makeshift ceremony on August 23, 1962 (less than a week after Ringo's debut with the band). The Beatles had a previously booked performance on their wedding night. That evening, John left Cynthia home alone.

Lennon never respected his marriage vows. Women were readily available and fungible for the band. As the Beatles grew in popularity, sexually charged fans met sexually charged Beatles with predictable results. Bob Spitz writes of the early years when Beatlemania was flowering, "They cursed, drank, and fucked their way around the globe."

Ringo married Maureen Cox on February 11, 1965, two weeks before filming on *Help* began. She too was pregnant at the time. George and Patti Boyd were wed on January 21, 1966. Paul had a five-year relationship with actress Jane Asher, that began in 1963 and ended when she came home and found him in bed with another woman.

John met Yoko Ono on November 9, 1966, at a private preview of a show featuring her art that was opening in London the next day. Yoko had been born in Tokyo and was seven years older than John. They were both married at the time. Twenty-eight months later, they would be married to each other.

Before Brian Epstein cleaned up the Beatles' act, John had frequently been drunk onstage. The band's success (and the high profile that came with it) precluded certain kinds of public conduct but enabled other excesses. He binged repeatedly; first on alcohol and sex, then on alcohol, sex, and drugs.

"I'd gone into these troughs [depressions] every few years," Lennon later acknowledged. "It was less noticeable when I was in the Beatles because the Beatles image would carry you through. You're protected by the image and the power of the Beatles."

John then referenced 1965, which followed the Beatles breakout year in America. "I was in the middle of a trough," he said. "You can't see it. But I'm singing. 'Help!' for a kick-off."

By 1967, John was tripping regularly on LSD, smoking grass, and snorting cocaine. He had become a drug addict. "Part of me suspects that I'm a loser," he said. "And the other part of me thinks I'm God Almighty."

Yoko pursued John after their initial meeting. In late 1967, he began to reciprocate her interest. They consummated their relationship sexually at his home in May 1968 while Cynthia was vacationing in Greece. She returned on May 22 (a day earlier than expected) and found her husband in pari delicto with Yoko.

Cynthia had known that John was unfaithful to her throughout their marriage. This was the final rejection. John soon went public with Yoko as his girlfriend and left home to live with her. After they started living together, he added heroin to his drug habits.

There was, in the eyes of many, an ominous aura about Yoko that contrasted markedly with the image of the Beatles. It's likely that the band would have broken up without her being in John's life. But her presence made the break-up uglier and more tension filled than it would otherwise have been.

"When John hooked up with Yoko so intensely," Paul said afterward, "it was obvious that there could be no looking back. I always felt that he had to clear the decks of us in order to give her enough attention. I was annoyed with him, jealous because of Yoko, and afraid about the breakup of a great musical partnership. It took me a year to realize they were in love."

"The old gang of mine was over the moment I met her," Lennon confirmed. "I didn't consciously know it at the time, but that's what was going on. As soon as I met her, that was the end of the boys. But it so happened that the boys were well-known and weren't just the local guys at the bar."

In late-spring 1968, the Beatles began work on a new album.

"I wasn't interested in following up *Sergeant Pepper*," John later said. "I don't know whether the others were or not. But I know that what I was going for was to forget about *Sergeant Pepper*. You know, that was *Sergeant Pepper* and that's all right, fine it's over and just get back to basic music."

Many of the songs on the new album had been written while the Beatles were in India. They reflected a wide range of styles from 1920s vaudeville ("Honey Pie") to a touch of reggae ("Ob-La-Di Ob-La-Da") to rock and roll ("Back in the USSR"). Hard-edge (almost punk) tracks like "Helter Skelter" mixed with sweet sounds like "Julia," "Dear Prudence," and "I Will" (which evoked memories of "Till There Was You"). On "I Will," Paul sang double-track harmony with Paul. That can't be done in a live concert. George came into his own as a songwriter with "While My Guitar Gently Weeps."

The new album was titled simply *The Beatles*. The album sleeve made it clear that this wasn't *Sergeant Pepper* or *Magical Mystery Tour*. Unlike its immediate predecessors, it was pure white (not multi-colored psychedelic) with a small embossed title and print number. Because of the sleeve, it was popularly known as *The White Album*.

The studio was tense during the creation of *The White Album*. John insisted on bringing Yoko to the recording sessions. Yoko, in turn, irritated and alienated virtually everyone there (including Paul, George, and Ringo) with her intrusive presence and demands.

"We were all trying to be cool and not mention it," Ringo said later. "But inside, we were all feeling it and talking in corners."

As the recording sessions progressed, Yoko became more and more intrusive, acting (in the words of one participant) like a "fifth Beatle."

Worse; John (who was a drug addict by then) was a brooding, often hostile presence.

"The two of them were on heroin," Paul later recalled. "This was a fairly big shocker for us, because we all thought we were far-out boys but we kind of understood that we'd never get quite that far out."

John's addiction was reflected in his music.

"He was getting into harder drugs than we'd been into," Paul told Barry Miles. "So his songs were taking on more references to heroin. Until that point, we had made mild rather oblique references to pot or LSD. Now John started talking about fixes and monkeys. It was a harder terminology, which the rest of us weren't into. We were disappointed that he was getting into heroin because we didn't really see how we could help him. We just hoped it wouldn't go too far."

The White Album was released in the United States on November 25, 1968. Four days later, an album by John and Yoko entitled *Unfinished Music No. 1: Two Virgins* was released in England. The music was awful and diluted the Beatles brand. Equally damaging, the front sleeve featured a full frontal nude photo of John and Yoko.

"They showed me this cover," Ringo later reminisced. "And I said, 'Come on, John; you're doing all this stuff. And it may be cool for you; but whichever one of us does something, we all have to answer for it.'"

The White Album was followed by yet another creative turn. The group decided to film the process of writing, rehearsing, and recording a new album. Filming for *Let It Be* began on January 2, 1969.

"I thought, 'Okay; it's a new year and we've got a new approach,'" George later recalled. "But it soon became apparent that it wasn't anything new. It was the same as it was the year before when we were last in the studio. It was just going to be painful again. It was very unhealthy and unhappy."

Yoko was intrusive. John was high on heroin much of the time.

"What happened," Paul said, "was, when we got in there, we showed how the break-up of a group works. We didn't realize, but we were breaking up as it was happening."

At one point in the filming, George and Paul got into a snippy exchange.

"It was just a very difficult stressful time, being filmed having a row," Harrison later noted. "I got up and said, 'I'm not doing this anymore. I'm out of here.' So I took my guitar and went home."

George returned the following day, but with a new direction in mind:

"I thought, 'I'm quite capable of being relatively happy on my own. If I'm not able to be happy in this situation, I'm getting out.'"

On January 30, the Beatles performed in public as a group for the last time. The occasion was an unannounced rooftop concert above the studio where they'd been working on *Let It Be*. For forty minutes, they previewed their new project.

"I'd like to say thank you on behalf of the group and myself," John told the crowd that gathered below. "I hoped we passed the audition."

But *Let It Be* was so lacking in quality that the decision was made to delay release of the film and album. Instead, the Beatles gathered together for one last hurrah. In April and May 1969, they recorded *Abbey Road*.

Each of them understood that this was probably their last collaborative effort.

"I think, before the *Abbey Road* sessions," Paul later reminisced, "it was like we should put down the boxing gloves and try and just get it together and really make a very special album."

It wasn't easy. There were times when the atmosphere in the studio was akin to a cold war.

"I don't think John ever felt he was better than me," Paul said later. "And I don't think I ever felt I was better than John. It would have been fatal in a collaboration for either of us to ever think that. [But] by the time we made *Abbey Road*, John and I were openly critical of each other's music, and I felt John wasn't much interested in performing anything he hadn't written himself."

Parts of *Abbey Road* were genius, displaying the Beatles' mastery of their art as songwriters, singers, and musicians. Its two best-remembered and most-praised songs—"Something" and "Here Comes the Sun"— were written and sung by George.

The album was released in the United States on October 1, 1969. Five years earlier, Frank Sinatra had labeled the Beatles "unfit to sing in public." Now Sinatra called "Something" "the greatest love song of the past fifty years."

"At the point we finished *Abbey Road*," George later said, "the game was up. I think we all accepted that."

But the end game wasn't pretty.

In 1968, "Hey Jude" had been released as a single and, within a year, sold the staggering total of six million records. In February 1970, artistic considerations were cast aside with the release of an album that returned to the pre-Beatles industry formula of packaging around a single hit. *The Beatles Again* was a mix of recycled old songs and new mediocrities with "Hey Jude" thrown into the mix.

Several months later, *Let It Be* was released as a film and album. By then, Paul had said publicly that the Beatles were breaking up. Adding to the ugliness was the fact that Apple Corp Ltd (which the Beatles had formed in 1968 in an effort to gain financial and artistic control over their music) was devolving into a financial mess.

"We've all accused one another of various business things," Paul told the media. "We tend to be pretty paranoid by now, as you can imagine. There's a lot of money involved."

On December 31, 1970, Paul filed suit to formally dissolve the Beatles' contractual partnership.

Speaking of the break-up, George later said, "The Beatles gave us the vehicle to do so much when we were younger. But it got to the point where it was stifling us. It had to self-destruct. I wasn't feeling bad about anybody wanting to leave. I wanted out myself."

"It was like the wind-down to divorce," Ringo added. "A divorce doesn't just happen. There's months and years of misery. On a lot of days, even with all the craziness, it really worked. There were still good days. We were still close friends. Then it would split off again into madness. I couldn't put my finger on one reason why we broke up. It was time and we were spreading out."

"We'd come to the end of our tether," Paul said. "We'd done all that we wanted to do. It was like a marriage. You love each other, but you're getting fed up. Then we'd solve it. We'd realize we love each other and it's all cool. But then we'd argue again."

John put it more simply: "We couldn't play the game anymore. We'd come to a point where it was no longer creating magic."

When the Beatles split up, there was worldwide mourning. True to form, Lennon took a contrary view.

"It's not a great disaster," John said. "People keep talking about it like it's the end of the Earth. It's only a rock group that has split up. It's not that important. You have all the old records there if you want to reminisce. We were a band who made it very very big. That's all."

VI

When Paul announced on April 10, 1970, that the Beatles were breaking up, each of the band members was in his late-twenties. The public assumption was that, in one way or another, they would reunite as a group at some point in the future. From time to time, there were rumors of a Beatles reunion and concert tour. Finally, John put the rumors to rest, asking rhetorically, "What's the point? To be more famous?"

After the band dissolved, its members weren't Beatles anymore. When they went out on their own, their individual strengths were clear. But so were their limitations and flaws.

Ringo has lived the past four decades as a celebrity with forays into various entertainment ventures. "When I'm ninety-five and it's This is Your Life time," he has said, "they'll still be referring to me as 'ex-Beatle'. It does have it's advantages. It's still the best way to get a good table at a restaurant."

John, Paul, and George each sought his own separate musical identity after leaving the band.

"I am not the Beatles," John proclaimed. "I'm me. The Beatles are the Beatles. Separately, they are separate."

Lennon's solo career took off with *Imagine*, then fell to earth as he wrestled with personal demons. On December 8, 1980, he was shot to death by a deranged gunman outside his home in New York. His murder, regardless of what the calendar said, was the last assassination of "The Sixties." The great icons of that era had been John and Robert Kennedy, Martin Luther King Jr, the Beatles, and Muhammad Ali. Of that group, only Ali was left untouched.

"You make your own dream," John told his followers. "That's the Beatles' story, isn't it? That's Yoko's story. That's what I'm saying now. Produce your own dream. If you want to save Peru, go save Peru. It's quite possible to do anything. But don't expect Jimmy Carter or Ronald Reagan or John Lennon or Yoko Ono or Bob Dylan or Jesus Christ to come and do it for you. You have to do it yourself. I still believe that all you need is love. But I don't believe that just saying it is going to do it."

George's solo career faded after a promising and commercially successful start. He died of brain cancer on November 29, 2001.

"I'd like to think that all the old Beatles fans have grown up and they've got married and they've all got kids and they're all more responsible, but they still have a space in their hearts for us," George said. "The Beatles will exist without us. The Beatles will go on and on."

Paul launched a new group—Wings—after the Beatles broke up. "It's hard to follow my own act," he acknowledged. "But I only had two alternatives. Give up or carry on."

Since then, Paul has written music in various forms. He was knighted in 1997 and continues touring to this day.

"When I write, there are times—not always—when I hear John in my head," Paul has said. "I'll think, 'Okay; what would we have done here?' And I can hear him gripe or approve."

Over the decades, the Beatles have been interpreted and reinterpreted many times. They came to the United States in February 1964 and disbanded six years later, leaving large footprints for such a short period of time. They were four disparate personalities who blended together (and at times conflicted with one another) to create extraordinary music. Some of their creations were self-indulgent and ordinary. Others were genius. Some were in between.

If they had never sung a note, their legacy as songwriters would endure.

The Beatles' music was marked by an intensity and honesty of feeling. They expanded the notion of what popular music can convey and were the most influential performing artists of their time. The safe thing for them to do would have been to keep doing what they were doing once they reached stardom. But they were determined to get better and not just repeat what they'd done before.

One can point to the contributions of this Beatle or that Beatle as being superior to those of the others. Paul rebutted that line of thought when he declared, "It was like the four corners of a square. People would say, 'John and Paul were the important ones.' I say, 'No, no, no! It's a square. Without any of those corners, you collapse.'"

The Beatles evolved hand-in-hand with The Sixties and were in the forefront of a new cultural wave. To have the success and power that they amassed at such a young age, to be in the spotlight and at the vortex of one's era, can be a heavy burden. So much meaning and hope was piled on their shoulders. But they carried that weight well. Their reach extended far beyond their chosen profession. They created and personified a spirit. They changed the way that people felt about the world and also about themselves.

Good music reaches everyone's soul.

Echoing John, Paul once said, "The basic thing in my mind was that, for all our success, the Beatles were always a great little band. Nothing more, nothing less. [But] there was a very good spirit behind it all."

That spirit was an important part of the journey through life for an entire generation.

Most creative artists throw pebbles in the water and hope that the ripples spread. The Beatles threw boulders.

Confronting Racism

In 1991, I found myself increasingly troubled by the view expressed in some circles that good race relations were almost entirely the responsibility of white people. With that in mind, Jack Newfield and I set out to interview a cross section of black leadership in America. We chose eight individuals from various walks of life—Jesse Jackson, Mary Francis Berry, Roger Wilkins, John Lewis, Charles Rangel, Sterling Johnson, Arthur Ashe, and Harry Belafonte. When we were done, Penthouse *devoted a full twenty-two pages to our findings. The interviews appear here in full for the first time.*

Many things have changed in the decades since then. The presidencies of Ronald Reagan and George H. W. Bush are long gone. Barack Obama is now president of the United States. But I find it disheartening how many of the issues we discussed in 1991 remain unresolved.

1991 Introduction to "Confronting Racism"

Ever since the first slave ship docked in 1619, race relations have been America's special torment.

Now we are experiencing a tale of two cities. This is the best of times and the worst of times; a season of light and a season of darkness; a time of hope and a time of despair.

More black Americans hold political office than ever before. A black man is governor of Virginia. New York, Los Angeles, Philadelphia, Chicago, Baltimore, and Seattle have all elected black mayors. Philadelphia, Mississippi—where Andrew Goodman, Michael Schwerner, and James Chaney were murdered during a 1964 voter registration drive—now has a black congressman. General Colin Powell is chairman of the joint chiefs of staff. Bill Cosby is a television superstar. More blacks have entered the middle class than ever before, as doctors and lawyers in suburban homes.

Yet at the same time, an increasing number of black Americans live in poverty. The life expectancy for a black male born in Harlem is shorter than that of a child born in Bangladesh. Black income is half that of whites. Blacks still suffer from discrimination at the hands of banks, unions, and real-estate developers. The pathology of crime, drugs, and broken families has created a permanent inner-city underclass. Recent studies show that 23 percent of all black American men in their twenties are incarcerated, on probation, or on parole. The leading cause of death among black men between the ages of eighteen and thirty-four in this country is homicide.

For some, the glass is half-full. For others, it is half-empty. Reality has become a Rorschach test perceived differently by black and white. Events like the trial of Washington, D C, mayor Marion Barry, the rape of a jogger in Central Park, the claim of rape by Tawana Brawley, the death of Yusef Hawkins in Bensonhurst, and other racially charged incidents have underscored this differing perception as a measure of America's racial polarization.

Whites can't imagine black anger and suffering. Blacks can't imagine white fear and resentment. Blacks say racism leads to crime. Whites say crime leads to racism.

We have come through slavery, the Civil War, the civil rights movement of the 1960s; and still our racial dilemma is unresolved. And if the 1980s were a decade of greed, many fear that the 1990s will be a decade of further polarization and racial violence.

In an effort to confront this dilemma, we set out to interview a cross-section of America's black leadership. Our goal was to listen and learn; to get a perspective on racism, its causes, and its cures. The eight men and women we interviewed are part of history and have a profound sense of history. Their views on racism in America are important for all of us to hear and understand.

Mary Frances Berry is an educator, author, and attorney. In the past, she has served as chancellor of the University of Colorado at Boulder, assistant secretary for education in the United States Department of Health Education and Welfare, and chairwoman of the United States Commission on Civil Rights. When we interviewed her, she was president of the Organization of American Historians and a professor of history at the University of Pennsylvania. ★

Mary Frances Berry

Q: How do you define racism? What is its degree of virulence in America today? And is there any difference between white racism and black racism?

BERRY: I guess the way I define it is, not only being prejudiced and making judgments about people without regard to evidence one way or another based on their race; but I would also add to it, having the power to make decisions about that person's future. So it's more than just simply not liking somebody or being prejudiced toward somebody. The implication of it is power to somehow affect. I think that racism in policy terms has to be defined that way. What's the difference between white racism and black racism? Nothing in terms of being prejudiced against somebody, making judgments about them. But in terms of power to decide and power to control and power to influence life chances, they're different degrees of that. There may be black people who have lots of power to decide people's lives, but that is more exceptional than not. So I would add that power component to it. It's virulent in either case, but it's a question of power.

Q: Do you think that the manifestation of racism in the white community today is a backlash to black assertion or a sign of the black movement in America losing ground and losing strength?

★The author profile preceding each interview in this section reflects the interviewee's status as of 1991.

BERRY: That's an interesting question. One of my colleagues on the Civil Rights Commission made a statement one day in which he said, "You know, if blacks keep demanding things, then it's going to cause more white racism." This was a heartfelt comment on his part. And I thought, "Wait a minute. Do you mean to say that, if blacks didn't demand anything, there would be fewer manifestations of racism?" Well there's a sense in which that is probably true. I do think that, if blacks were less assertive in a lot of ways, some negative and some positive, that there would be less of this sort of thing. But that would just mean we wouldn't be dealing with it. It would still be there, the power to decide and all that.

Q: Have you looked at any of the campus situations involving racial antagonism?

BERRY: Yes, I've been out at Michigan and I teach at Penn, and we've had a few things happen there over time. I read all the reports, and I've been around campuses. That part is really disappointing; the campus part. I find that more disappointing than anything, because I really did believe when I was a student at Michigan that in twenty years nobody would be doing any of this stuff anymore. And now you have it on the campus. Part of it is the assertiveness of the minority students. Black students, Hispanic students; in some cases, Jewish students. There's a lot of anti-Semitism too on campuses. And part of it is the desire to keep people in their place. So what you've got is a very aggressive student body. Black students are very aggressive. They didn't grow up the way I did, and they are not that old. They don't understand that there was a time when you couldn't be aggressive at all. Otherwise, you could get killed. And they think it's perfectly normal to be aggressive about where they go, what they do, what they say to people, what they demand, and so on. And then people who they encounter are irritated by it.

Q: Do you feel that black students are more aggressive and demanding than white students?

BERRY: They're all aggressive and demanding. My point is that black students used to come to a university with the idea that we're here and we're happy these people have us here; isn't it wonderful. If we're real nice, maybe they'll let us stay. That used to be the case years ago when you had a handful of black students. There still aren't that many, but they're enough to be visible going to predominantly white institutions. And now you have black students coming to campuses, and they say, "I'm a student, I'm here. What's here for me to enjoy? What can I do?" And they demand things from professors. They're no more demanding than the white students. It's just that many white students believe that black students ought to be nice and grateful; that they ought to be happy they're there. Be grateful, and as one white student told me, "They ought to understand that they're here so we can interact with them, so we can find out what they're like." Students tell me that. They're quite naive, and they're trying to be nice. They're not trying to be difficult. They say, "I just want to be able to touch them, talk to them, and so why don't they let me. That's what they're here for; for me to feel." And the black students are saying, "I'm not here for you to feel," and the separatism is reinforced.

Right now, one of the major tendencies among black students that I see on campus is what we would have called in the 1960s just plain black nationalism. And since they know no history—none of the students know any history—they don't know that anybody did this before. So when I hear them talking, if you didn't know the time warp, you would just say these are some cultural nationalists from the 1960s walking around on the campus now.

Q: How would you assess the degree of racism in universities in terms of hiring, admissions, corporate investments, and the like?

BERRY: Well, I think the people who run universities—faculty and administration—are pretty good and a lot better than they used to be about admitting black students, Hispanic students, and so on. The problem is what happens in the classroom once they're there, and what happens in the interaction with other students. Admissions officers are out looking for people. They're trying to get diversity on the campus. But it's the campus environment that the people who run the universities can't seem to do very much about, primarily because presidents don't run universities. People think they do, but they don't. The university is run by faculty and students, and it's a collegial environment. You can't tell people what to do, and there's all kinds of freedom of speech. So when they argue—the black students and the white students—the white students say, "Not only are we letting you in here and my buddy isn't here, now black student, you won't even relate to me and let me learn about you and learn what you're like and feel your hair. They let you in so I could learn about you, so what in the hell are you doing here?" And that makes the black students mad, and they get mad at each other.

Q: What about the question of quotas, both for admissions and hiring faculty?

BERRY: Well, everybody—I shouldn't say everybody, but almost everybody—in a predominantly white university who is on the faculty or in the administration knows in fact that they don't have quotas for admission [as opposed to affirmative action]. But when students get into arguments with each other, they argue about whether they should be admitting as many students who are black or Hispanic. There's even arguments about Asian students, whether they should be admitted on the campus. The argument really isn't about quotas, because they don't discuss it from that standpoint. The argument is, "If the university didn't reach out to try to get some black students, my buddy from my hometown would be here. Because you know, in my high school, for years, a certain percentage of the kids went to Penn, and now my buddy couldn't get in but they have these black students here." And the black students are saying, "Well, why should your buddy get in here when your buddies have been coming here for years and we have a right to be here too." So the quota thing misstates it. It's that, even if you have one person there, if my buddy didn't get in, it's one too many. It's not that twenty-five got in, but why are they admitting any of these people.

Q: What would you say is the primary issue for black students on American campuses today?

BERRY: Money. Most of them complain that whatever amount of money they're getting to go to school is not enough, or they have too many loans. That's the main thing you'll hear. Got all these loans. You'll hear it from all the students, but you'll hear we've got more than anybody else. When we get out of school, we won't be able to do anything. The other thing is the environment on campus, where white students treat them as objects, which they don't like. The third thing is that many of them think that in classes, still, there's a presumption on the part of professors that they're dumb or stupid. You know, you're probably some affirmative-action admittee, and you don't know anything. There's this tension always at that level. And then there is a lot of aggressiveness on the part of white students. The fraternities have been a big problem. So you get a lot of overt physical harassment and intimidation on campus.

Q: What about curriculum?

BERRY: Curriculum, of course. They say the same thing that we said in the '60s and '70s; that the curriculum doesn't have enough about us, and the courses ought to be revised. There is this big issue, for example, about whether history should be taught to glorify one's ancestors. They say that it's not a question of glorifying ancestors; it's just a question of including us, and you're not doing enough of that. We're not saying glorify us, but you folks aren't including us. So let's revise the curriculum; let's argue about what we're going to read, which are old issues. We fought all this stuff before; it's not new. But they think it's new, and they're fighting very hard about it on the campuses.

Q: How do you feel personally about all these issues on campuses that you've touched upon?

BERRY: You obviously have to have diversity on the campus. If you didn't, it would be less interesting for everybody. And the students are better off having to interact with each other, even when it's painful, than they would be if they didn't do it. As far as the curriculum is concerned, I think it's true that most universities could do more to have a curriculum that is more inclusive, and I think that most faculty members will agree with that when they're not having a fight. People are trying very hard, but there's a lot more that needs to be done. And you don't need the kind of people like, I was in a faculty meeting at a university where a distinguished white professor got up in a debate among faculty about what to read in the English curriculum. And he said that he didn't want the works of Toni Morrison included in the literature courses, because it would pollute Shakespeare to have such inferior works placed into the curriculum. This is at a faculty meeting. Most of the people in the room thought he was crazy, but he had five or ten people who agreed with him. They had quite a big argument about this, which is silly. I think that most people who are intelligent know that teaching certain things and reading certain things is of course influenced by excluding people. We've excluded all kinds of Jewish literature from philosophy over the years, and all kinds of other things have been excluded. I think that it's very painful. We need to be more inclusive.

Q: Statistics show racism and racist incidents on the rise in the past two years. To what extent does black America bear responsibility for that and have an obligation to deal with it?

BERRY: If you want to know what black people can do to try to reduce the level of racial hostility, whether it results in incidents or whatever; the answer to that, I suppose, is, until every black person in America is clean and neat and non-threatening, many people will find any black person they see threatening. That's unfortunate but true. You read all these stories about black people who can't get cabs, and I know it's true. I can't get a cab right out here, and I'm a female in front of an office building. I ask one of the white people—we have white people who work here—to go out and get a cab for me. So I think that what we can do is work toward a day when we're all nice wonderful-looking people who don't do anything to anybody, or who appear not to do anything. And we can also keep denouncing people in the black community, like the Sharptons, people who are ridiculous. Maybe that will help. But I really don't know what the answer is.

Q: Why has the black leadership in this country been so reluctant to denounce Al Sharpton?

BERRY: I don't know. Nobody's asked me. If anybody ever asked me, I'd denounce him. There are some people I won't denounce, but him? I really can't figure out what he's doing. Sharpton, I mean, I don't know what his problem is. Maybe in New York, you guys regard him as a leader. But that guy, he's a charlatan. Everybody knows that. I thought people knew that, but I guess some people regard him as a leader.

Q: Why is it that so many people seem to be following Al Sharpton?

BERRY: Now that's a better question. He obviously touched some nerve somewhere. There are large numbers of African Americans who do not believe that there is opportunity in the United States, and who believe that most politicians aren't going to do anything for them. Their daily lives are something you don't understand and I don't understand, because we don't live them. And if we had to live the way they live, Al Sharpton might look like a pretty good guy. Because at least he's articulating their pain and their suffering and their disbelief and discontent with the system. So to be serious about Al Sharpton, while I would regard what he does, what I've seen of what he does, as buffoonery, to those people the guy represents leadership. He's a guy who's saying what they'd like to say to somebody. Kiss off, he's saying to the system, and that's what they'd like to say. So if you want them to stop caring about Al Sharpton, then what you do is make them believe that there is opportunity and make them somehow believe that something can happen in their lives.

Q: Do you think the failure of elected politicians creates the vacuum that Al Sharpton fills?

BERRY: Right. See, the thing that one has to understand is that the civil rights movement promised to many Americans, and to black Americans in particular, that politics could be a way to solve your problems. That the standard American way of now you can vote; now you can elect people; and now if you've got any problems, take them to the guy or the woman; they'll take care of them. But that promise was not fulfilled. And there are many people who feel that electoral politics doesn't change anything. If you vote, nothing happens; that yes, we got the right to vote, but hey, what does that have to do with the drug problem or the bread on my table or the crime in the streets. That's why many people don't vote in the black community. You have a large number who don't, who laugh at politicians, and who don't care. So they say, "Well, all of that work and all of that promise, politics is not the way. Maybe this guy Sharpton, at least if he tells people off and kicks them in the shins, maybe they'll do something because we're giving them trouble." It's the failure of electoral politics to make people feel they have real opportunity that left that vacuum.

Q: What about [former Washington DC mayor] Marion Barry? How do you feel about him?

BERRY: I feel very sorry for him. Sorry for him, because I know what he did before he did all this bad stuff. Sorry for him and embarrassed for him, because the situation he found himself in was ridiculous. I think he ought to have resigned earlier from the mayor's office; even when I wasn't sure what he had done, because the whole thing had gotten out of hand. I feel sorry for him. He's a tragic figure, and it does show how, when people abuse cocaine and alcohol, what can happen to your personality. It's really too bad what he did to the city and what he did to himself. That's how I feel about Marion.

Q: How would you compare black political leadership in this country in the 1960s and early 1970s with the black political leadership today?

BERRY: It's different, because the role is different. You're talking now about people who are by-and-large in electoral politics. Electoral politics is a very different world from protest politics. All the assumptions are different. The people who were leaders in the 1960s were outsiders trying to get in. And when you're out trying to get in, your assumptions are completely different and that requires a certain kind of leadership. What has happened now is that some of these people are on the inside; more people are getting on the inside. And electoral politics is not a good way to have someone stand for something. I know very few elected officials who stand for anything; I don't care what color they are. And so what's happened to most black politicians is that they've ended up being just politicians and are happy to do that.

You get a mayor of a city, like Andy Young became mayor of Atlanta, and if you go out in the neighborhoods in Atlanta, poor people will ask, "What did he do for us while he was mayor?" There are people, members of the Congressional Black Caucus, most of whom are concerned about the same thing that every other politician is concerned about—staying up there as long as they can, getting re-elected, chairing a committee, without having any commitment beyond the rhetorical to doing anything about issues and taking risks. So we no longer have leadership that likes to take risks. We don't have leadership that's committed to the goal of the overall elevation of the black community. We have people who use a lot of rhetoric and are in it for themselves, but that's just like other politicians. There is, in general, a decline in leadership ability in this country. And in the black community, we've done that about as well or poorly as everybody else. We don't have anybody, really. It's hard to find people you can look up to. I think that, as far as moral authority is concerned, people who are not in elected office are the people that I would think are leaders.

Q: You're pretty tough on black elected officials.

BERRY: Let me put it this way. When politicians are doing what politicians are by definition supposed to do, then I admire their ability to be good at it. So [congressman] Bill Gray, I admire for being good at what it takes to get ahead in electoral politics. I admire [Virginia governor] Doug Wilder for being good at what it takes to get ahead in electoral politics. I loved [former Chicago mayor] Harold Washington and admired his ability to do what it took to make it in electoral politics. All those people, I admire for their ability to do what is necessary. My point would be that little of it is relevant to the problem of the mother in the crack house and the crack baby and the people who are stealing stuff.

Q: Did you think differently in the 1960s, when the emphasis was on voter registration? Did you think then that traditional electoral politics would be a major avenue of progress?

BERRY: Yes. I think most of the black community believed that, if we could just get the right to vote and we could all vote and we could get some more elected officials, all this would change; that when we were able to vote and elect our own people, they would do right. And now what is happening is, people like to have elected officials. They're happy that Bill Gray is there. But everybody knows now what we didn't know then, which is that it doesn't mean the fundamentals are going to change. Politics can do some things; it's just that the fundamental things aren't changed very much by politics. And that isn't surprising. Probably, everybody else knew it before we did.

Roger Wilkins served as assistant attorney general of the United States from 1966 to 1969. Thereafter, he was a member of the editorial board of the Washington Post, *a columnist and member of the editorial board of the* New York Times, *associate editor of the* Washington Star, *and chairman of the Pulitzer Prize Board. When we interviewed him, he was a professor of history and American culture at George Mason University in Virginia.*

Roger Wilkins

Q: You wrote an op-ed column in the *Washington Post* that was critical of [Washington, DC, mayor] Marion Barry while his trial was going on. And one of the questions that has come up a lot with black leaders is, what is the limit of solidarity? At what point are black leaders prepared to criticize each other?

WILKINS: Well, I don't think that black people ought to go out of their way to criticize other blacks, because white people work overtime doing that. Of course, you criticize black people when they deserve it, but you do it in a way that is intended to be constructive. That's my view. Obviously, you can't live by the principle that black people are beyond criticism, because that would mean you have no standards, and no community can get healthy and remain healthy without standards. So I believe that it is perfectly appropriate to criticize people, and I also believe that it's appropriate to disagree with people.

As you know, I am a very good friend of Jesse Jackson's and have been a member of his inner circle in both of his campaigns. I think he's a great figure and that his contributions to American politics are historic. That doesn't mean he shouldn't be criticized. Surely, I criticize him in our private conversations and raise questions about things. That doesn't mean that I won't someday decide that I have to write something critical about him.

My own judgment was that, over the last few years, Mayor Barry has been very harmful to this city and harmful to race relations in the city. There were a lot of people who took the view that this was an internal black community matter; that it was inappropriate to criticize him because he was being unfairly besieged by the media, which is generally white-owned, and by a prosecutorial system that not only is principally white but also Republican. And it's true; the media was unfair in my view, and the prosecutorial system was, in my judgment, disgraceful. But just because other people were wrong and behaved unprofessionally or even in a racist manner didn't make Barry's behavior better. It didn't excuse it. Two wrongs don't make a right. And it seemed to me that it was a disservice, first of all to other black people, not to criticize Barry; not to say to other black people that there are higher standards; and not to say to my own children, there are higher standards than this. It seemed to me that it was incumbent upon me to say that. And secondly, of course, the white community had to know that there are black people who are not blinded to standards of decency and honorable public service.

Q: You've also said that Ronald Reagan helped create a climate where once again it was acceptable for white people to hate and give in to their prejudices. Do you feel that within the last few years that sort of response has also become more acceptable in the black community?

WILKINS: What, to hate white people?

Q: Yes.

WILKINS: Never in my lifetime has there been a time when there was a lack of suspicion in the black community about white people. And never in my lifetime has there been a time when there was a lack of hostility in the black community toward white people. What I think you have now is a greater degree of bitterness, because dreams have been bashed. The black poor are demonstrably poorer than they were a decade ago with fewer reasons to hope for anything. People who are wallowing in hopelessness are not going to be restrained in their language; particularly when they bear the brunt of the society's contempt. They will hurl back invective and contempt at the people who deprive them of every opportunity to have a shred of dignity and hope in their lives. So yes, they say unkind unpleasant things.

Q: Do you think that there's more antagonism between black and white in America today than there was in the 1960s.

WILKINS: That's so hard to measure. The nature of the society is so different. You talk about the 1960s. Hell; I went to places in the South in the sixties where I was afraid I was going to get killed. I'm not afraid that I'm going to get killed in the South today, so the answer is that it's not nearly as bad there anymore.

But the North is the home of hypocrisy. When the North came face-to-face with the best principles that it applied to the South, it blinked. I knew people who were capable of writing thunderous editorials telling the South how to reform itself. The *New York Times*, for example; the *Washington Post*. They did great, always telling the South what to do. We loved to read it. But I have a picture of the metropolitan staff of the *New York Times* in 1966; all white. When it came time for the movement to come North and the North had to examine its own racism, it was not very comfortable and not very gallant. And we always said, you know the South. White people in the South hated blacks as a race, but loved us as individuals. And northerners loved blacks as a race, but hated us as individuals. In the South, a lot of white people had relationships with black people. Side by side; they were close to each other. White people could form close relationships with black people, and there were great kindnesses and love between lots of black southerners and white southerners. In the North, segregation was rigid; stratification was rigid. So it was easy for white people in the North to talk about racial justice, but they didn't confront blacks in their daily lives. Maybe the shoeshine guy or something like that; the guy who ran the elevators in their building; but nobody of consequence. When it came time to integrate, white people in the North thought the only task of integrating was to inject a few black people in the picture; the picture of the metropolitan staff, for instance. Just hire a few black people. But these black people must adjust. It never occurred to white people that they had to adjust to the black people. It never occurred to them that black people brought anything of value. It just occurred to them that whatever differences black people had, those differences were called defects that had to be fixed. As one black reporter told me, "My editor always says my judgments are clouded by my blackness. It never occurs to him that his judgments are clouded by his whiteness."

Black people ran into heated racism in the North. And that's not to say there aren't a lot of terrific white people in the North. But I think that the North has always been less honest about its race relations than the South. Also, money and power have basically been concentrated in the North. And by and large, white people aren't prepared to share money and power in any significant way. No place where I have been in my lifetime—and I've been to a lot of fancy places—are white people prepared to share money and power with black people in any significant way. There's a token here and there, but nothing of consequence.

I worked at the *Washington Post*, and this city is full of black people. The *Post* has, as far as I know, one major black editor, and that's one more than they had when I left sixteen years ago. The *New York Times* has none. They offered me a major editing job in 1977, but I turned it down. That's the history of major black editing jobs at the *Times*. Let me tell you something. A major journalist from the *New York Times*—a very famous journalist for the *New York Times*—told me a story. He went to a party one night at the home of Abe Rosenthal, who was then the executive editor of the *New York Times*. Abe's apartment in those days was on the top floor of a building on Central Park West. It was a penthouse. He took this journalist out to the balcony; he puts his arm around him; and he says, "You see this; this is all our town." And he sweeps his hand forward toward Fifth Avenue and south toward the lights of midtown. This journalist, being something of a wry fellow, said, "Yeah, Abe; and this is our town," sweeping his hand left and up toward upper Fifth Avenue and up toward the Bronx and Harlem. And Rosenthal said, "No, no, no! This is our town." Abe Rosenthal is not my favorite guy, but I don't think that Abe is much different than other major news executives. I think, in a private moment, he kind of gave you his priorities in that little conversation. Racism is a deeply ingrained part of American culture. It's as natural as water running down a hill.

Q: What can be done at the grass-roots level by black Americans to combat the racial antagonism in this society?

WILKINS: I don't know that racial antagonism is the big issue. The issue is to save our kids. The big-city school systems are terrible, and we're losing kids. I think that one of the things we need to do is to flood the school system with volunteers; with middle-class volunteers. All of us who are successful need to go into schools and figure out ways to help them. That will do several things. First of all, it will make schools better. Second, if enough of us men do it, black kids will see males who have succeeded at something other than street life. And one would hope that it would politicize us about education to a degree that we would become fierce and powerful advocates for much better urban inner-city education. We need a lot of that kind of community organization that we had in the 1960s. There was a lot of very effective idealistic community organization going on. People really pouring their lives and souls into it. And I think we have to find ways to get back to that. As much as I love what Jesse has done on a national level—and I think he's really broken things open—the gut-wrenching politics are still local. And the more we find black people getting involved locally in nitty-gritty ways; you know, really going into child-care centers that are dealing with kids who are born addicted or into neighborhood housing or half-way houses, wherever it is; the more we do it, the more we will uplift our politics; the more we will start to sharpen our demands about what society really needs to do in order to make life more bearable and better for people. I really think that what black people need to do is go back to some of the self-help traditions that we developed in the nineteenth century after slavery when we were adrift and alone. I think that basically the black poor are adrift and alone, and I think we need to help ourselves.

Q: Why did the sixties revolution fail?

WILKINS: It didn't fail. Just because it didn't complete the process of repairing three-and-a-half centuries of legalized racial oppression of one kind or another, doesn't mean it failed. You cannot look at Colin Powell and say it failed. You cannot go into a bank and see black bank tellers and say it failed. You cannot see black bus drivers and black engineers and black accountants and black college professors and say it failed. You cannot walk into the Hilton or Hyatt or whatever is the best hotel in Jackson, Mississippi, and say it failed. My uncle [Roy Wilkins] testified once before the Senate Judiciary Committee. John Pastore from Rhode Island asked,

"What do you people do, Mr. Wilkins, when you drive through the country?" And my uncle told them, you call ahead and you stay with friends. And you have a strong bladder, because you may not he able to go to the bathroom. That testimony was given in 1963. Less than thirty years later, if I want to drive from here through the Deep South, through Texas up to California, I don't have to worry about that. I can stop wherever I want to; eat wherever I want to. Don't have to worry about somebody killing me, as one would have worried with a fancy car with northern license plates on it thirty years ago. So you can't say it failed. It just didn't do the complete job.

Q: What is your agenda to get from here to there? What are your priorities?

WILKINS: It isn't any different now than it used to be, except that I understand the country better. We came of age in an aberrational time, the 1960s. Change looked inevitable. For guys who followed baseball from 1947 on, terrific wonderful social change looked inevitable. 1947 [when Jackie Robinson joined the Brooklyn Dodgers] was followed by 1954 and the Supreme Court decision, and those changes were followed by the 1960s. The country was feeling rich, powerful, and expansive. A lot of people said to me during the 1960s, "We can buy justice out of economic growth. Nobody has to lose." And when Americans are feeling powerful, expansive, and rich, they're more apt to be compassionate and fair.

Well, America is not going to feel powerful and rich again for a long long time thanks to that guy Reagan and the people he brought with him. Dishonest negligent people. Those people were criminally negligent; they really were, from stem to stern. It's just the most disgusting administration that we will ever see. It ranks right up there with Harding and Grant.

But if I had a magic wand, we would change the way Americans look at their nation. We would make Americans aware of the fact that we're throwing away the country; we're throwing away the cities. I said years ago, the best way for society to commit suicide is to raise savages who are unconnected to the rest of us by anything but rage in the middle of its islands of civilization, which are the cities. That's what we're doing. And I said, leave aside my humanitarian values; this is a utilitarian judgment. This is why America must change these policies. If not to save a soul, at least to save a civilization.

Poor people beat on me like crazy, because they said I believed that poor black people are savages. I don't believe all poor black people are savages. But I believe that, if people are raised like savages, some of them are going to be savages. And the cities are a lot worse now. The *Washington Post* ran a story a year or so ago, detailing how the libraries, the public libraries in this city, are becoming unusable. Prostitutes plying their trade in some lavatory restrooms. Male homosexual prostitutes plying their trade in others. When your civilization is so unraveled that the public libraries are becoming unusable, you know you're striking right at the core of the civilization.

Q: Why hasn't there been more visible and vocal outrage within the black community at the people who are pillaging the black community? From the drug dealers to the muggers?

WILKINS: Well, I don't see a great level of outrage and hostility toward the pillagers of the public treasury in the white community either. I mean, white folks' taxes got stolen by the people in the HUD scandal and S&L scandal, and I don't see a hell of a lot of outrage in the white community. That's number one. Number two, no people hate drug dealers more than the people in poor black communities. I mean they hate them. They still say what my grandmother used to say: "They ought to put them under the jail." That's what my grandmother used to say, and that's what people still say. And you certainly see periodically reported local community efforts to drive drug dealers out of peoples' neighborhoods. So I don't think that there is any passivity in the black community about these things.

Don't ask black people to rise up in wrath when the white people are letting M. Danny Wall [chairman of the Federal Home Loan Bank Board, who was forced to resign as the savings and loan scandal spiraled out of control] walk around like he's some kind of real human being. I mean, come on. I was at the White House Correspondents Dinner. Back tie dinner. I look up, and Charles Keating [chairman of the Lincoln Savings and Loan Association, who ultimately served five years in prison for his role

in the scandal] is walking through there with a black tie on. Some journalist invited him. So don't talk to me about black people not being outraged. That son-of-a-bitch Keating doesn't belong in polite society. Some
societies do shunning; some people deserve shunning. I don't see white
people shunning that son of a bitch, so I don't know where you get this
stuff that black people don't have an appropriate amount of outrage about
bad things.

I mean, as I was driving here to meet you guys, I heard a news program that announced President [George H. W.] Bush's War on Drugs is a
year old. I just hope that he can report more success after a year-long war
on Saddam Hussein [the 1990–1991 Gulf War] than he can on this war
on drugs. But Bush pronounced it a great success. He got up there and
said it was a great success, according to this radio report. Now, no black
person who lives in a black neighborhood can take that white man seriously. I live in an urban renewal neighborhood, but there are black poor
people who live very near me, and there's an open-air drug market a half-
mile from my house. I drive that way every night to take our babysitter to
the subway. They announce a war on drugs, and the drug czar [William
Bennett] says he's going to make Washington, DC, the big example. Every
night, I drive through there, and they're selling drugs. I'm used to them
selling drugs, and periodically there's a murder. Well, this jerk in the White
House is standing up proclaiming victory, and this loud-mouthed wind-
bag Bennett, his drug czar, says, "Oh yeah; we're winning the war." Well,
black people look at that and really get enraged, because we know these
guys haven't put any money for treatment into it and we know they're
just standing up there making political points for white people, because
they sure can't be talking to black people because black people know the
truth. So there is giant rage.

Q: Is that what people like Al Sharpton have tapped into to give them
their following?

WILKINS: They've tapped into the white media. They've tapped into
how to get a headline in the New York Post, how to get on the local news.
And as far as I can tell, Sharpton's major constituency is the white media
in New York. Now you ask the question, what is it that he's tapped into

as if there's a mystery. A third of black people are in poverty. Harlem is a mess. The South Bronx has bottomed out. The earning power of young black men without a high-school diploma has declined precipitously since 1969 to the point where they're not able to earn enough to keep a family of four above the poverty line. And nobody gives a damn. For eight years, we had an administration [the Reagan administration] that was unremittingly hostile to them. What have they tapped into? What are you talking about? There is pain and anguish and anger and an unresponsive society that makes it very difficult for moderates or even immoderate mainstream blacks to deliver.

I called Ronald Reagan publicly an ignorant savage. And to my people, he was. People ask, why aren't black leaders more responsible? I have never seen any bunch of people more irresponsible than those white people who ran this country in the Reagan years; more irresponsible toward blacks and the poor; irresponsible with a malignant hostility. When Ronald Reagan would see the Congressional Black Caucus only once—and that was an introductory meeting at the beginning of his first term—and then wouldn't see them again; when he gave short shrift to all other black leaders who had a legitimate constituency in the black community so that these people couldn't deliver anything; of course, guys are going to get up and yell and express random anger and frustration. Of course, they're going to get a response. And Bush is not a heck of a lot better than Reagan. It's enraging. And it's cruel. But unfortunately, in America it's not unusual.

Q: Do you have any insights into the system whereby the mainstream media decides which black leaders become visible and which ones don't?

WILKINS: I wrote a very powerful strong objection to Ben Bradley today about that ocean of print about Al Sharpton. And I said I couldn't figure out why they did it. But knowing how the editors of the style section of the *Washington Post* think, or seem to think, they may have thought presenting a black buffoon would be just the thing to amuse their upscale readers. And as we know, there is a long deep rich cultural history in the United States of presenting black buffoons to amuse white people. So I think that's part of it. And I think part of the psychology is, it's a way to trivialize blacks. If you put Sharpton out front day after day, then you

don't have to deal with the more profound critics of society. You know
what black America has to offer. And you know that, in New York City,
you could go to a thousand people before you need to get to Al Sharpton
to get a rich full textured layered analysis of what's going on in the black
community.

Let me just tell you, when I was in New York writing for the *Times*,
an editor on the metropolitan section of the paper said to a black reporter,
"I'm tired of seeing these quotes in the paper of black people talking like
college professors. I want some 'deese' and 'dems' and 'disses' in there." So
I don't know a lot about the mechanism, but there you go. It helps trivialize real grievances, deep grievances, profound grievances that the society
is absolutely unwilling to deal with. If you have Sharpton on the air all the
time, then you don't have to deal with the catastrophic housing problems
that black people have. You don't have to deal with the catastrophic problems that produce kids who ritualize mugging in order to get into gangs.
You don't have to deal with the schools that these kids go to. You don't
have to deal with the fact that the doctors in Harlem Hospital and the
AMA are telling you that the life expectancy of black males in Harlem is
worse than in Bangladesh. You don't have to deal with that stuff. You can
dismiss Al Sharpton. And by dismissing Al Sharpton, you can dismiss the
whole thing.

Q: What will the next generation of black leaders be like?

WILKINS: I don't know. Our generation grew up in the civil rights
movement, understood it, ingested its values, lived by its values. We'll be
dead soon, all gone, and a whole new generation of trained black people
is going to come along who don't have any memory of that at all. Because
of the civil rights movement and the values of the people who were our
parents' generation, we knew, most of us, no matter who we were or what
we did or how high we rose, we didn't achieve what we achieved just
because we were cute or bright. Although cute and bright we may have
been, some of us made it because we stood on the shoulders of giants.
And we understood that we owed great debts to the past and had great
obligations to the future. Kids come along now and don't understand that
struggle. The struggle is not nearly as clear for them, because they have no

memory of segregation; only confusion about hostility as a result of affirmative action. Ultimately, they get their Harvard MBAs, Stanford JDs, or whatever, and a lot of them think, "I got it on my own; I don't owe anybody." That scares me to death. Our generation knew that we owed something to people who were poorer than we were. We knew it, and lots of us, a huge percentage of us, acted on it, lived our lives that way. But I'm afraid that the current generation is much less imbued with that philosophy.

Charles Rangel has been an assistant United States attorney, counsel to the speaker of the New York State Assembly, and counsel to the President's National Advisory Committee on Selective Service. Since 1970, he has served in Congress and is now the ranking Democrat on the House Ways and Means Committee.

Charles Rangel

Q: Do you believe that race relations in this country are worse now than they were five years ago, or is it just that the problems have become more visible?

RANGEL: I have not noticed that they are worse, nor have I seen an improvement.

Q: How would you divide up the responsibility for race relations between the white community and the black community? In other words, to what extent does the black community have a responsibility to work toward better relations? To what extent could the black community be doing more? How could the white community be doing more?

RANGEL: I don't see where the so-called black community can give a high priority to improving the relationship with the white community. I rather think that the black community spends so much of its time just trying to survive from one day to the next, trying to find a decent home, paying the rent, keeping the job, keeping the kids out of trouble, trying to get the kids an education, avoiding being shot, avoiding kids getting on drugs. Survival is the number one priority that black folks have in this country, and most of them can't afford the luxury of attending meetings with people around tables in order to see how we can better understand each other. There has not been an equal relationship between black kids and teachers, black kids and police, black kids and landlords, black kids and the media, black kids and television. And you can strike out "kids" and put in the black community. Trying to improve the relationship is like you climbing in the ring with Mike Tyson. This is not the place for you to wonder how you two can develop a better working relationship.

Q: What is the right priority for the black community?

RANGEL: The right priority is to try to get a strong economic and political anchor in this country, and there is no question in my mind that better racial relationships would follow.

Q: To what extent do you see racism as a barrier to the black community achieving good jobs, good education, the economic and political anchor you're talking about?

RANGEL: Well, you can only reach that point if people are starting off with equal opportunity, and the barrier is that black folks seem caught in an economic and political situation where they don't have the same ladder extended to them that has been extended to other groups. If a guy is an addict and an alcoholic and is homeless and jobless and happens to be black, he can't say that he's not getting a job because he's black. But he has been born under different circumstances and his opportunities are different from someone who was raised in a community where the schools are higher achievers and the community is more supportive and crime is less and the goals that people see and are able aspire to are greater.

Q: How does society facilitate and encourage economic equality?

RANGEL: Well, they are not going to do it because it's the right thing to do. It's abundantly clear that the mush and the flag-waving of Ronald Reagan is far more important to most Americans than paying taxes and redistributing the wealth in such a way that there are schools of equal standards throughout the United States and good housing and good job opportunities. There are not enough people who care about it happening, and that's true whether you're talking about [Secretary of Housing and Urban Development] Sam Pierce or Dan Quayle or George Bush or Ronald Reagan.

It just seems to me that, if you want a productive America, the way this thing is going to happen is that the European Common Market, a united Germany, an expanding economic power like Japan; it's going to force America to review where we've placed our priorities, where we're spending our money. And I guess the answer will come from chief executive officers who find out that spending forty and fifty and sixty thousand dollars a year on some bum in prison is stupid; especially since they're not trained to do anything except become better criminals and avoid the law, and most of them will be returning to jail in three to five years; that our rehabilitation programs don't work because the resources are not there to develop skills for people to take jobs; that we're spending so much of our company profits in taxes to pay for cops and judges, social workers, court attendants, that it's really one of the most unproductive inputs, and there's no productivity that comes out of it in terms of a labor force; and we're just not doing the job in our schools.

Now, whenever business people and capitalists take a look at what is happening with human and capital resources and see that they're not getting anything out of it, it turns the country around. And this is especially so when you can't afford the luxury of hiring and talking only with people who look like you. This is what happened in every war that we've had. There has been a reduction in job discrimination based on the need for manpower. And I see the day coming, if it's not already here, when our economists say that we will not continue to be a world leader in trade as long as we're losing in terms of education, high school dropouts, drug addiction, health care, and prisons.

Q: So you think hard times can create a crisis that will force economic equality?

RANGEL: Equality? I don't know. But there's no question in my mind, with the population we have, that we don't have enough money to be able to afford people living off of society as addicts and criminals and inmates and patients; that we will have to redirect our attention to keeping people healthy and away from drugs and crime as a matter of public policy and as a matter of national security.

Q: How bad was Ronald Reagan for black America?

RANGEL: Ronald Reagan was bad for America. Ronald Reagan is a stain on the pages of history. Ronald Reagan was able to dismantle a caring government and make a direct appeal to the worst instincts in America. The greed for lower and lower taxes is an addiction, and once you get used to it, it is very difficult for anyone to tell you that an increase in taxes is good for you and your family. It is difficult, except in times of war, for you to be persuaded that there is a need for additional money for health and education and housing. Ronald Reagan combined lower taxes for some people with a devastating multi-hundred-billion-dollar cut in domestic services and then went on to triple our national debt until now it is more than five times what Ronald Reagan inherited. The third largest budget item is now interest on that debt. Ronald Reagan has been able to do and to lock into place something that Republicans have tried to do since Roosevelt, and that is to get Congress out of the pursuit of happiness for people, and to have people believe that our problems are basically those of local and state governments and charitable organizations and churches, and all we have to do is provide capital by giving tax incentives for the rich and increasing a military force to protect America. So it is one of the meanest periods in the history of the United States. It's very bad. The whole political arena has become so clouded and fuzzy with self-interest. It's difficult for good people to come forward. I don't see the Tip O'Neills, the Hubert Humphreys, the Harry Trumans, the John Kennedys. It is bad, very bad. Anytime you find that Dan Quayle is vice president of the United States, that shows you the level that we're dealing with.

Q: Do you believe that the media in the United States holds black elected officials to a higher standard than white officials?

RANGEL: I believe that reporters reflect America, and that there is a double standard in the United States of America between black and white [in many areas of news coverage].

Q: Mayor Dinkins alluded to this when he talked about crime coverage, particularly in New York City; that the media assigns a higher headline value to white middle-class victims.

RANGEL: There is no question about that, and it is shocking to believe that his statement could be challenged. I mean, the murders, the rapes, the robberies, the muggings, the assaults that take place in poor communities in New York City and around the country hardly get on the police blotter. I guess some people have forgotten that Dinkins comes from that community. But certainly, if we heard on the way home that Mrs. Jones was raped in a park in Brooklyn by some black folks, there would be no monitoring of the trial. The only reason that the Tawana Brawley hoax was successful is because they threw a white guy in there to make it reach the level of excitement that it did.

Q: You made reference to the Tawana Brawley hoax. What effect do you think that had on black-white relations?

RANGEL: I don't think it had any effect at all. The people that were getting the headlines in those stories; maybe some white folks woke up in the morning and said, "Now I'm not going to like any blacks because of them." But those who said that had already prejudged black folks, so I don't really think it had much to do with anything. The real question should be, "How could so many people lack such confidence in the law enforcement of America that they could believe, and in some cases still do believe, that Tawana Brawley was the victim of a rape. You have to look at the fact that, in some of the communities that these people come from, people have not been able to get jobs and they need something to live for and sometimes their cause becomes something that they are fighting against. I don't know why the papers never really talked about that. Tawana Brawley, when you match her with the statistical data in New York, is just another alleged crime.

Q: What is your solution to the drug crisis, since that is one of your fields of expertise?

RANGEL: I truly believe that you have to get at the reasons why people are willing to risk dying in order to feel the pleasures of drugs. Most of the people who have taken that risk feel they have nothing to lose, and that is because society has not given them many alternatives.

Q: What would you say to those who argue in favor of the legalization of heroin, crack, and cocaine?

RANGEL: First of all, I would say that you would find it much more constructive to relieve the pain by providing decent shelter for families, access to education, health care, and other opportunity. Because the more that people have something to lose, the more they are inclined not to do drugs. Also, legalization would be a disaster, because it's clear that the more available drugs and alcohol are, the more people would experiment with them. And as I've said many many times, once you start legalizing drugs, then certainly you have to take into consideration that people will buy them.

Q: What is the most effective way to get across to the populace the message that the primary victims of violent crimes and street crime are black?

RANGEL: Why do we have to get that across to them? Why would they care? Why should we educate whites that blacks are killing blacks? Why is that so important? What we should educate the whites to is that they can't afford the luxury of not providing for decent schools and decent housing. That you can't mistreat people and ignore people and think that their explosions are going to be confined to their own cell or their own alley or their own street. This is what you tell white America and white folks; that the whole lifestyle of the economy is changing because the focus is on jails and law enforcement and it's not really on investing in people. And whenever we try to invest in people, it's a fantastic success.

Q: Do you think that, on balance, the Great Society programs were a success?

RANGEL: Absolutely. No question about it. I use the GI Bill as a classic example of how education has made it possible for better job opportunities, and the expanding of civil rights made many people better able to assume higher responsibility. Unfortunately, many of our would-be community leaders followed the job opportunities and went to other places where they could provide better opportunities for their children than they'd had for themselves, and many of the poorer communities were left barren because we didn't have continuing Great Society programs. All we've got now are kids being raised in welfare hotels and on the streets, where the only successful people they see is some stupid kid with his teeth capped in gold pushing dope and a white cop driving around in a police car.

John Lewis served as chairman of the Student Non-Violent Coordinating Committee (SNCC), director of community organization for the Southern Regional Council, director of Voter Education Project, director of domestic operations for Action Agency, and city councilman at large in Atlanta. Since 1987, he has represented Atlanta's Fifth Congressional District in the United States House of Representatives.

John Lewis

Q: What can we do—and by "we," I mean black and white—to improve race relations in this country and get people working together again?

LEWIS: More than anything else, there is a need for leadership. Leadership at the highest level of government. I think one of the things that the president of the United States can do—hopefully, he will do—is make a commitment in support of the need for us to put the question of race behind us. And not just make a statement, but encourage people throughout the year to do what we can as a nation and as a people to eradicate racism. Encourage business groups, the academic community, the religious community, to conduct programs, seminars, workshops on race relations. I think our young people need to know the distance that has been come, but at the same time the distance that we still must travel. There's still a need for organizations in the black community, the white community, the Jewish community, and others to deal with the whole question of race.

Q: How do you feel about the breakdown of the coalition between blacks and Jews that was so central to the civil rights movement?

LEWIS: I think it's one of those tragedies, really, because during the 1960s there was no better working relationship than the one between blacks and Jews. I say to young people—blacks and young Jewish students and others in Atlanta and around the country—that we have a history of working together and somehow we must rebuild that coalition. In many communities all across this country, you still have a black-Jewish coalition, a black-Jewish dialogue, where there are ongoing efforts by blacks and Jews to work together. To give you an example; Bill Gray from Philadelphia, along with the Jewish community there over the past few years, has organized a group of black and Jewish students who traveled from Philadelphia to Israel for two weeks, and then to West Africa for two weeks. Last year, the same group that went to Israel and West Africa came to Atlanta, and we took them on a tour of the South. They saw some of the rural South. They went to Tuskegee; they went to Montgomery; they went to Selma, in addition to being in Atlanta.

Q: What do you see as the issues that will be the foundation of a new coalition?

LEWIS: Well, I don't see any meaningful changes in the future based simply on race. I just don't see what we might call a civil rights movement similar to the 1960s. I think, if we're going to see major social and economic changes in the years to come, those issues must be issues that affect blacks and whites alike. One of the major issues today affecting the whole country is this large number, millions of young black men, who are growing up, coming into young adulthood with very little formal education, without a sense of purpose, without a sense of direction. The black community, black organizations, cannot handle that problem alone. This is a problem for the total society, white America, the federal government to get involved in. The problems within our large urban centers—drug abuse, gangs, and other anti-social behavior—it's all related. And there must be massive intervention on the part of the national government. It's in our best interest as a democracy. It must not be looked upon as a black problem. I think we've made progress; we've come a distance. But the sad fact is that there is still a terrible distance we must travel. There are just too many people, human beings in America, who have been left out and left behind, that the movement passed by. With all of the changes, with all of the legislative action, the Civil Rights Act of 1964, the Voting Rights Act of 1965, the Fair Housing Act of 1968, the rulings of the Supreme Court; there are just too many lives that have not been greatly impacted. There are still people affected by racism. There are certain places in this country where the conditions are still not much different from 1960 or 1965.

Q: Have we lost ten years under Ronald Reagan and George Bush?

LEWIS: I'm afraid we've lost ten years plus, really. At one time, I thought, as a nation and as a people, that we were ready to take that great leap; we were ready to move much faster. And I think, with the election of Reagan, that movement was arrested. You know, Rosalynn Carter said during the Reagan years that she felt the Reagan administration made people feel comfortable in their homes with their prejudices. And I think that's what happened during those eight years. Despite economic conditions, a president, a leader, a political leader, a major moral leader or social leader can inspire people and bring out the very best in people. Robert Kennedy was able to do that. Martin Luther King, Jr was able to do that. I think often about what this country would have been, and maybe what the world would have been, if Martin Luther King, Jr and Robert Kennedy had lived; what type of life we would have today. I think we would be much further down the road toward a society free of the disease of racism and violence; that we would have less poverty, a greater sense of community, a greater sense of family. There would be a greater sense of purpose, a greater sense of direction within the American community. We all lost something in the loss of Robert Kennedy and Martin Luther King, Jr Some of that hope, some of the optimism—a great deal of that hope, I should say; and a great deal of that optimism—died with them. And we have not been able to renew much of that hope and optimism.

Q: If Dr. King were alive today, what do you think he would be doing and saying?

LEWIS: I think he would be speaking out against the violence in our inner cities. He'd be leading the campaign against drugs. He would be calling upon the nation to lay down the tools and instruments of war and violence. And he probably would still be saying that we need to spend billions of dollars on something like a domestic freedom budget; a domestic Marshall Plan to rebuild American cities.

Q: Are drugs and inner city violence a greater threat to black Americans today than racism?

LEWIS: Oh, yeah. I said a few days ago, when I was leading a group of about two hundred young black men through a housing project here, that I felt the epidemic of drugs and the proliferation of violence related to drugs was probably the greatest threat to the black community since the days of slavery. We found a way to fight segregation and race discrimination. It took a lot of time and a lot of effort and a lot of legal work, but we were able to use our bodies as living witness against this system of segregation and racial discrimination. How do you organize and mobilize a community to say that we want the drugs out and to teach people, educate people, that this is not the way, that there is a better way.

Q: Would Dr. King, if he were here today, be focusing his energies in the North or in the South, in the cities or in rural areas? Where would his priorities be?

LEWIS: I think, if Dr. King was alive today, he would be spending a great deal of his time appealing to people in the large urban centers in both the North and the South, but especially in the North. You know, today there is a sense among black Americans that, in places like Atlanta and maybe even in parts of Alabama and Mississippi, the opportunities for blacks may be greater than in the North. So you have this unbelievable migration of young professional blacks from the North to the South. So I think that Dr. King would be trying to find a way to give people a sense of hope and greater opportunity in those places where people are leaving from.

Q: Could you comment generally on the link between crime and racism. Which is the chicken and which is the egg; or do they feed off each other?

LEWIS: That's a hard one. I think, if people are forced to live under certain conditions, and if it's racism that created the conditions, it helps breed violence and crime. Just the way we build our cities, when we cut people off from one another and isolate so many people in these unbelievable housing projects; where we ghettoize people and pile people on top of people; whether we are conscious of it or not, whether it is a racist decision or not; many of the situations in which people find themselves sap all of their human energy and their sense of optimism. It breeds despair and it breeds conditions that give way to violence and crime.

Q: What particular pieces of legislation do you think would make a difference?

LEWIS: I think we need a massive job training effort. I was very hopeful, with the cold war being over and behind us, that we would be able to reach some type of budget agreement on deficit reduction and start spending billions of dollars, taking money out of the highway trust fund, out of the airport trust fund, where we have billions of dollars, and build up what we call an infrastructure trust fund to generate jobs and economic development across the country. It could train millions of American citizens, especially young men, to start rebuilding America; our highways, our sewage systems, our waterways. During the eight years of the Reagan administration and so far during the Bush administration, we've heard very little if anything, except from [Secretary of Housing and Urban Development] Jack Kemp, about urban America. And urban America is literally, it's like it's dying on the vine. The cities are rotting. They're dying, and we're talking about spending five hundred billion dollars or more to bail out the S&Ls [savings and loan associations]. But we need to be spending billions and billions of dollars to bail out the people who are trapped in our large urban centers. I think—I really believe this—I think that Martin Luther King Jr and the civil rights movement saved America, at least the southern part of America, from becoming like Northern Ireland or Lebanon. And we've made progress. I've said over and over during the past few years, we have witnessed what I like to call a non-violent revolution, especially in the South. But it doesn't mean that we cannot and will not go through another period of social upheaval and social conflict.

Q: To what extent do you see racism in America today as a barrier to progress?

LEWIS: Racism is still a barrier. Despite all of the progress we've made, the scars and the stains of racism are still deeply imbedded in almost every corner, in almost every segment of American society. Race affects almost everything we do. Whether a person moves up in an organization, whether a businessman is successful or not; it can be based on race. Whether a particular school system or school district gets money, computers in their classrooms, and other resources that are needed to enhance the quality of education; I think it's based on race.

Q: Are there other societies that you think have dealt with the issues of race more successfully than we have?

LEWIS: No, not at all. See, I think we're so different. I think we have to travel down this road by ourselves, really. We are involved in an experiment in America. We have to make it work; I believe that we can make it work; and it must work. There may be some setbacks; there may be some interruptions, disappointments here and there. But you know, we're on that long march; we're on that road. We're traveling down that road toward a society based on equality and equal opportunity. We're on our way toward the building of a loving community; that open society, that interracial democracy. We may slow down and walk and sort of march in place, but I think we're on our way. There are going to be different forces rising up from time to time, trying to slow down that effort or interfere with that effort. But as a nation and as a people, there won't be any turning back.

Jesse Jackson served as executive director of Operation Breadbasket, president of Operation Push, and president of the National Rainbow Coalition. As a candidate for the 1984 Democratic presidential nomination, he won 3.5 million primary and caucus votes and 465.5 convention delegates. Four years later, he was a candidate again, gathering 7 million primary and caucus votes and 1,218.5 convention delegates.

Jesse Jackson

Q: To what extent, if any, do you feel that black Americans have contributed to the climate of racial hostility that exists today?

JACKSON: Let me first say that blacks are inheriting a backlash. This generation is receiving the backlash from the last generation's progress. The cycle is this. 1865, the Emancipation Proclamation. Then Reconstruction, which amounted to the affirmative action plan of that period. Eight black Congressmen were elected in South Carolina; a black governor was elected in Louisiana. Then came the reaction to the Emancipation Proclamation. The position was the Emancipation Proclamation was not a vote; the president decreed it. If we'd voted, slavery would never have stopped. By 1890, the thing had swung so far back that, in the civil rights debate of 1896, you had *Plessy versus Ferguson*, the apartheid decision. We went from slavery to apartheid in thirty-one years. Then 1965, the Voting Rights Act. Lyndon Johnson said when he signed it that perhaps it lost the South for twenty-five years. The racist whites said, if we had voted on the Voting Rights Act, it wouldn't have been granted, but them Kennedys and them Johnsons and them Warrens, the Supreme Court, they took advantage of us. Reagan played on the same thing that happened a century ago. By 1990, the civil rights debate saw the president vetoing the Civil Rights Act, and calling de Klerk [F.W. de Klerk, South Africa's last apartheid-era president] and [Nelson] Mandela moral equivalents. There's a cycle here, and many blacks are reacting to the backlash of white intolerance.

Q: Let's rephrase the question. Do you feel that black Americans have in any respect contributed to this climate of racial antagonism that exists today, or is it entirely the responsibility of white America?

JACKSON: Well, one can argue that the high level of killing in places like Washington DC, Chicago, and Los Angeles is secondary racism. That self-hatred has been ingrained so deeply that this is racism. And one cannot for a moment justify that kind of violent and self-destructive thing. All of us have ethical responsibilities. And the extent to which blacks or browns or anybody limits their moral authority to become morally equivalent with decadence, that's not good. That's why comparing yourself to the worst of your oppressors' behavior is never a good trade-off, because one authority that the oppressed must never give up is their moral authority because ultimately right is might.

Q: Can you meditate on the political dynamic between black crime and white racism, which is now becoming a problem for Mayor David Dinkins in New York and in different places around the country as a barrier to the Rainbow Coalition. And how do you deal with it politically?

JACKSON: Number one, there is a double standard in the judicial system between the haves and have-nots generally. Thousands of poor people— black, brown, white, and female—who don't have money for court, who are not released on personal recognizance, are in jail waiting for trial, learning the ropes of criminal culture. They're being criminalized in the process. You might call them political prisoners, because they are prod- ucts of the politics of poverty. And then look at people with money who have committed far greater crimes, able to buy time and eventually never go to jail. There are more whites on drugs than blacks, but blacks spend more time in jail for it. A kid was shot in the back in Teaneck, New Jersey. And the police, on payroll with their uniforms on; not wearing Klan robes and hoods where they hid their faces, but in police uniforms showing their faces, rallied. At the rally, they were selling T-shirts from police headquarters—"He had a gun." That's an ominous sign of racial violence. When the four kids were shot in the subway [by Bernhard Goetz] and people like Joan Rivers on the Johnny Carson show wanted to fly to New York to stand up for Goetz; do you recall that? Just hysteria, hysteria, hysteria. And of course, there is the killing [of a young black man] in Howard Beach. These overt acts of violence and the lack of justice against the perpetrators is a source of great pain.

Q: You've mentioned cases in New Jersey and New York, which are one side of the racial coin. Those cases justifiably outraged the black community. But the other side of the coin is the Central Park Jogger case [where a white woman was brutally beaten and raped] and the high-school girls who were going around sticking pins in white women on Broadway. And certainly, in the Central Park Jogger case, there was a wave of white outrage that was accentuated when people such as Al Sharpton started suggesting that the woman had actually gone to the park seeking drugs and sex and maybe her boyfriend had beaten her. How do you feel about that?

JACKSON: I feel that we must never try to defend the indefensible. Raping people is wrong, whoever does the raping. But they must be tried in court, not in the media. My bottom-line point is that we can never justify unethical behavior or use ethnicity to cover up ethics. But we do know that whites have the institutional strength with which to make a stronger case when their rights are violated. It is a source of hurt to us, really, when we look at the number of our youth in jail for stealing cars compared with the S&L [savings and loan] thieves who are still walking the streets. I mean, people do make these correlations.

Q: You have indicated in the past, and I think appropriately so, that it's wrong for a person to vote against a candidate simply because he's black. What about the phenomena of people voting for a candidate, such as yourself or David Dinkins or Doug Wilder, because he is black. Is that also a form of racism?

JACKSON: No. Racism is a set of beliefs that one group is inherently superior, usually chosen or ordained by some deity or some master race. Some superior race theory. Racism is a belief that another group is inherently inferior; that the inherently superior group has the right to the first and the best of everything. The out-group gets the worst and the last of things. The logical conclusion of that is the glorification of the in-group and the elimination of the out-group. And it follows into you should not marry the inferior race or work on the same job with the same opportunities as the inferior race. It runs all down the line.

Many whites have had inherent racial fears bred into them deeply about black people; starting with our Constitution. When the founding fathers looked at African descendants and asked how should we handle them, they concluded that we were less than people and more than animals; three-fifths of a human. That three-fifths of a human definition lasted as a matter of law for many years, and then was replaced by one hundred years of apartheid. Now you look at our income and life options. The three-fifths ratio has not been altered measurably. It is deeply embedded into our culture. So if blacks react to whites out of fear that they will not be fair or cannot be trusted, there is a material basis for that fear and a justifiable pride in blacks who stand up. If Doug Wilder represents that breakthrough, if [Seattle mayor] Norm Rice or Jesse Jackson represents that breakthrough, then the black wave of support is for someone around whom they can build security.

Historically, we've had no security options; only this lesser of two evils thought, when neither candidate would campaign for black support, but we had the right to vote. Republicans write us off, Democrats take us for granted. We have no options. And that's different from believing that another group is inferior and undeserving. Blacks vote for white governors, white senators, white presidents, white judges, all the time. When whites vote 40 percent for Doug Wilder, it's like something has happened to him. No, something happened to them. You get my point? The expectation that whites will support blacks is extraordinarily low. The expectation that blacks will support whites is extraordinarily high. Even that's a racist assumption.

So I would like to think that blacks voted for me because, when we were living under the laws of apartheid, I went to jail to break up the laws of apartheid. And if you benefited from that, then I have earned your support. No one else can match that. I marched for the right to vote, and now that you have it, I've earned access to it. Who can match my record on that? I have fought corporations for racial justice and general equality and led boycotts to make them be fair. Who else can match that? I represent a chance for your children to have a breakthrough to make America better. Who can match that? So it is an affirmative thrust. Then I would say to whites, if our farmers want fair prices and our workers want fair wages, who has stood with you at the farm auction, at the plant gate? And although there may be a conflict in culture and race, when they take away your urban job, not from black to white, but from America to Taiwan where all the tennis shoes are made, when they close your family farm and the corporate barracudas beat up on family farmers, when they pull the plug on you and the lights go out; all of you, black and white, look amazingly similar in the dark.

Q: You've said in the past that the mind of America was becoming more integrated; that you got seven million votes in 1988, and that was double what you got in 1984. Do you see that as meaning race relations are getting better in America?

JACKSON: It's a tale of two colors. Some aspects of American life are the most multi-racial and multi-cultural that they've ever been. Some aspects of American life are retreating to fear and hatred and violence. So you can't use one set of numbers to define the trend. Racial injustice is a source of real division, and it's compounded by three things: One, people tend to be more generous when they feel that they are rising and less generous when they think they're sinking. This is the first generation of whites ever who are projected to be less well-off than their parents. There's a sense of material sinking, and with that sense of material sinking, people are less generous, more anxious, more hostile, more defensive, and they feel that the out-group is a threat to them or taking something from them, and so the economic crisis is a factor in the racial tension.

Combine that with reason number two; the fact that we live in a multi-cultural society with virtually no multi-cultural preparation in our school system. We don't even learn how to live with people who have a different language and culture. What does it matter if you give someone an airplane for a gift and give them no aeronautical training? What does it matter to have the gift of a multi-cultural society and no training in multi-cultural education? That's the second thing, this lack of education. I went to Bensonhurst and talked to youth about how half of all human beings are Asian and half of those are Chinese; that we're just one-third of our hemisphere; that two-thirds of our neighbors speak Spanish or Portuguese; that we are 6 percent of the whole world. When Gorbachev and Bush meet, they represent only one-eighth of the human race; that's a minority meeting. That there are more people in India than in the United States and the Soviet Union combined by 200 million. That most people in the world are yellow, brown, black, non-Christian, poor, and don't speak English. You could just see them coming alive. Our children are not taught that. And the media plays a role in this. Blacks are projected in five very deadly ways every day. We're projected as less intelligent than we are, less hard-working than we are, more violent than we are, less universal than we are, and less patriotic than we are. A substantial number, probably 50 percent, of our ground soldiers in Saudi Arabia are black or brown; willing to die for our country. That side of our story is never projected. That's an injustice, and therefore a source of the tension.

The third big reason is that we've received some very definite race-conscious political signals from the White House in the last ten years. Reagan ran a very race-conscious campaign. Use of the welfare queen, this black woman who's not going to work who is going to create a budget deficit for us. You reduce the budget deficit fears to the welfare claims. Then he implied that Dr. King was a communist, but that we would not know until twenty-five years later. He opened his campaign up in Philadelphia, Mississippi. Most people conveniently forgot that. There's not even a railroad there. It's only known because Schwerner, Goodman, and Chaney were killed there. And when he gave his speech there that day, the Klan endorsed him. I met him in my office on August 5 of that year and challenged him on that point, and he denounced any association with the Klan. That was a month after he made that speech in Philadelphia, Mississippi. So the president went from Philadelphia, Mississippi, to laying a wreath at Bittburg, to no resistance to Johannesburg in a straight ideological line. We lived under that for eight years. Then Bush succeeds him with [a racially charged campaign commercial featuring] Willie Horton, a venture with South Africa in Angola, invading Grenada, and invading Panama.

So really, the last ten years we've had a very low level of commitment to racial justice and equality coming from the top of our nation. When this guy David Duke ran for senator in Louisiana, the Republicans ran to publicly distance themselves from him. Oh, this guy's reputation embarrasses us. But run a test on the Republican national chairman, the Republican president, the Republican vice president, and David Duke. Remove all names, and just start asking questions. Where do you stand on the joint venture with South Africa in Angola? Where do you stand on Grenada? Where do you stand on invading Panama? Where do you stand on affirmative action? Where do you stand on African studies in our schools? My point is, if you do this like when you're in college and they give an exam and all the grader has is your ID number, not your name, because they want to be fair; look at where Duke stands. When the 1990 civil rights bill was being debated and Ted Kennedy brought it to a vote, the senator from Utah, Orrin Hatch, and Robert Dole hit the floor screaming at the top of their voices, "Unfair, unfair! You're taking advantage of white men." David Duke would have done no less. Bush vetoed the 1990 Civil Rights Act. David Duke would have vetoed it too. Bush and Willie Horton; it's David Duke. Just remove the names and all the photo op sound bites; just get ten critical civil rights positions. Remove the names and put president, David Duke, Dan Quayle, whoever else, and just lay them up there. Don't call no names, don't make any value judgments, just look at them. That leadership is casting a shadow of fear, rather than a light of hope, across our country.

I heard from a fairly reliable news person that the date of the sting on Marion Barry was set for January 15th [Martin Luther King, Jr's birthday], but that several blacks who were involved argued against it because it was symbolically such a sinister thing to do. And we do know that the recommendation from [Attorney General] Dick Thornburgh's office to veto the 1990 Civil Rights Act came on April 4; the anniversary of Dr. King's assassination. That's like hitting us in the heart.

Q: Do you believe there's a plot to target black political leaders for criminal prosecution?

JACKSON: Well, there are about forty indictments of black leaders right now in Alabama. What we won at the ballot box, we've started losing at the jury box. Dave Dinkins won in New York, and his opposition decided that they would beat him at the jury box. It took Dave a quarter of a million dollars to stop an investigation; a quarter of a million dollars. Look at all the indictments. [Philadelphia mayor] Wilson Goode, no conviction. [Newark mayor] Ken Gibson, no conviction. [Detroit mayor] Coleman Young, lots of indictments, no conviction. [Pennsylvania congressman] Bill Gray is on the rise. Move in on him on Labor Day weekend, looking for a ghost payroll. Couldn't find it; that didn't work, and they started an IRS investigation retroactive eight years. The Barry trial inherited some of this atmosphere, this environment; these broad sweeping investigations, indictments, seldom convictions, but almost always great disruption. And it didn't just start. Try Marcus Garvey, mass organizer, IRS. Try Paul Robeson. Try Martin Luther King Jr IRS, that didn't work. Sex charges, FBI sending tapes to his family, and the FBI memo saying their role was to disrupt, discredit, and destroy black leadership. My point is that there is a material basis for racial fears among blacks being hurt by whites at the highest level. Willie Brown said in a forum two weeks ago; he said, "I'm Speaker of the House, I'm the most powerful politician in the state of California, and I can't take it too seriously, because every day I wake up, I fear they decided to get me last night. Everyday I wake up." Me too.

Sterling Johnson is a former New York City police detective, who served as executive director of the city's Civilian Complaint Review Board and later as executive liaison officer for the federal Drug Enforcement Administration in Washington, DC. In 1975, he was appointed special narcotics prosecutor for the City of New York, with jurisdiction over the investigation and prosecution of felony narcotics offenses committed within the five boroughs of New York. Subsequent to our interviewing him, he became a federal judge.

Sterling Johnson

Q: Why has the drug problem ravished the black community in this country more than the white community?

JOHNSON: First of all, we don't know if that's true. That is the perception, but is it correct? I don't know, because I don't know how deep the problem is. I don't know how many doctors are taking drugs, although there are a lot of drugs in the medical profession. How many airline pilots? How many people on Wall Street? These people are not visible, but we know for a fact that the users of drugs are about 70 percent white. The drug industry, the illegal drug industry, is about 150 billion dollars a year. And minorities don't generate that type of income to sustain it. Most of the people who are using drugs are people who are employed, and some people term them "casual users." These are your male whites, your female whites. The other 30 percent are your minorities, blacks and Hispanics, and they are so visible because they're out on the street corner. They rob and mug and, when they do that, it makes headlines. But the person who has a drug problem and is a physician; you never hear about him. The guy who works in a brokerage house and embezzles to support his habit doesn't make the headlines. Also, many members of the black community have no hope of getting out of poverty. They can't make a decent dollar because they don't have the background. And if they do have the background, maybe racism prohibits them from getting ahead. So you tell a person to go to McDonald's and turn over hamburgers for four or five dollars an hour, when they see someone else making a thousand dollars a day by working as a look-out on the street.

Q: Do they really make that kind of money?

JOHNSON: Oh, yes. I recall in the 1970s, before we had the problem as bad as we have it now and the main drug was heroin; one guy told me that he was selling one hundred thousand dollars a day on one block in Harlem.

Q: One hundred thousand dollars?

JOHNSON: One hundred thousand dollars. And there was very little overhead. One hundred thousand dollars a day. So yes, they make money. There was a time when they made so much money, this was before you had the money-counting machines, that they didn't count the money. They weighed it. It was an old adage that, if you had twenty-two pounds of hundred-dollar bills, you had a million dollars. The scale might be off a little, but so what. You just kept counting and counting.

Q: Do you think that drugs are as great a barrier to black progress in this country as racism?

JOHNSON: I think that in some respects maybe even more of a problem. There is racism in this society. But you can have a young kid in Harlem. He's in his own community, in his own little world, and he really doesn't experience racism. It's all around him, but he doesn't really experience racism; and if he does, he doesn't know what it is. But he goes out on the street and sees the other kids selling drugs, taking drugs. He experiences that particular phenomenon. Racism in America might prevent a black American from advancing to a certain level. Drugs in America, in a community, not only will not let him advance at all, but will tear that community and his family down. Both are evil, but I think that drugs are more evil.

Q: Is the drug problem out of control?

JOHNSON: I personally think it is. It definitely is not under control. We can't provide treatment on demand. There's no education. Law enforcement is totally underfunded. America has 6 percent, or one-sixteenth, of the world's population and we consume 60 to 70 percent of all the illegal drugs. We consume more illegal drugs than anybody else in the world. I would have to say, yes, it's out of control.

Q: Do you think the drug problem will get worse?

JOHNSON: Unfortunately, I do. It exploded around 1985. The ratio used to be, 80 percent of the drug abusers were male and 20 percent were women. Now it's 50-50. In 1985, many of these young women started using crack. They became pregnant; they gave birth. This September, these kids are going to be five years of age and entering our public schools. What are we going to do with these kids? We don't know how to handle these kids. There's a new drug called ice. It's all over the west coast now. There's a bumper crop of heroin in the heroin producing areas, southeast and southwest Asia, that's going to be making inroads in New York City and the rest of the country.

Q: Can it be brought under control?

JOHNSON: I hope so. If it's not, I hate to think what this country is going to be like. Because they say that, by the year 2000, the minorities in New York will be the majority in New York. They're going to be coming into the job market. They're going to be our future leaders. They're going to be your mayors, your city council people. They're going to be on Wall Street. They're going to be your airline pilots. And if a substantial percentage of the population that's going to be in these key positions are drug addicts, I'd hate to be around at that time.

Q: What is the role of law enforcement in combatting the problem?

JOHNSON: Law enforcement is a discipline that is utilized when all other disciplines in this drugs business have failed. When treatment has failed, when religion has failed, the family, the community; then they come to law enforcement and say, "Hey, you take over for these other disciplines that haven't worked." I've been in law enforcement for over thirty years. We need law enforcement, but as far as drugs are concerned, it's not the only answer. I think you need more treatment, prevention, education. And until we get serious about the drug problem and address these other disciplines, we're always going to have a drug problem. We can't attack this problem on a single-faceted level. It's got to be done all at one time, like the moving parts of an automobile. Treatment, prevention, education, and law enforcement. We need law enforcement. Yes, concentrate on law enforcement. But these other disciplines, you have to do that also.

Q: We obviously need better education; we need better treatment programs. Do we also need more jails?

JOHNSON: Yes; you need more jails, because you've got to have enforcement. You're going to have to put people in jail. As long as there is a demand, there's going to be people supplying that demand, and you're going to have to arrest people, and you're going to have to have more jails. But I think the key to it comes at the beginning; to stop people from using drugs. You must have education, and you should start when you start picking that young child up and you're talking to them about love and everything. Talk to them about drugs. Because I firmly believe as a law enforcement official, if we stopped every ounce of drugs aimed for these shores today, tomorrow we'd still have a drug problem, and that's because of America's insatiable appetite for drugs. If you stopped all of these drugs, you'd have some entrepreneur who would make a synthetic drug, and they can make these synthetic drugs now. As I said before, I'm an enforcement official, but I preach education, treatment, and prevention.

Q: Should the military become involved in fighting drugs, intervening shipments?

JOHNSON: I think the military should become more involved. You've got a resource here, and we're not using it. But I think the key to it is not so much interdiction, because drug smugglers are limited only by their imagination. For instance, they swallow these balloons. People can swallow a hundred balloons, and have a kilo-and-a-half of drugs in them. What's this thing that they have in hospitals that will go through the body? What do you call it? Not sonogram, but they can look and they can see these little balloons. Then they sit you down and put you in a room and wait until you're ready to defecate and the balloons come out and they arrest you. But like I say, they're limited only by their imagination. They now have balloons that you can't detect with this x-ray machine. I call them the first stealth condoms. So going back to the role of the military, I just got back from the Pentagon. One of the things they're doing is they have some equipment that might be available to local law enforcement. Audio surveillance equipment, visual surveillance equipment. One of the problems that law enforcement complains about in a lot of major cities is a communications problem. You go underground in the subway, and you can't use your walkie-talkie to the guy above ground. One of the things that they can do is to put a satellite up here for the northeast corridor and let us use these satellites. So can the military get more involved? Absolutely.

Q: How serious is the problem of marijuana use in this country as opposed to crack or cocaine or heroin? My impression is that most of the recreational drug use in this country is marijuana, and many people draw a distinction.

JOHNSON: I take the position that there is no such thing as a recreational drug. Right now, other drugs are so serious that we don't have time to devote to marijuana. The marijuana cases that we have are cases where a person is arrested for robbery and has marijuana, so he's charged with the robbery and possession of marijuana. We don't have the resources to go out and investigate and prosecute marijuana cases. The other problem we have is that, in New York state, marijuana is a Class D felony. That means you can get up to seven years in prison, but you can also get probation. So why waste all of your enforcement energies prosecuting a case like that when you can spend it getting someone who's doing heroin, crack, or cocaine.

Q: What impact would the legalization of marijuana have on the drug problem?

JOHNSON: Devastating. What message would you be sending to young people when you talk about, "Say no to drugs, but you can use marijuana." And if you're going to legalize marijuana, then why shouldn't a country like Colombia or Peru or Bolivia legalize cocaine? And another country legalize heroin? I think the big thing is abstinence from all drugs.

Q: How do you feel about the prosecution of crack-addicted mothers who give birth to crack babies?

JOHNSON: It's a difficult question, and I personally think that, if it were me, I wouldn't do it. Because you know, one of the purposes of doing this is to protect the welfare of the child. But if that mother were to say, "I want treatment; I don't want to take crack; I don't want to give my baby, who is in my body, this crack," there's no treatment on demand. They can't get treatment. Should you prosecute a case like that? I personally don't think so. We also have a problem with mothers and alcohol. Same problem, different drug. She's an alcoholic; she's sick. Would we prosecute that mother because the baby is exposed to alcohol as a fetus? We don't do that. So I don't think that I would do it.

Q: How do you feel about sports figures who have gone through rehab and come out okay. Do you think they're good role models for youngsters?

JOHNSON: Well, first of all, I really sympathize with anyone who does have a drug problem. It's a tragedy. But for people to go into these programs for thirty days, I don't think that's enough. Do you know David Stern, the basketball commissioner? One of the things they do in the NBA—and I assist them in doing it—is they bring their rookies into an orientation program. These are young kids right out of college. Most of them never graduated, and now they're millionaires or multi-millionaires. They're taught how to handle the press. They're taught how to select someone who is going to invest their money. They're taught the danger of associating with females who might lead them astray. They're also taught the evils of drugs through education programs. I assist them in doing this. We need more of that as far as sports and entertainers. The other sports don't have that type of program, and I think they should.

These athletes don't know the impact they can have as role models on young people.

Q: How do you feel about the pro-drug messages that are in some of the rap music?

JOHNSON: I'm a music lover. I love all music. I do not like rap music. First of all, I don't understand it. And I think this is a case of people who call themselves entertainers but they're just making money. If I was a black entertainer myself and I had an opportunity to make a record, I would not make a record that sent a message saying use drugs. I would not do it, because I would owe it to my brothers and sisters to stay away from it.

Q: How serious a factor are these videos and records in drug consumption?

JOHNSON: We've got a lot of kids who don't read and write, but they do watch television and listen to music. You ask them where Kuwait is, and they couldn't tell you. But if you ask them—and I can't understand a word; they talk so damn fast—what did this damn rap thing say, they can give it to you word by word. So it's very important. Go down the street and you see the kids with those loud things going, blasting the eardrums. Sure, there's a cause and effect. But this didn't start with rap music. The Beatles went, hey, it's all right to get a little high here, a little high there. And then, one day, you don't have a problem; the problem has you.

Arthur Ashe rose to prominence as the first black superstar in men's ten-
nis, capturing the men's singles championship at the United States Open
in 1968 and at Wimbledon in 1975. Later, he authored A Hard Road
to Glory *(a three-volume history of the African American athlete) and*
served as president of Artists and Athletes against Apartheid.

Arthur Ashe

Q: How important do you feel sports have been and continue to be in
breaking down racial barriers and combating racism in this country?

ASHE: I think the importance of it has varied according to geography,
which section of the country you're in. It has varied according to how
well society in a particular place has reacted to integration. It varies with
educational attainment. And I think it varies with the assertiveness of the
athletes themselves. My best example is in the South. *Brown vs. Board of*
Education, the Supreme Court decision, was rendered in April of 1954. I
was eleven years old, in Baker Elementary School, and I remember hearing the scuttlebutt, "Oh, my goodness; in September, five months from
now, we're going to be going to school with white kids." And it never
happened. The point I'm making is, to the extent that you could find
some vehicle for socialization to ease the integration process in the South,
no question, sports was important. Extremely important, because it was
the one place in the South—in public gatherings at high-school stadiums,
college stadiums, or wherever—where once things started, you really
didn't care who was sitting next to you. You might care who your daughter or son married, or who was in church next to you, or at your club. But
in the stadium, you didn't care who sat next to you.

Q: It has been said that Sam Cunningham [who scored four touchdowns
in one game for USC against the University of Alabama] did more for
integration in Alabama than anyone.

ASHE: No question about it. It was that famous football day at the
University of Alabama in 1970. USC had an all-black backfield; and obvi-

ously, Alabama had an all-white team. And USC ran all over Alabama. Bear Bryant just sort of, I think his quote was, "Well, I guess we'd better start recruiting some of those colored boys." Yeah, that was a big day.

Q: What is the state of major sports in America today? What more should they be doing in racial areas?

ASHE: Well, I definitely think they should be trying to recruit more minorities into positions other than athletes on the field. We now have some black owners of a professional franchise, the Denver Nuggets. I think baseball has a lot of unrealized potential in the black community that it lost some years ago. As I understand it, even by baseball's own estimate, only about eight percent of the fans at baseball games are black. That could be a lot higher if they marketed it correctly. It's still the national pastime. People will still, under the right conditions, go out and watch it. But you can't take it for granted that they're going to show up just because their teams are doing well. I also would like to see more—although we're start-ing to see more—minority faces among the television sports commenta-tors, both anchors and analysts. I think the biggest thing they could do is put in place a mechanism or a process whereby a lot of the present athletes are counseled in making that transition from professional athlete to civilian. There are a lot of black athletes who made a lot of money in the past, who retired, who are now broke. We're talking broke. Their marriages, if they had any, are busted up. Some of them are on drugs or they're alcoholics, and there needs to be a lot of things done in that area, where they come in and learn to live in a manner that can be sustained. The San Francisco 49ers are doing this. Harry Edwards works with the 49ers. I think he's also working with the Giants and the Warriors. And they think that's one of the reasons why the 49ers win; because they work at cultural harmony on that team. People really pull for one another. It's not just because they've got Joe Montana and Jerry Rice and Ronnie Lott and Roger Craig.

Q: What sort of moral obligation do you think today's African American athletes have?

ASHE: That's the central question. I believe they have a moral obligation to assist, and don't just assist blacks. It's a play off the adage, "From those to whom much has been given, much is expected." And if you're already doing that well, there is definitely a role that you can play to help the situation. If you don't do it, I think that's a serious omission. It doesn't require much sacrifice on your part because, let's face it, most of the things that athletes do are symbolic. They show up at this, and they go to that hospital, and they're signing autographs. It's like Dwight Gooden and this kid who was burned up and spent all that time in the hospital. His idol was Dwight Gooden. Dwight Gooden spent a couple of hours with him at the hospital. But it's not as if Dwight Gooden is spending five hours a week on some project where he's really immersing himself. He's not doing that. Very few of them are doing that, even though they can certainly afford it. The athletes today, really very few of them, seem to have a moral or historical consciousness about how they got to where they are.

The most famous statement—I'm sure you read it—that is bandied about now is the one that Vince Coleman made about three years ago. It was on the heels of the Al Campanis statement [about blacks "lacking the necessities" to be Major League managers]. Major League Baseball was celebrating Jackie Robinson's fortieth anniversary, and Vince Coleman was asked, "What did Jackie Robinson mean to you?" And Vince Coleman's answer was, "I don't know nothing about no Jackie Robinson." It was said in a way that meant don't bother me; that stuff doesn't even matter to me; I could care less who Jackie Robinson was. It was almost like, all I care about is doing as well as I can so I can make as much money as I can. And I say it has gone too far. I mean, it's okay to be an individualist if you're responsible. But some of these athletes, black athletes, don't want to be role models. They are loath to speak up about social issues. It's like pulling teeth to get them to show up at some political function or fundraiser. I'm not saying that it's true of all of them, but it's very difficult. You would not have had to do that with Jackie Robinson, or even Wilt Chamberlain or Jim Brown, who has been very outspoken on a lot of things. Of course, Muhammad Ali was like that. You had the black Olympians; John Carlos and Tommie Smith in 1968 in Mexico City. This generation just seems to be out for themselves, although obviously there are some exceptions.

Q: If Joe Louis, Muhammad Ali, Jackie Robinson, Arthur Ashe, Jim Brown, and Althea Gibson had never come along, how different would American society be today?

ASHE: It would certainly be different. I think white society really would not have known the true limits of expression in some endeavors; because we've literally, especially with the major sports, changed the very way those sports were played. I mean, we changed the orthodox approach to offense and defense completely when we were allowed to play. Up until World War II, we were really only allowed to go as far as we wanted to in boxing and track and field. And even in boxing, there were qualifications for the heavyweight title. Jack Johnson, of course, won the title in 1908 and lost it in 1915, and it was 1937 before another African American fought for it. But in that five-year period right after World War II when we started to enter football, basketball, and baseball, we changed those sports completely. I mean, we literally just took the standard orthodox way of coaching and devising strategy for those games and said, hey look, those things are obsolete; throw them in the trash can, because you haven't been playing them right all along. We literally changed them, basically through speed and a bit more daring and creativity. Before Bill Russell, nobody blocked shots in basketball. Nobody got up in your face and just swatted it away. And of course, Jim Brown did what Jim Brown did on the football field. Within five years, we dominated the stolen-base category in baseball; and even though that's just one category, it changed the way you scored runs on a baseball diamond. Julius Erving, Connie Hawkins. You had to write the strategy books all over again. Sports have given white Americans a reason to cheer for us. We don't have a counterpart to Lee Iacocca. We have Thurgood Marshall; but we don't have a George Bush; we don't have a Henry Kissinger; we don't have a J. P. Morgan. Our heroes across the board, the people who are well- known, are entertainers and athletes and the odd soldier.

Q: Why is it that black Americans have come to so dominate basketball, football, and some other sports?

ASHE: There are loads of role models. There's a lot of money to be made, both relatively and in absolute terms. The major team sports are also the sports stressed in the public-school systems, where 97 percent of all black students go to school. So the facilities, the coaching, and the competition are right there. The relative cost of some other sports makes them almost prohibitive, but the major team sports don't cost you a dime. Also, we have a cultural proprietary interest in some of those sports now. We've come to think of some sports and some positions in sports as ours. If you're a cornerback or wide receiver or running back in football, those are black positions. If you're white, you've got to be damn good to get one of those spots. In fact, I think the most damaging, probably the saddest commentary on how our society has twisted its interpretation of events is that now, within the last fifteen to twenty years, there are literally thousands of white coaches telling their young white athletes that there are some positions that they can't even buy. Don't even bother trying to do this, because blacks are better. Whites don't even try for sprint positions on high-school teams; they don't even try. Or if you want to play football; look, you've got to be a lineman. You can't be a safety. Maybe you can be a linebacker. Maybe you can be a quarterback. But a running back, cornerback, wide receiver, safety; forget it. Basketball, forget it. You want to try out for the US Olympic team; if it's a sprint event or jumping event, forget it. Try the half-mile or the mile or the ten thousand meters. There are a lot of people who believe that, and that's sad. Statistically, it makes absolutely no sense that, in a country the size of ours, where black people are 11 percent of the population, that we get all of our sprinters from 11 percent of the population. Statistically it makes absolutely no sense to me, but it happens.

Q: What are the barriers that still exist in sports, such as black ownership of franchises or black general managers?

ASHE: Those are not barriers. I think the barriers are more psychological than real now. I really do. The other day, we were sitting around putting on a piece of paper the names of black Americans who could put $10 million on the table and, if they lost it, wouldn't blink, wouldn't bat an eye. That is, they could afford to. Bill Cosby, Eddie Murphy, Whitney Houston, Oprah Winfrey, Reggie Louis who runs Beatrice Foods, John Johnson of Johnson Publications, Berry Gordy, Richard Pryor. I've named mostly entertainment figures, with the odd interloper from other areas thrown in. And my question is, why haven't you all started your own studio? Why don't Eddie and Bill and Oprah and Whitney put $60 million in there; $10 million each from six of them. You start with $60 million, and you can go to any bank you want with the lineup you've got there, and you can start your own studio. Why don't they do it? You want to buy a professional team, no problem. It wouldn't even cost $60 million. You put $20 million on the table; you can get financing for the rest of it. See, it's more psychological than a matter of trust among the people.

Harry Belafonte broke new ground for black Americans as a recording artist, concert singer, actor, and producer. As part of his lifelong struggle to advance human rights, he has served on the board of directors of the Southern Christian Leadership Conference, as cultural advisor to the Peace Corps, chairman of the Martin Luther King, Jr Memorial Fund, and a goodwill ambassador for UNICEF. Among the many awards he has received are the Dag Hammarskjold Peace Medal and the Martin Luther King, Jr Peace Prize.

Harry Belafonte

Q: How would you define racism?

BELAFONTE: I would define racism as an invented mode of social response that works toward the detriment of a group of people. And it comes in many forms, because it isn't just one bacteria at work; it's several. But the overall thing is an invented form of social response or social behavior that works to the detriment of a group of people. And the operative word is "invented," because I don't think people are born with racist attitudes. It's acquired, and its acquisition and the development of it has so many layers and so many interpretations that no one dynamic can eliminate it and no one definition can satisfy what it really is. Racism has had so many institutions of respectability responsible for some of its most intense expression. The church and the Christian forces of the world legitimized the slave trade because it put large profits into the state and into those who were supportive of the church. That set up a whole dynamic. And when I look at an immigrant coming from Europe, who comes here with no money, just raw off the boat; one of the first things he realizes in this country, from the day he lands, is he's already better than black people. And he begins to play a role in that, which already puts him in an adversarial position to the blacks who he might meet, who are economically on the same level. And it sets up this reciprocity of hate and social conflict. To define racism is not an easy thing to do, because its tentacles go so many places that you have to define it each place you see it for people to understand fully.

Q: How deeply ingrained in the black community is racism?

BELAFONTE: I don't know how you can be the victim of something that is as oppressive as racism and not begin to develop mechanisms in response that become racist as well. How can you eternally love white people without some sense of discontent or hate or anger toward them as a group, when the group of white people have been so responsible in the daily practice of racism, behaving in a way that supports and reinforces the institutions of racism. So, for example, black people who suffered at the hands of rents that were gouged from buildings that were traditionally owned by Jews developed an anti-Semitic bias. The world already had an anti-Semitic formula. Blacks were just able to find a specific one for their own kind of racism, because there was this economic exploitation in the face of their economic helplessness.

So I believe that there is a great deal of racism that exists within black consciousness and black subconsciousness. But I believe that, in blacks, it is perhaps the most swiftly healed. I find in many instances that blacks who begin to have access, blacks who begin to understand that there is a legitimate basis for an interdependency with other races and other people, are the first to play that chord of harmony, because their basic thrust is to find harmony, to find brotherhood, because they've lived for so long out-side of the regions of brotherhood. Americans can sit down and talk about our British allies. They can talk about our French allies. They can talk about a host of things that give them a sense of community, a sense of brotherhood, a sense of fraternity. Blacks don't have that. When we talk about our West Indian brothers, we can only relate as victims. We can't relate as people who come with power to reinforce each other. We can't call on a black Margaret Thatcher to interface with our black George Bush to arrive at some common objective and therefore get a sense of fra-ternity within the tribe. We come together all the time in a desperate hope so that we can use our resources in the face of all this weakness, in the face of all this destruction, in the face of all this stress, and carve out some goal for ourselves. I'm not suggesting that there is no black frater-nity. But there is another kind of fraternity; a fraternity of power, real applicable power; not spiritual power, practical power; everyday physical power, banking power, buying power. In terms of our personal power, we have a resource because our struggle, our pain, gives us a way in which to come together that is not quite the same for anybody else who never had that experience. So we have a resource that is terribly powerful. We just haven't learned how to apply it.

Q: How would you evaluate the current tensions between black residents and the Korean deli owners [who were subjected to a boycott led by black community organizers] in New York?

BELAFONTE: I think clearly, on a people-to-people level, there is a lot about that conduct and that experience that is a negative. For black people to be confronting another people around what is expressed as a racial definition is sad and unfortunate. There is the claim that these people have come into our community and robbed us of our revenue. That rather simplistic definition has caused a lot of mischief.

I think that the ability of any entrepreneurial force to move into the black community, to develop a dynamic in that community, should be the right of almost anyone. But part of the problem is, as I said before, most immigrants come into this country, and even if they come into this country penniless, they already understand from the get-go that they are more favored; they have more opportunity and more possibilities than blacks, so they're coming already with an attitude. They're coming already with something in place which says, hey, I don't have to relate to your interests and your problems, because your own country doesn't do that, so why should we get bogged down with that in pursuit of our own goals and objectives as the new-landed immigrant. Blacks strongly resent that. They strongly resent the Cuban community in Florida. And what that has done to race relations in Miami is even more insidious than what's happening in Brooklyn with the Korean grocers. All those perceptions begin to play, so when you get an incident in the community that has to do with price-gouging or rude treatment of those who buy in your store, that one problem takes on the dynamic of the total social problem and at some point becomes non-negotiable, because you're no longer speaking about the Korean grocer and the black woman who may have been insulted. You're speaking about the whole question. And since there is no leadership for the whole question, since there is no leadership for the whole dynamic, then people become vigilantes.

With the Korean grocery store, we've got to get people together at a table to talk, to come to an understanding about their commonality. And once you get the commonality thing; it's like when I went out to Bensonhurst right after the Yusef Hawkins shooting. I said to the Italian community that came together at the invitation of [State Assemblyman] Frank Barbaro; I walked in and asked, "Why do you hate us so much, the universal hate. What is it?" And those people began to express personal grievances. "We have no community center," the Italians said. "Our drop-out rate is enormous. Our kids are unemployed." Their perception is that all this welfare money is going to blacks and they don't have it. And I said, "Well, stop and listen to this. We have no community centers. We have a high drop-out rate. We don't have this and we don't have that, and we think you have it. And that's why we're pissed off at you. Now, if we don't have it and you don't have it, who has it and why are we at each other's throats?"

Q: What is the level of racism or race discrimination that you see in the entertainment industries where you have spent your career; movies, records, clubs, concerts?

BELAFONTE: I find that racism very clearly exists in our ability to make films that deal with the serious inside workings of black history and the black experience. That these projects are shunted off as "economically not viable" might be the excuse given at the table of negotiations, but it is not the truth. You're not going to tell me that, if we do our *Julia*, if we do our *Missing*, and if we do our *Cinema Paradiso*, if we do the black equivalent of all of those and do it on a basis that is economically astute, that we're not going to be able to have a viable competitive product in the marketplace. I think that institutional racism has denied us that because the line is, "We don't want messages in our pictures. People don't like messages. If you want to send a message, then go to Western Union."

Q: What about making *Mississippi Burning* with a white FBI agent as the hero, or making the Biko movie from Donald Wood's point of view? Do you have to have a white person to tell the black story through?

BELAFONTE: That's the other side of the coin. To have our history and our roles articulated to the appreciation of masses of people can only be done if we have a Tarzan figure in place to tell the world what Africa is really like. And that's just not acceptable. Invariably, that carries distortion. And the greatest distortion is that there is an impotence in black people and, unless there is a white force with benevolence ready to embrace us, we cannot articulate or move for ourselves in heroic ways. I think that it is incumbent upon blacks to understand this manipulation and to seize the initiative as a group to make an infrastructure so that attitude can no longer prevail. But we as a race are too apart when it comes to the ability to sit down and discuss with a sense of mutuality what our objectives should be and go ahead and deliver them by pulling together as a collective. We still are very competitive with one another. There are a lot of people who don't even talk to one another. There are a lot of people in this country, who are black and who are superstars, that I never hear from. I've called a lot of people to come onboard to do things artistically, to do things politically, to do things socially, and they just don't take the call anymore, because they don't need that disruption in their lives; because they're either afraid or they're impotent. In most cases, it's both because you don't have fear without impotence, and you don't have impotence without fear.

Q: Can you talk a bit about the role of the black artist, the role of the black star, the role of the black super athlete, in raising the consciousness of America and as a role model. Yourself, Bill Cosby, Eddie Murphy, Diana Ross, anybody you want to talk about.

BELAFONTE: I think any black celebrity, regardless of profession, carries the burden of responsibility to articulate those things which will most impact upon the hopes and aspirations of black people in some very positive way. To clearly become a force and a vibration that will rip away the facade, rip away the chicanery, rip away the cosmetic that gives one the sense that all is well with black people because these people have the role of celebritiness despite what's happening to the larger masses of black people. Anybody who is a celebrity has to come to some balance about what and who they are, and use that role to say, my celebritidom, my celebritiness, should not be equated in any way with the success of black goals in America. If anything, we should use that power to look closely at what's going on with the rest of the black people in this country and make a difference. Why do we have this power? Is it exclusively to per-petuate our own images and our own fortune? Or is this meant to be used in the service of a much broader social objective? For us to not come to grips with that aspect of our power is to really and truly diminish us in a major way in terms of much that we could be achieving.

I can't go anywhere in the world—nowhere, I don't care where it is—and not find young people who know Michael Jackson; people who have heard of Eddie Murphy. Everybody's seen Bill Cosby. The cinema and all that it does, let alone all the other things that are happening when you get into a certain socio-identity with the rap singers and all that is beginning to happen with what I call the real folk culture. All these resources continually impact upon people's thinking, the ability to mobi-lize forces around who and what you are. And if those forces will begin to consistently deliver information and consciousness-raising to issues that plague us rather than just exploit that environment toward selfish gains, then I think we will make tremendous headway.

Certainly, no one used their power more fully than Paul Robeson did with this gigantic international impact and visibility that he had and then turn it toward the political objectives of Africans, the Caribbean populace, and black Americans. Those of us who became effective in the arts com-munity afterward—myself, Sidney Poitier, Charlie White as a painter, James Baldwin as a writer—all of us were the beneficiaries of Paul Robeson's existence. He set a mood and set objectives for us to emulate. He was our mentor. None of us would be as articulate or as committed if we hadn't seen the dignity and the integrity and the power of what Robeson did. The fact that more didn't do it is a sorrowful comment, but there are many who were affected by that and will tell you clearly that he was the centerpiece. My God, think about that dynamic if many more of us were able to understand that and use our influence.

Q: Do you feel that you have more artistic freedom, more freedom to express yourself professionally, than you did before. How has the enter-tainment industry evolved over the past twenty-five years?

BELAFONTE: I have to answer that in a number of ways. First, I do believe that there is a lot of opportunity and choice out there for me artistically. But that has existed for a long time in the face of a host of other dynamics. I made my relationship with people directly with the public. Even when media was unavailable to me, I went around to the concert halls of the world, sometimes the first black artist to appear in a lot of countries, and developed a durable constituency. So when things were denied to me, I could always pick up and go to Buenos Aires, or I could go to Japan. I could go to France or England or Africa, and find a constituency, so there were always things open for me. And in that openness I could afford to be as outspoken as I cared to be. The only thing that has eluded me, but not in every instance, is the ability to do it with the entire industry serving my interests. I had it when I first started out with the success of "Banana Boat" and the West Indian folk music rage. But to have been able to prevail for forty years and still have people come to the concerts on a sold-out basis and to still have people interested in me and interested in what I say is a remarkable journey and a dynamic that is quite unique in the face of who and what I am politically.

As a matter of fact, most people don't even know the extremes of my behavior politically and the work I did with Martin Luther King. It's true that I wasn't in all the pictures. I didn't rush to hang onto Dr. King's arm to ensure that every picture in the world that was taken would be with me and Dr. King. Most of the time, I was back at headquarters, mapping out strategy. You don't get much publicity that way. But on the other hand, the absence of publicity was one of my greatest weapons. People trusted what I was about. This is all in answer to your question "Do I have a platform?" Yes, it's there. When I go out and I sing at any institution in this country, the only thing that stops the public from getting to me is the price of the ticket. It's true that I'm not heard on the top-forty stations, and it's true that I'm not seen on all the talk shows. It isn't that I'm not invited to the talk shows. I decline going until I have something unique to talk about. Familiarity carries no edge to it. But I don't know of anybody who does what I do and has my platform, and at the same time sells a hundred million records or whatever those numbers are today and gets three hundred million dollars. Somehow, the two are incompatible.

Q: One issue that has emerged in recent months is the whole question of the limits of solidarity among black leaders. At what point, in order to have some standards, do you publicly go outside the family and criticize or disagree with another black leader?

BELAFONTE: First of all, I think that it really and truly is no longer in the best interest of black people to look at our lives and our options in life from the exclusive perspective of color, although that has to play a very rich part in the mix of ways in which to look at our problems, our hopes, and our aspirations. To define our goals as a community solely from a racial perspective is to deliver ourselves to conclusions and commitments that are based exclusively on race without any regard to what that does to us. I think the time has long since passed for the earlier credibility that such a view might have attracted when we were new at the game.

Before Dr. King, there were less than three hundred elected black officials in this country. Now there are seven thousand or thereabouts. And I don't know that seven thousand black elected officials have been able to deliver to the black community what one would have suspected. Certainly twenty-five years ago, if somebody had told me that there would be seven thousand elected black officials on all levels of the spectrum of politics—and that's just the elected officials; it doesn't include people who are appointed to positions, whether it's federal courts, state courts, the chief of staff of the United States Armed Forces; and then you look at all the people who have gotten corporate positions and roles that are enjoyed by certain black personalities—one would have had to conclude that, by this time, the plight of the almost thirty million black people in this country would be in a very different place in terms of our ability to direct the energies and goals of this country. Not just black aspirations, but a national view, domestic and foreign.

The black voice in this country should have long since been a powerful force in foreign policy; certainly as powerful as the Jewish voice in foreign policy as it relates to Jewish interests. So I think that the whole question of goals and objectives for the deliverance of black expectations can no longer afford the negative luxury of looking at things solely from a racial point of view. Now it's very difficult to ask a community that suffers so vigorously at the hands of racism and racist institutions and the tradition of racist behavior in this country to become so insightful and so sensitive to the sophisticated way in which all of this machinery works to be able to seize that morality and look at black aspirations in that very sophisticated way. But to not do so, or not to put that language in our vocabulary as a new thrust on how to do business, will eternally keep us locked into positions that reinforce opportunists who are black and who use the language of progressive politics and progressive aspirations on behalf of the black community to pursue corrupt interests and selfish interests and withhold from the black community its abilities to develop leadership and challenge the larger society about our goals and our rights.

Also, to plow all of our resources into one personality, one person, and endow that individual with the ability to move and shake in a way that we ask that one individual to solve all of our problems is totally incorrect. And we have a capacity for doing that. Jesse Jackson is an example. I think there are a lot of things that black people have brought to Jesse Jackson and have kept almost exclusively as a focus for Jesse to do. And it has seriously impaired our ability as a people to look around the field and see if we shouldn't in fact be developing ten or twenty other people to walk out as personalities, as individuals, as thinkers; men and women who give us a broader selection of possibilities, a broader selection of choices. I don't think that any one individual is going to be endowed with the ability to do it all, or to pull everyone together. No matter how tenaciously they work to carve out that role for themselves, it should be unacceptable to us. I'm not talking about when a messiah comes into our midst, like a Martin Luther King, or a Malcolm X, or a Nelson Mandela, who are men endowed with such exceptional gifts that their presence wasn't even just to the interest of black people; it was to the interest of the universe, their position was so universal. But with that exception, which has to be noted, the people who come with less credentials than that, like the Jesse Jacksons and other mere mortals, should not be endowed with the hope or the commitment from us as a people to do that work. They can't do it.

Q: Do you think that another presidential campaign by Jesse Jackson would be a diversion or a necessary step toward building something? If Jesse asked you, "Should I run again?" what would you say?

BELAFONTE: I'm not sure what my answer would be, because I'm not sure whether or not Jesse's running for another shot at the presidency is what we should be about. I think we have a responsibility as citizens of the United States of America to be sensitive to who is the president. But with all the resources that have been spent on Jesse Jackson attaining the presidency, I'm not sure the presidency is what we should have our eye on. I'm not saying that we shouldn't have that in the mix, but to have that as an almost exclusive focus? An alternative would be a leader who carries us to places that are well beyond the narrow confines of the presidency. Martin Luther King and Malcolm X didn't have to be president of the United States in order to make an impact on this country and on political policy. That's the kind of leadership we should be looking for; not endowing our resources to an individual on this rather narrow goal that then keeps us exclusively to that at the loss of being able to mobilize the streets, mobilize people, go after goals in a certain way that doesn't have to fit whether or not it is designed for the presidency. I think, when you run for the presidency, you have to make too many compromises. You have to be too narrow in what you do. You have to play some kind of a partisan role. And we should not be looking exclusively toward partisan relationships. We should have somebody out there endowing people with the right to go across the board and to do what has to be done, both unilaterally and independent of party politics and party commitment

Q: What in your view would Dr. King be doing if he were here today?

BELAFONTE: I don't know that Dr. King would do anything differently than he did when he was here. He would be addressing that virtue, that force, that power, that gift toward the objectives of the day. That hypothetical always throws me into a bad kind of head because, were he here, we wouldn't be where we are. But if Dr. King were emerging today for the first time with the world in the shape that it's in, I think, clearly, running for the presidency would not be his objective. I think he would support the idea that, as a people, we should have that right. But should it be our main objective at the moment? The truth of the matter is that I don't believe that even blacks themselves are going to be wholly committed to what that really means in getting a black person elected. We can't do it without white America, and white America is not ready. You can give me the statistics and what not, and we could sit here and massage that back and forth. But I think the bottom line is that a black president in the near future is not going to be a realizable objective. Now hold that for a minute, and let's look at a black president who's going to have the kind of a platform that we as a people should be addressing in terms of what any president should be credentialed to do on our behalf. I say, well, not only is it going to be impossible to find a white person to do that; you're certainly not going to elect a black person or person of color to do it. There is no way for Jesse Jackson or anybody else to become president of the United States and go up against the will of the Pentagon, the will of the military-industrial complex, to make rules and regulations regarding the use of NATO and all kinds of alliances, most of which are going to be directed toward the exploitation and redirecting of our newfound imperialist power since there is no longer the Soviet Union to monitor ourselves against. So for any leader to take that role; is white America going to feel safe with a black taking those kinds of risks, and not feel somehow as if this guy is not loyal to America; he's too busy trying to protect racial interests around the globe.

Q: Do you think Nelson Mandela has a role to play in dealing with racism in America?

BELAFONTE: I don't think there has been any force in this country since the death of Martin Luther King that has brought such a dynamic to black thinking and such stimulation to black feelings as Nelson Mandela, because people not only saw in him the Messiah quality, but they also could instantly measure his forthrightness and his dignity as a man who stood with a directness and a power and a sense of purpose. They saw in him all that is absent in our own leadership; all that is absent in our own dialogue; all that is absent in the way in which we behave. They were able to measure our leadership and our absence of it based upon what Nelson did, and that was very cathartic. I have people today, and I'm sure it will be there for a long time, who say, I can never go back to where I was. That's why I'm encouraging Nelson to be very consistent in how he relates to America, and in particular black America, because I think we are a great resource for him. And he is certainly a great resource for us. He should not get so caught up in things that he misses the momentum that he has created here. We have this mutuality that should be looked at. He clearly is an instrument against racism, against oppression; clearly is an instrument that says we have a moral power here that is far greater than anybody else; because when we say we're learning to live with our oppressor, nobody can say that with greater force than us. I think he brings an energy here that I would like to see nurtured, and I think he sends fear through a lot of the black leadership. I watched it wilt while he was here. One thing that Nelson Mandela forced everybody to be, no matter how hard you tried not to be, you had to be who you were when you sought to do business with him. If you were a deviant, if you had a hidden agenda, if you were corrupt, if you were wonderful, if you were greedy or desperate; all that came out if you were around him long enough to try to do your thing. And I watched the black community, not only see the best of itself but see the worst of itself. A lot of people were very exposed when Nelson was here because of the moral force, the ethic, the political power, and the political clarity that he brought.

Q: How did you feel about Jesse Jackson's presence in South Africa when Nelson Mandela was freed?

BELAFONTE: I feel that, clearly, Jesse Jackson's presence anywhere where people are in a life and death struggle to come to grips with oppression; that wherever these people exist, Jesse Jackson's presence should only be at the behest of the people in that struggle, the people who have a right to control their own destiny. And if that has not been negotiated clearly and fully and you do not come with that mandate, then I think your presence can only be a negative and can only have a dynamic that is not in the best interest of the goals of these people and therefore to the goals of all people who are committed to a sense of camaraderie and a sense of support for liberation struggles in the world. When I speak to people in South Africa and to the ANC and to the PAC and to the UDF, most of them will tell you that Jesse Jackson's presence there was not in their best interest nor to their liking. Jesse has to understand that. Jesse will come and he will interpret. He will ask, "What harm did I do?" From the point of view of a lot of South Africans, there is a benevolence that comes from Jesse Jackson which is as rude to them and as unacceptable to them as white benevolence. How dare you come to interpret for us what we should be about. If you'd like to sit and consult and have a partnership in this thing, if you'd like to give us the benefit of your wisdom, that's one thing. And we will tell you the dynamic under which that can be done and the arena in which that that can be played out in. But don't come and stand on our platforms and grab our hands and hold them up and get the photo opportunity of doing those things in the name of being devoted to our cause. We don't buy that. More and more people are beginning to resent that; and more and more people are beginning to be vocal about it. The problem is that a lot of black leaders who feel exactly that way are reluctant to say it, because they're somehow trying to hold the tribal interests together and not become factionalized. To a degree, that is understandable. But there has to come a point where people understand it no longer serves our long-range interests and goals. A lot of people are questioning, is Jesse truly out there to lead in the highest sense morally, or is he out there for personal power and for personal gain? That is the question that has to be asked.

Q: What do you believe is the answer to that question?

BELAFONTE: I think that Jesse should, first of all, be given the opportunity to interpret very clearly why does he behave this way. And based upon that answer, we can then clearly draw some conclusions. I think we're all intelligent enough to be able to dissect what the meanings are that he gives us. He has never answered the question. It's about the rights of people to a certain kind of morality and self-determination. But I have to tell you that, when it comes to the basic things that are being uttered by Jesse, I have no problem with Jesse and his position on most of the questions from a political-philosophical point of view. It is the methodology and what he does with it and what he turns that into that creates the problem for a lot of us.

Q: Do you believe that Jesse Jackson is seeking to discourage other black leaders from rising to challenge him in authority and prominence?

BELAFONTE: How conscious it is, I can't say. But is that the fact of what's happening? Yes; it's out there. I think that a lot of people who could perhaps achieve certain objectives and certain goals do not get the opportunity to pursue that, nor does their constituency pursue it with them, because a lot of that is immediately co-opted by something Jesse may or may not do. I've seen too many communities where people have started a dynamic within that community. Then some things happen, and Jesse moves in and gets the high ground. The reporters come in. They do their thing for two or three days, or two or three minutes, whatever the case may be. Then all that stuff is gone, and the community is left somewhat devastated because it doesn't understand clearly what its program is anymore. The leadership being developed inside that core has now been shadowed by this other dynamic. Whereas, if nobody ever went into it and let it grow at its own pace, there would be a whole bunch of other leaders, a whole other way in which the media would have to deal with it and look at this thing as a serious force. I have to be concerned about my own mode of behavior in relation to that. I always look at how to prepare the platform for those who can articulate and are going to be there on an everyday basis and to be consistent with the needs of that community. And I think that Jesse should wait for the invitation to come and sit at some reasonable table of negotiation and discussion as to what his presence will do, and then move on that basis; not just do it without having talked it through and done it at the behest of the people who are the victims of what he says he's speaking to.

In 2001, I visited with Al Sharpton for a wide-ranging conversation.

Al Sharpton

Ten years ago, Reverend Al Sharpton was regarded by the establishment as a bad joke. Sharpton was almost comically short and heavyset
with long processed hair; given to wearing powder-blue leisure suits and
a faux gold medallion around his neck. Writers for the *New York Times* dismissed him as a "rotund preacher with a semi-automatic mouth" who
"straddled the worlds of news and entertainment, religion and community
activism, the media and the mob." Even within the black community, criticism was harsh. One of America's leading black educators, Mary Frances
Berry, called Sharpton "a charlatan." Respected journalist and scholar
Roger Wilkins labeled him "a black buffoon."

Times change.

For a lot of people, there's still a threshold issue regarding Sharpton.
In 1987, he took up the cause of a fifteen-year-old girl named Tawana
Brawley, who claimed she had been abducted and raped by a group of
white men who smeared her body with racial slurs written in excrement.
Sharpton made Brawley an icon of victimization for a crime that most
investigators believe never occurred. And until Sharpton admits that his
Tawana Brawley crusade was a hoax, many observers say that they will
never be able to fully respect him.

"I hear that all the time," says Sharpton. "And my position is, if I were
going to be politically expedient, I could have said a long time ago that I
was duped. But I do not believe that Tawana made it all up. I believe she
was violated. I believe something happened, the details of which Tawana
has given."

Does Sharpton believe that "something" happened with white
aggressors?

"That's what Tawana said," he answers. "And I don't disbelieve her.
There may be some things that I said about people in the case that got in
the way of the broader cause of what Tawana Brawley represented. And
clearly, it has cost me some political capital. But I can live with myself."

Regardless, Al Sharpton is now a major player in the human rights movement and the point man on a host of issues in the black community. It's a remarkable road that he has travelled.

Sharpton was born in 1954 to a middle-class family in New York. "My parents were very religious," he remembers, "so I grew up in the church. Before I began to form values and beliefs of my own, I was in an environment where the assumption was that God exists."

Sharpton gave his first sermon at age four at the Washington Temple Church in Bedford-Stuyvesant. At age nine, he was ordained as a Pentecostal minister. "Then, when I was ten," he recalls, "my parents had an ugly separation that was very traumatic for me. We'd lived in Queens in a comfortable middle-class environment. And all of a sudden, I found myself with my mother in Brooklyn. She went on welfare and worked part-time as a household domestic. And I had to appeal to the God I'd been taught to believe in. It forced me to confront my own beliefs, and that faith sustained me."

After his parents' separation, Sharpton turned to political activism. At age fifteen, he was chosen by the Southern Christian Leadership Conference to serve as youth director for Operation Breadbasket in New York City. Two years later, while still a student at Tilden High School, he founded an organization known as the National Youth Movement.

In 1978, still operating beneath the media radar screen, Sharpton made his first run for public office, campaigning in Brooklyn for a seat in the New York State Senate. However, he was removed from the ballot after a court ruled that he was not a resident of the district in which he was campaigning. Nonetheless, he remained a loud presence, with his battle cry of "No justice; no peace" resounding through the streets of New York. In 1986, when a young black man named Michael Griffith was struck and killed by a car while trying to escape from a mob of club-wielding whites in Howard Beach, Sharpton was the most visible and vocal of those demanding justice. Several months later, when New York City mayor Ed Koch held a New Year's Day meeting with twenty-three black leaders at City Hall in an attempt to ease racial tensions, Sharpton condemned the occasion as "a coon show." Shortly thereafter, he denounced New York City police commissioner Benjamin Ward with the words, "He's of our color but he is not of our kind."

Then came Tawana Brawley.

In 1992, and again in 1994, Sharpton campaigned for the Democratic senatorial nomination in New York. In 1997, he entered the Democratic primary for mayor and came within one percentage point of forcing a run-off against the eventual nominee, Ruth Messenger. Meanwhile, Sharpton's self-described mission as an advocate for the powerless and the oppressed continues. And even the reverend's harshest critics concede that sometimes there is a basis for his complaints. In point of fact, it was Sharpton who brought to light the brutal sodomization of a Haitian immigrant named Abner Louima in the back room of a New York City police precinct house and spearheaded the public demand for justice.

Sharpton's current duties revolve around his position as founder, president and chief executive officer of the National Action Network, which is headquartered in New York and has satellite offices in four other cities. The National Action Network is, in Sharpton's words, "a civil rights organization geared toward economic justice, political empowerment of disenfranchised citizens, a fair criminal justice system, and a moral agenda of equity for the twenty-first century."

Sharpton is married with two daughters, who are now entering adolescence. Gray pinstripe suits have replaced his powder-blue leisure suits of the past. And even his most vocal critics acknowledge that, while the messenger might be flawed, Al Sharpton has tapped into something powerful.

Q: The perception of you has changed enormously over the past decade. You're now a major player in the human-rights movement. Have you changed; has the rest of the world come toward you; or have both of those things happened?

SHARPTON: There's been growth on both sides. In the late 1980s and early nineties, the media decided that I was a great caricature with no serious following. Then, in 1992, I ran for the Senate and got 166,000 votes. And all of a sudden, there was a new understanding that what I was saying mattered to a lot of people. And at the same time, I started taking myself more seriously. A turning point for me came on January 12, 1991. I was leading a march in Bensonhurst, and a man—a white man—came through the crowd and stuck a knife in my chest; almost killed me. During my time in the hospital after that, I thought about how I was going to be remembered. I'm very much concerned with the long run. The broad sweep of history is more important to me than contemporary analysis. And I realized I'd been living in the sound bite and the drama of the moment. I decided to take things more seriously; that the issues were more important than my own vanity. So over the past ten years, I've grown a lot. I don't think I was ever a buffoon. But I'd done some things that allowed people to look at me in that way, and I decided to move beyond that. And another thing is, people tend to forget that I grew up in public. And when you do that, when you make mistakes as we all do, everybody sees them. I'll put it to you this way. George Bush [the second President Bush] says that he discovered God and maturity at age forty. If America can forgive George Bush for drunk driving and everything else that George Bush did in his twenties and thirties, then America can forgive Al Sharpton for having used showmanship tactics in pursuit of human-rights causes.

Q: You've always been very adept at using the media; particularly television. And a lot of people have criticized the way you've done it although, as you once noted, you didn't hold the media at gunpoint and force them to cover you. Let's talk about that a bit.

SHARPTON: Two things on that. Number one, I grew up in New York. That meant I was organizing and fighting issues in a town with Broadway lights, Wall Street, the Statue of Liberty, the United Nations; so you have to develop a strategy to get attention on your issue. Had I come out of some small Midwestern town, I might have been different. But I understood that you've got to do something dramatic and different to get attention in New York. Second, I was raised by Jesse Jackson, who was good with media. I had a father-son relationship with James Brown, who promoted himself as a major artist for four decades. How does one grow up around those people and not learn how to deal with media? I would have been incompetent if I'd been around those guys and not learned how to use the media. A lot of guys in the movement say I came out of the Dr. King school but Jesse's class. And that's true. So my position on the media is that you have to find a way, usually dramatic, to break your issue. Now what I had to learn over a period of time was to not let the drama get in the way of the message. So let's say there's a situation where, in the late-eighties, I might have said something or done something outrageous. As I developed over time, I realized that doing something like that might get in the way of what I was really trying to say and show people about. So by the time I got to the late nineties and police brutality like Abner Louima and Amadou Diallo, I'd learned to be dramatic but not lose the issue. I had to learn that mix of how to be dramatic enough to get to the top of the news, but where I don't do it in a way that obscures the cause that I'm trying to represent.

Q: Do perceptions of the Tawana Brawley case hamper your effectiveness or in any way interfere with your message of social justice?

SHARPTON: In my opinion, no. There are many people who disagree with me on the Brawley case. But they understand that you can't take two decades of public work and weigh it against just one case. And there are also people who use the Brawley case against me because they're just looking for a way to not deal with the issues I raise; and if it wasn't the Brawley case, it would be something else.

Q: If a fifteen-year-old girl came to you today and asked what the Brawley case was about, what would you tell her?

SHARPTON: I would tell her that it was about a girl her age and two attorneys [C. Vernon Mason and Alton Maddox]. This girl was missing for four days. She then came forward and said that she had been abducted and violated by four law-enforcement officials. And since Tawana said that the perpetrators were law-enforcement people, she and her attorneys wanted me to demand that there be a special prosecutor to investigate the case. That's what I did. I felt that I had an obligation to fight for her to get a fair hearing. I didn't have convicting evidence. But you do what you do and say what you say based on your belief. I fought for what I believed to be true.

Q: How do you explain the judgment that Stephen Pagones [one of the accused men] won in the libel action that he brought against you?

SHARPTON: I think Pagones is the one who has to explain it. He said that I conspired against him and ruined his life. And the verdict was $60,000, which clearly doesn't say that his life was ruined. So I feel the verdict he got was wrong, but clearly it wasn't the multimillion-dollar verdict that he was looking for.

Q: You've said that a truly spiritual man is honest about his flaws. What flaws have you seen in yourself over the years?

SHARPTON: Vanity. A lack of discipline. Responding out of anger. Doing what I think is politically expedient. Saying something that I know will make a good sound bite on the evening news but isn't necessarily the best way to communicate the truth. Giving in to the temptation to seize the moment instead of working to define the hour, which is a much more difficult task. You know, part of being a good minister is to minister with yourself and deal honestly with your own flaws. And a lot of that for me was maturity and spiritually coming in tune with the idea that, if I'm going to be effective, I have to deal with my own sins. As a boy preacher and a young activist, I grew up on stage with hundreds and sometimes thousands of people looking on. Under those circumstances, you're given to vanity. But real spiritual purity is learning that you can't have a ministry where you're feeding on the applause of the crowd. You have to feed the needs of the crowd. That might not always make the crowd happy. It might not make them applaud. It might not be the sound bite that some guy who's looking for a story on the evening news wants from you. But I know the difference between saying something because it's cute and it's going to make the news, as opposed to saying something that needs to be said and is giving voice to something important that has been ignored and will give people a broader understanding of a good cause. You know that song they sing in church: "If I never reach perfection; Lord, I tried." Well, I'm trying.

Q: One of the complaints regarding your work is that there are times when you seem to have a double standard; that you don't hold the black community to the same standard of behavior as the white community. People ask questions like, "Why doesn't Al Sharpton voice more outrage at the drug dealers who are pillaging the black community?"

SHARPTON: That's a misconception. I do those things; they just don't get the same coverage in the media. I'm the same Al Sharpton who went and painted crack houses and closed crack dens in the black community. I'm the same Al Sharpton who runs programs at the National Action Network dealing with the criminal element in the black community. But that's not what the media is interested in. We have a whole office at the National Action Network that deals with nothing but corporate responsibility. It's called the Madison Avenue Initiative. How much do you hear about that? So do some people see me as one-dimensional? Yes, but it's because of the media coverage. They assume that I'm sitting there in the middle of the night with a walkie-talkie waiting for a cop to kill a kid, and then I run to the scene and make an issue of it. But that's not how I operate.

Q: Explain what it is that you've tapped into with your core constituency? Why do people believe in you?

SHARPTON: It's everyday life. Social justice is when society operates with the same rules for everybody. But too many people in this country live under circumstances where the system doesn't equally protect them. Their schools don't operate the same. Parents know that their children need an education to survive, but their kids sit in overcrowded classrooms and graduate from high school reading and doing math four or five years behind the national average. Their health care is different. They can wait in a hospital emergency room for hours and never get care. The whole reality of their life, from the sanitation services in their neighborhood to the criminal justice system, is markedly different from the prosperous American families that they see on their television sets. If they call the police, they don't know if the police will defend them or if the response will be that they become a suspect or a victim. They feel the inequity that, when they or a loved one faces a criminal proceeding, they're more likely to be incarcerated and incarcerated for a longer period of time than other people. And it's not just the black community. There's a growing feeling in the Latino and Asian communities, and there's more awareness of it now in those parts of the white community that don't have means. It goes to the mother whose child has a Legal Aid lawyer; and she knows the lawyer will give her child only a limited amount of time, but she can't afford a better lawyer. They're all feeling the economic reality that, if you don't have money, the criminal justice system works differently for you and the system as a whole works differently for you. I speak to that reality. I tap into the reality that many people feel when they aren't being treated equally and fairly. And when I give voice to their feelings, they support me.

Q: Looking back over the past twenty years, we've had three presidential administrations and now George W. Bush. How would you critique them?

SHARPTON: Ronald Reagan was a good-natured charismatic comfortable figure for many Americans. Unfortunately, his grandfatherly air deceived the public into accepting a reactionary agenda and some of the most antiquated regressive social policies we've ever seen. The rolling back of civil rights; the championing of trickle-down economics. That was Reagan. George Bush wasn't as charismatic as Reagan, but he was just as committed to undoing the achievements of the 1960s. Bill Clinton was a major disappointment. A lot of his policies were just one step away from Reagan and Bush and led to the ideological destruction of the Democratic Party. Clinton clothed it sometimes in a liberal veneer, but the facts speak for themselves. As far as Bush Jr is concerned, I expect we'll see a lot of what his father did; trying to bring America back to the 1950s, which is why we've got to be just as committed to fulfilling our own fathers' dreams.

Q: How do you feel about Bill Clinton's decision to rent office space in Harlem?

SHARPTON: I want Bill Clinton to go to the window of his office and look across 125th Street at the boarded-up businesses and homes that did not enjoy the Clinton years of prosperity. I want him to look at the thousands of people who are off the welfare rolls as a result of his welfare reform bill who can't get jobs. It's poetic justice that Bill Clinton is coming to Harlem, because some of the downside in Harlem today was created by the negligent policies of his administration.

Q:There are people in the black community who refer to Bill Clinton as our first black president. Could you comment on that?

SHARPTON:That is more socio-cultural than the reality of Bill Clinton's programs.Yes, he plays the horn.Yes, he came from a family that had dysfunctional problems that we see sometimes in the black community.Yes, he knows how to go to a black church and behave.Yes, he knows how to hang around black people comfortably. But Bill Clinton's policies have not been helpful to the black community. More people went to jail under Bill Clinton than under Ronald Reagan, and a disproportionate number of them were black. So when we divorce policy from personality, it's a real stretch to call Bill Clinton our first black president.

Q: Comment, if you will, on the role of religion in American life today; and in particular, the religious right.

SHARPTON: I preach at two or three different churches every Sunday, so I'm not talking as an outsider here. Organized religion in America today has, in many ways, become a very cold business. It's more about institutions than the relationship between God and humanity, and it has become an impediment to people finding God. I see a denominational corporate attitude rather than a true desire for spiritual uplifting. It's "these are our dogmas" and "these are our rules." It's about building megachurches and competing to see who has the largest edifice, rather than asking ourselves what's the most good that we can do. It has nothing to do with people discovering God and discovering the goodness in themselves. And the religious right presents a particular challenge. Dr. King and his contemporaries had the high moral ground.They had the Bible and, in some cases, the flag. But the right wing in the 1980s and 1990s kidnapped the Bible from the movement.The religious right has taken some bits and pieces of religious rhetoric and used them in an attempt to justify some of the most reactionary and repressive politics that we've ever seen. In my view, the Christian right isn't so Christian. A lot of what they advocate is against helping the poor and against developing children's minds and against civil rights and civil liberties. On abortion, they love you till you're born. So I think that young people in the church must rediscover the social good of religion in practice. In my study of the Bible, I found Jesus on the streets far more often than I found him in the cathedral.

Q: What do you realistically expect to accomplish over the next four years?

SHARPTON: The realistic goal would be to build and rebuild alliances in the progressive community across racial and economic lines. Even if we don't come forward and embrace one another, George Bush will give us the opportunity to back into one another. I'll give you an example. Usually, the forces that are anti-black are also anti-Semitic, and vice versa. Usually, the policies supported by blacks are supported by Jews, and vice versa. Look at what happened in Florida. There was a robbery of democracy; the systematic robbery of peoples' right to vote. And it was Miami, Dade and West Palm Beach—blacks and Jews—who were disenfranchised leading to the selection of George Bush rather than the election of Al Gore. So we need to look at common interests, build a common agenda, and sit down with the fact that, unless we rebuild our coalition, we're not going to solve any of our individual group problems. That can lead to the turnover of Congress in 2002 and an unprecedented voter turnout in 2004.

Q: Talk to me about Clarence Thomas.

SHARPTON: I can't imagine what goes on in Clarence Thomas's mind. Someone who lives under the prerogatives of the movement he scorns; that kind of madness is hard for me to fathom. You know, in 1995, I led a march on his house. Some people said I was getting too personal. But what I wanted to show was, here's a man living in the suburbs, in an interracial marriage, sitting on the United States Supreme Court; all three of which are the result of the civil rights struggle that he now condemns and votes against. I cannot think of a more despicable person than someone who gains from a movement and then commits himself to destroying that movement so others are unable to enjoy its fruit. Clarence Thomas is a result of the civil-rights movement that he now votes against. And because of some madness in his being, he feels obligated to serve and give cover to the most reactionary forces in this country, who now say, "We're not racist; look at Clarence Thomas; he agrees with us." It was a huge mistake that all of us made. Those of us in the black leadership, including me, quietly gave lip service to the fight against Clarence Thomas. But we were not aggressive, and it was a mistake. We should have fought outright. And instead, Clarence Thomas was allowed to use his skin color and his rhetoric—"high-tech lynching" and all that—to put himself in a position to do maximum damage. We should never again sit back and allow someone to do that based on skin color. And there was also the whole question of Anita Hill. We should never have treated her testimony as a women's issue that we weren't going to confront. History will not be kind to us for failing to aggressively fight Clarence Thomas's nomination.

Q: Colin Powell?

SHARPTON: On one level, there's a great deal of pride that someone could rise in the military like that. But you have to question his policy commitments. I did not agree with a lot of Colin Powell's activities in Somalia and the Persian Gulf. I don't see him as Clarence Thomas, but many of us intend to put a lot of pressure on him. For example, on the issue of debt forgiveness in Africa; the fact that Colin Powell is black doesn't mean that we shouldn't confront him on that. The embargo of Cuba; our whole way of dealing with the Caribbean. We should not have the Clarence Thomas disease where, because of the color of Colin Powell's skin, we give him immunity from dealing with some serious foreign policy questions.

Q: What about Colin Powell's position on gays in the military?

SHARPTON: I strongly believe that you cannot limit anyone's civil rights without limiting everyone's civil rights. If it's gays today, it will be blacks tomorrow and Latinos the day after. The problem is—and I've had arguments about this with a lot of my peers in the clergy—number one, we should not be homophobic. But beyond that, you cannot argue against someone else based on religion or skin color or sexual preference without realizing that those arguments will someday be resurrected and used against you. Once you legitimize a prejudice, it can be used against anyone. And certainly, those of us who have experienced and survived prejudice should be sensitive to that.

Q: Condoleezza Rice?

SHARPTON: Again, I don't think skin color should give immunity. I've never met Ms. Rice. But we can't have a double standard where we allow someone in a sensitive position to use skin color to do damage. Right now, under Bush Jr, we're looking at international racial profiling, where parts of the world have huge debts, little trade, and little or no investment, while the rest of the world is treated in a whole different way. Now the worst part of this will be if, because we have someone up there like Ms. Rice who is black, no one looks at this as a policy that is anti-African or anti-Caribbean. So it will be incumbent on black leadership to press both Mr. Powell and Ms. Rice very hard and very openly on these questions.

Q. You returned recently from a trip to Sudan, where there are reports that thousands of people have been taken prisoner and sold into slavery during an ongoing civil war. Could you comment on what you found?

SHARPTON: I felt compelled to go to Sudan because, if you're going to fight to end oppression, you must be consistent no matter who the oppressor is and no matter where the oppression exists. But in a million years, I could not have prepared myself for listening to hundreds of women and children who had been abused mentally and physically tell their story of being held in slavery in the twenty-first century. If this sort of slavery was going on in Bosnia, if white women and children were being sold into slavery, there would be a national outcry in America. The United States and the rest of the world would not sit by passively if this was happening to other than African people. There is a moral catastrophe here, and we're running around arguing whether this is a sectarian issue or a civil war and whether its slavery or indentured servitude. The fact that people are enslaved is the issue, and I'm committed to doing what I can to expose this horror to the world so it can be eradicated. You know, it's sad. The Christian right has showed more concern on this issue than some of our own civil rights leadership in America. And I know the Christian right has its own sectarian agenda, but that doesn't matter. You don't leave an issue like this to those who you claim are on the wrong side of other issues. And I should also say that I see this as a litmus test for the Bush Administration in general and Colin Powell in particular. We need sanctions against those who are involved in this slave trade, and we need sanctions against those who turn their heads while they know this is going on. We should not allow major oil companies to operate in Sudan and still be listed on the stock exchange and trade with America. Also, I would appeal to Islamic nations and Islamic people around the world to join with us, because true Islam, like true Christianity, has to oppose slavery. I don't want to get into a sectarian battle here. Just like some people distorted Christianity to justify slavery in America, there are people now who distort Islam in an attempt to justify slavery in Sudan. But true adherence to any religion has to stand against slavery and man's inhumanity to man.

Q: How do you feel about [Oklahoma congressman] J. C. Watts?

SHARPTON: J. C. Watts was elected as a Republican and a conservative. He's sincere about what he's doing. I just think that he's wrong on most issues. Also, I personally took issue when J. C. Watts started talking about civil rights leaders as poverty pimps. And the irony of it is, when George Jr got into office, the first thing he did was push for giving public funds to faith-based organizations. Now, which is more poverty-pimp oriented? Fighting to have the government open the door for qualified people or getting direct government money? The same people, who yesterday were accusing us of being poverty pimps, are now all standing on line to get faith-based federal funding.

Q: Are you troubled by the glorification of professional athletes who are less-than-good role models?

SHARPTON: What troubles me is that, thirty years ago when I was young, the symbol of athletes interacting with social issues was Muhammad Ali standing up against the war in Vietnam. And today, the symbols are Mike Tyson and Ray Lewis having been charged with personal criminal acts. I have no way of knowing whether Mike Tyson and Ray Lewis were guilty or not. But to go from Ali in the sixties to people acting like beating a murder rap is of some social good shows me the problem of our times. You know, I was asked several times to go to the O. J. Simpson trial. Johnny Cochran is a friend of mine. I don't know if O. J. Simpson did what he was accused of doing or not. But I never went, because I did not see the case as a civil-rights issue. I felt O. J. was entitled to a fair trial. I felt that the jurors did what they did based on the evidence as they saw it. But I did not feel that O. J. Simpson was there on a civil-rights case. And I think it's so cheap that our cultural figures expect us to rally around them with regard to personal difficulties that have nothing to do with the broader issues. It's all about personal circumstances and that saddens me.

Q: What did the revelation that Jesse Jackson fathered a child out of wedlock several years ago do to you personally and to his standing as an effective leader?

SHARPTON: Jesse's family and my family are very close. We've spent a lot of time together, so it personally pained me because of what his family had to go through. But I admire Jesse as a father figure and a mentor. And I honestly believe that his service and good works outweigh any personal frailty. So yes, he erred. And there are people who will try to use it against him, just as they've always tried to use things against social activists. But I think Jesse should be forgiven, as Bill Clinton should be forgiven. It's Jesse, more than anyone else, who has felt the pain of his error. And I think that, ultimately, he'll be fine.

Q: Let's talk about a few hot-button issues. Affirmative action?

SHARPTON: Affirmative action is a conservative remedy for a serious problem. It's absolutely necessary, and it has not yet run it's course because the playing field is still not even.

Q: Capital punishment?

SHARPTON: I'm totally opposed to capital punishment under any circumstances. I even went to Jasper, Texas, and opposed capital punishment in the James Byrd case [Byrd was brutally murdered by three white supremacists]. Given society's capacity for error, particularly in the criminal justice system, I do not believe that we can afford to open that door to the possibility of being wrong. And I believe that's true even with the most horrific crimes. Also, I'm opposed to capital punishment on moral terms. I believe that only God gives life and only God should be able to take it away.

Q: School vouchers for private schools?

SHARPTON: I would much rather see that money put into public education. My children go to private school. And for people like me who want their children to have a certain kind of religious training or other kind of teaching, fine, but we should pay for it.

Q: Rap music?

SHARPTON: Rap is like electricity. It's not good or bad; it's how you use it. The same electricity that lights up your home can electrocute you. Some rap lyrics are bad, and some are positive. I'd like to see an end to rap music that's violent and misogynist and appeals to the negative in people. But I'm very much against censorship, because who becomes the censor? Who decides where the line is drawn? I'd rather appeal to the artists to do things in a way that's responsible.

Q: The legalization of so-called "recreational" drugs?

SHARPTON: I'm open to that discussion. I'm not for decriminalization, but I'm not necessarily against it either. We need to examine a lot of behavioral issues and decide whether or not to decriminalize them. As far as drugs are concerned, there are a lot of questions to be answered. Are they really criminal? Are they a health problem? Do we have criminalization because big business hasn't figured out a way to get its hands on the money. The National Action Network is planning a forum on the issue later this year. And I expect that, after our forum, we'll take a stand on the issue.

Q: Police brutality?

SHARPTON: It's a serious problem that permeates our society far more than most people realize. And it's not just New York. New York is more dramatic sometimes, because it's a high-profile city and we've had some outrageous stuff under Giuliani. But I can't think of a day when I don't get a call from some part of the country about a case of police brutality. We need federal guidelines on police behavior. We need national legislation on police training and police conduct and a national standard on how to hold the police accountable. And until we have it, we'll keep having cases like Amadou Diallo and Abner Louima in this country.

Q: Tell me some more about your feelings toward Rudy Giuliani.

SHARPTON: Rudy Giuliani did some good in cleaning up New York. But he absolutely polluted the spirit of the city. He practiced the politics of meanness; playing to one side of town and acting like the other side didn't exist. And he was arrogant about it; saying he knew how to handle black people and refusing to meet with black leaders. When Giuliani came in, he told everyone, "The day of Al Sharpton is over. We're not going to deal with Al Sharpton at City Hall anymore." He played to the crowd and pushed the perception that it's us against them. That might have benefited him politically, but it hurt the ability of the people in the city to come together on common goals. So with Giuliani, the positive things in his legacy will be obscured by his meanness.

Q: Tell me about yourself as a person. How would you describe Al Sharpton?

SHARPTON: I work very hard; sixteen, eighteen hours a day. And I'm very committed to what I do. I don't really have any hobbies other than reading. I'm very religious. And everything I do, I try to do within a moral framework. I don't always make it. Sometimes I fall short, but it's always a consideration.

Q: What sort of things make you happy?

SHARPTON: Personally, the development of my daughters. And achieving a goal. I'm very goal oriented.

Q: What makes you sad?

SHARPTON: When I see people living beneath their potential; when I see people who don't have proper motivation; when I see people mindlessly squandering opportunity and going in a direction that's bad for them and bad for society. Injustice also makes me sad and very angry.

Q: What do you see as your greatest achievement to date?

SHARPTON: I wouldn't point to a specific event. I'd say that my greatest achievement is being part of keeping the social justice movement alive in this country. And it's different now. In some ways, it's harder to keep the movement going. In the 1960s, the group was fighting to get into the system; public accommodations, the Civil Rights Act of 1964, the Voting Rights Act of 1965. But once we got in, it became more a question of individual accomplishment and how do we move up in the system. That's where you have your Bob Johnsons from BET, your Wall Street guys, black mayors, Jesse Jackson running for president. In other words, the civil rights movement of the twenty-first century is dealing with the maladies that came out of the success of the sixties. We wouldn't have had a racial profiling problem thirty years ago, because we weren't in the suburbs to be profiled. There was no question of black jellybeans and a glass ceiling at Texaco, because there were no black executives at Texaco. So it's gone into that next fight as a result of the success of the first fight.

Q: Will you run for public office again?

SHARPTON: Only if it will support a broader good and a broader public policy interest. After I ran for mayor, people said, "Run for a Congressional seat; they'll give it to you." But I'm not preoccupied with public office. In fact, I consider what I'm doing now far more important than most public offices. My fulfillment now is in being part of a broader movement.

Personal Profiles

One of my favorite interviews was a 1977 session with Ramsey Lewis.

Ramsey Lewis

For almost twenty-five years, Ramsey Lewis has reigned as one of America's foremost jazz pianists, with dozens of albums and seven Grammy Awards to his credit. He plays over one hundred concerts a year at five thousand dollars a concert. He's remarkably young looking for his forty-eight years; tall and slender with a warm smile, open face, and neatly cropped hair. As befits a man of his trade, he talks with his hands. He is a black man whose musical roots, like those of many fellow artists, can be traced to church and family origins.

RAMSEY LEWIS: My dad is a frustrated piano player. He has a good ear, but never received the benefit of proper training. As a result, he never got beyond church music. For years, he was choir director at the Friendship Baptist Church in Chicago. Anyway, he wanted to show the world that one of his three children could play piano, so he chose the oldest—my sister—and told her that she would have to take lessons. In those days, our church organist was the neighborhood piano teacher, and lessons cost fifty cents a half hour. I was four at the time, and seeing my sister getting to do something that I was denied didn't sit too well with me. I threw a tantrum, and finally my father said, "Okay, okay! You can go too." After the first lesson, I announced that I'd had enough. At age four, I wasn't about to practice. But my father said, "No, sir. You wanted to play, and now you'll stay with it." After two years, they let my sister quit; but I had to keep going.

Q: What were those early years like?

RAMSEY LEWIS: Torture. I started by practicing half an hour a day, which is a lot when you're only four. Then, every year, my father added an extra fifteen or twenty minutes to the daily schedule. Up until I was about eleven, I was forced to play piano. Then Ernestine Bruce, who was our church organist, decided that she had taught me all she could. She told my folks to take me down to the Chicago Musical College, where I began to study with a woman named Dorothy Mendelsohn. About the same time, I started playing regularly for our church choir. And more important, I was introduced to jazz.

Q: How did that introduction come about?

RAMSEY LEWIS: My father brought home some piano recordings by Art Tatum, Teddy Wilson, and Errol Garner. Tatum, in particular, blew me away. My training had been classical, and I had never heard anyone improvise like that. At first, I couldn't understand what he was doing; but whatever it was, I liked it. Then, a few years later, I heard Oscar Peterson for the first time. That's when I really fell in love with jazz. He had a flourishing overwhelming style that took me over. To this day, I love classical music. But there's a freedom and creativity about jazz which appeals to me even more. On any given day, I can get up and express my mood using any composition at all. It's different from classical music where, on a particular day, you go to the file cabinet and say, "I think Rachmaninoff will suit my mood today." With jazz, every piece can be played to a near infinite number of moods.

Q: Liking jazz is one thing. Learning to play it is another. How did you start?

RAMSEY LEWIS: Well, as I told you, I was the pianist for our church choir in Chicago. Our organist was a man named Wallace Burton, who had a dance band called the Cleffs. One day after church, when I was sixteen, he told me they'd lost their piano player and asked if I wanted to join them. I said "sure." That Friday, I went directly from school to some ballroom where the Cleffs would be playing that night. The other band members were already there, and Wallace said, "We're going to play some medium tempo blues. Can you do it?" I was really into boogie woogie back then and thought that's what the blues were all about, so I answered "Yes." He told me, "Okay, you take it first." The band hit a few introductory chords, I started boogying, and Wallace said, "Hold it, hold it! You don't know too much, do you?" I sat the next few songs out. Then, at the break, Wallace took me aside and said, "Don't worry; I'll teach you." That evening, my education in jazz began. If it wasn't for Wallace Burton, I'd be nowhere today. There were three basic forms that jazz artists used for improvisation in those days—rhythm, blues, and an adaptation of "fine and dandy." He got me started on each of them. Then I began working on style. It's one thing to play a particular note or chord, but there's a lot more to music than that. So what I did was, I tried to copy Oscar Peterson. I'd listen to his records. Then sit down and try to play one of his solos myself. All the time, I'd be thinking, "How is he using his fingers? What's he doing with that chord?" Then I did the same thing with records by Art Tatum, George Shearing, and Bud Powell. Over the next few years, I evolved from copying others to my own thing, until I reached the point where I had my own style.

Marrying at age eighteen, Ramsey Lewis worked as a clerk in a Chicago record store by day and played with the Cleffs at night. In 1955, he and two other members of the group—bassist Eldee Young and drummer Isaac Holt—went out on their own as the Ramsey Lewis Trio. For a full decade, they played small jazz clubs in black or "Bohemian" enclaves. Then, in 1965, they recorded "The In Crowd," which sold over a million copies and won a Grammy Award for the best small-group jazz instrumental recording of the year. *Time* magazine promptly labeled Lewis "the hottest jazz artist going." After ten years of trying, he had become the first jazz musician to meet with significant success in the multimillion dollar "pop" market which, from Bill Haley to the Beatles, had been dominated by rock and roll.

RAMSEY LEWIS: That first hit record—"The In Crowd"—will stay with me until the day I die. In a period of two months, we went from earning fifteen hundred dollars a week to three thousand dollars a night. I was in a state of glorious shock. Up until that point, we'd been pinching pennies hard. Don't forget, I had a wife and four children to support [there are seven children now]. On the road, the Trio had always stayed in cheap hotels. When we went into a restaurant, the first thing we looked at on the menu were the prices. With "The In Crowd," everything changed. Shortly after it reached the best-seller charts, we played a concert in Washington, DC. I remember it well, because that night we stayed in a hotel that Ella Fitzgerald had stayed in when she was in Washington. We were "big time." That evening, I ordered dinner from room service and didn't even ask about price. It was the greatest feeling in the world.

Q: But things with the Trio went sour soon after that, didn't they?

RAMSEY LEWIS: [After a long pause] Yeah, they did. We had some very good years together. [Lewis pauses again] They were better than very good. We went through a period where, as a group, we could play just about anything we wanted on the spur of the moment. We knew each other that well. We didn't even need a rehearsal. I'd just say let's play a certain song at a certain tempo, and it would sound like an arrangement. For ten years, we were like brothers. But in the end, we were more like a married couple who had lost the ability to communicate.

Q: How did the break occur?

RAMSEY LEWIS: Nasty. You know how marriages end up; screaming and fighting and cursing. It got to the point where, if one of us would say, "Let's talk about it," we'd talk for three or four minutes and then sit and scream for two hours. I remember nights on tour when we'd go on stage and not look at each other. It got that bad. So I look at it now as a marriage that didn't work out, and we had to get a divorce.

Q: Did you have sentimental feelings about the break?

RAMSEY LEWIS: At first, yes. There had been a lot of good moments with the Trio. But then I realized that conductors leave symphony orchestras, writers leave publishing houses, and the world goes on. And to be honest; after the break, I was more concerned with earning a living than I was with sentiment. A lot of people were telling me that I wouldn't make it without the original trio. The Ramsey Lewis "sound" was the work of three people, and I was a little concerned that everything I had worked for might go down the drain. So the week after the split, I went out, hired two new guys, and forced myself to keep playing. I wanted to know right away if I still had something to say that the public would buy. Fortunately, I did. That summer, Cleveland Eaton, Maurice White, and I recorded *Wade in the Water*, which was my second gold album. Then, in 1972, we recorded *Upendo Ni Pamojo* (Swahili for "love is together"), which represented the height of the Ramsey Lewis Trio as far as I'm concerned. After that, there was nothing more I could say in trio form, so I began to experiment with different formats.

In 1974, Ramsey Lewis recorded *Sun Goddess,* one of the best-selling jazz albums in history. However, the recording was bitterly assailed by some jazz purists as a sell-out for commercial gain. Gone were the soft lively tones of his earlier music. In their place, listeners heard ten musicians in a cacophony of sound. And, perhaps more important, Ramsey Lewis, who had once recorded albums before live nightclub audiences and spoken of the rapport which allowed his original trio to play "just about anything we wanted on the spur of the moment," had given birth to an album recorded partly in one city with voiceovers and horns added in another.

RAMSEY LEWIS: "Ramsey sold out." Yeah, I've heard that; but it didn't start with *Sun Goddess.* One thing I've noticed about so-called jazz purists is that, as long as you only have a small following, you're okay. But as soon as a truck driver gets off the job and he's got one of my albums under his arm, then they say, "Ramsey sold out." It happened to me, and I've seen it happen to other jazz artists like Dave Brubeck, Cannonball Adderly, and George Benson. In my case, the grumbling started back in 1965 with "The In Crowd." I did the song because I liked it. I didn't ask myself, "Should I do it," or "Has this kind of thing been done before?" I just did it. Then "The In Crowd" became a hit, and certain jazz people started saying, "No, no, no. You can't take rhythm and blues and use them to improvise on a popular tune." In reality, I had done the same thing on three or four occasions prior to that, but none of those records had been hits so it was okay. Those early recordings were approved, accepted, and certified by jazz society. It wasn't until I had a gold record that the criticism began. Sure *Sun Goddess* was different from what you might call traditional jazz.

All of my albums are different. Later, I released an album on acoustic piano with a symphony orchestra. That broke with tradition. Next, I did a solo piano album with eight or nine compositions of varying mood, character, and harmonic structure. That was different too. Obviously, when I record an album, I feel a certain commitment to the market place. That's why record companies pay me. But I'd never sacrifice professional integrity or quality for commercial considerations.

Q: How do you feel about having your albums recorded in bits and pieces, with horns, voices, and the rest added after the fact? Don't you risk losing the spontaneity that's so important to your music?

RAMSEY LEWIS: This is a problem that all jazz musicians have faced since the 1960s when twenty-four-track taping came into vogue. After that, the recording companies got carried away with the fact that they could separate sound. You know, the drums come out of one speaker, guitars from another. The public loves it; but for instruments to come out separately, they have to be put in separately too. Like most musicians, I'd prefer to do it the old way. I like a set-up where I might be playing an idea, and the drummer will respond in a certain way, after which the bass player will do something else, which will spark me to turn my music around. Unfortunately, if we recorded that way now, we wouldn't have separation and the public would say, "Ramsey didn't record that album very well, did he."

Q: Critics are always eager to point out what they don't like. Let's take an opposite tack. Which is your favorite album?

RAMSEY LEWIS: That's hard to say. I've worked on over fifty albums, and out of that group, there are half a dozen or so that represent turning points in my career. Others are special to me because of the way they sound or the way they were recorded. "Love Notes" is a good example. Stevie Wonder—God love him, he's a genius—wrote the title song on that album under incredible circumstances. One Thanksgiving weekend, he called me in Chicago and said, "I have a song for you." A few weeks later, after I had booked some time in a recording studio, he came by, sat down at the piano, started to play, stopped midway through his song, and said, "You don't like it, do you?" I said, "Sure, I do." But in truth, I didn't. And he could tell; he felt it. Then he said, "Wait a minute! Wait a minute! I've got something!" He fumbled around at the piano for a few seconds, ordered me to turn on the tape; and fifteen minutes later, he had written *Love Notes*. I had a five-man group at the time. After he taught it to us, we rolled the tape again and played it. It came out on the first take, just the way we used it on the album. It was so good, we didn't change a thing. So whenever I play *Love Notes* in concert now, that experience is in the back of my mind.

Q: Do you ever listen to your own records?

RAMSEY LEWIS: Not for pleasure. That might sound strange. But when I record an album, I spend two or three months listening to it every day, being critical, looking for mistakes, going back to clean up this or that. By the time it's finished, I really don't want to hear it anymore. Also, if I start listening to a lot of Ramsey Lewis albums, I'm going to start copying myself and my music won't grow with the times. Maybe, once a year, I'll take an old album out and play a few favorite songs like "Love Notes" or "Distant Dreamer." Stevie Wonder wrote that one for me too. But that's about all.

Q: What sort of music do you listen to?

RAMSEY LEWIS: All types. I listen to rock, and I listen to blues. I listen to classical music, religious, folk, and opera. I'm trying to get into country music, but I have a few problems there. Obviously, I also listen to jazz.

Q: Do you compose too?

RAMSEY LEWIS: Not really. I'm a pianist, not a composer. There aren't many people who can do both well. Duke Ellington probably did more for jazz than any person ever. He was a fabulous composer. But let's face it; he wasn't the world's greatest piano player. Art Tatum and Oscar Peterson were genius players, but their writing was less than brilliant. I think you have to do one or the other. I practice playing the piano for five or six hours a day when I have the time. That doesn't leave much room for composing.

Q: What do your practice sessions entail?

RAMSEY LEWIS: Right now, it's mostly independent fingers and technique. Playing the piano well requires more than two hands. It takes ten fingers. There are a lot of piano players who can't use all their fingers all the time. And to avoid that problem, I go through very strenuous technical drills to make certain my hands remain even and my fingers are independent. These hands are my tools. They're my best means of expression. And if I get an idea that my fingers can't execute, I'm in big trouble. Also, when they do execute it, I want that idea to sound the way I heard it in my head. I don't want my left hand a little behind the right. I don't want to be forced into a situation where I have to simplify an idea in order to be able to execute it.

Q: Your hands are very important to you. What would happen if you contracted arthritis or some other ailment that kept you from playing?

RAMSEY LEWIS: I suppose the first thing I'd do is consider slashing my wrists. After I got over that, I might lecture, write a book, or teach. But it's really impossible for me to visualize myself not playing the piano. It's been my entire life. I use it to express my moods, my feelings, past experiences, and just about everything else. It's a hard question for me to answer because music is what I am. Without it, I'd be at a terrible loss.

Q: One last question. What's it like to be famous and have a group of followers across the country who think you're wonderful?

RAMSEY LEWIS: I don't deny the fact that it's a positive feeling. I like the approval of other people, and I derive real pleasure from the joy and pride it brings my family, especially my parents. But like the Jason Robards character in *Julia* said, "Fame is a paint job." So I'm constantly reevaluating myself and searching for ways to make myself a better person.

Also, you have to remember that a lot of what I do now is a bore. Living in hotels day after day, chasing taxis, riding 747s. It's a real grind; and doing a hundred and sixty concerts a year, I'm subjected to a lot of that. When I'm on the road, I miss my family; I don't sleep as well; and I get tired. Fortunately though, one thing has never changed. Wherever I am, whatever the conditions, I still love walking on stage, sitting down in front of an audience, and playing the piano. I love doing that. I really do.

*This article, written in 1984, was a celebration of one of Columbia
University's finest professors.*

Richard B. Morris

What is a university?

Classroom buildings, when not in use, are sepulchral in nature.

Students quickly come and go.

School traditions are meaningless without a vibrant present-day entity
to keep them alive.

The essence of an academic institution is its faculty. For two hundred
years, Columbia has been fortunate. Nobel laureates, United States
Supreme Court justices, and American icons too numerous to mention
have presided over its classrooms.

Today (July 24, 1984), sixty years after first coming to Columbia,
Richard B. Morris is eighty years old. Henry Steele Commager has said,
"It's impossible to explain with any semblance of brevity what Richard
Morris means to us all. He is an extraordinarily versatile and prolific
scholar. His devotion to teaching and writing has enriched thousands of
students, colleagues, and friends. The craft of the historian has irrevocably
changed as a consequence of his legacy."

Morris was born in New York, raised in the Bronx, and graduated
from the City College of New York. He began graduate work at Columbia in 1924, and later recalled, "Columbia in the 1920s was a very rigid,
very strict and stuffy place in which students were not cordially welcomed."

Carrying a dual course load in history and law, he received a doctor-
ate in 1930 after authoring *Studies in the History of American Law*—a book
that focused on seventeenth- and eighteenth-century America and included
a pioneering chapter on women's rights in Colonial America.

"There was a serious gap in the scholarship of that time," Professor
Morris remembers. "No one was attempting to show the relationship
between American history and American law." To bridge that gap, he later

studied twenty thousand cases from the colonial era and wrote the seminal work *Government and Labor in Early America*.

Morris spent nineteen years as a faculty member at the City College of New York and returned to Columbia in 1949.

"I loved teaching," he recalls. "It was an opportunity to help students and encourage them to see a new point of view. And the 1950s were a Golden Age for historians at Columbia. The students were brilliant, very mature, anxious to make up for years lost during the war. My colleagues were men like Allen Nevins, Henry Steele Commager, and Richard Hofstadter. All of us within the department had enormous freedom. No one told us how to teach or what textbook to use."

In 1959, Morris was named Gouverneur Morris Professor of History and chairman of the History Department at Columbia. Six years later, he authored *The Peacemakers*, a Bancroft-Prize–winning study of the negotiations that ended the Revolutionary War. Over time, he has received three Guggenheim Fellowships and served as chairman of the board of trustees of the John Jay Homestead in Bedford, New York. In 1973, on reaching Columbia's mandatory retirement age, he was awarded a three-year lectureship that extended his teaching career through 1976. At its close, he was elected president of the American Historical Association. Still active, he maintains an office in Columbia's Butler Library, where he supervises the editing of the John Jay Papers, which will be published in four volumes.

One could go on, but there comes a time when citing achievements and publications is cumulative and irrelevant. Henry Graff, who succeeded Morris as chairman of the History Department at Columbia, speaks as others do of his predecessor's indefatigable energy and contagious good humor.

"Richard Morris," Graff observes, "has always known who he is and what he's about. Through his work and the conduct of his life, he has shown us that there is no better or more important work than the work of the historian."

Professor Morris would agree wholeheartedly with that assessment of his profession. But somewhat ruefully, he observes, "Not enough historians are interested in writing anymore. They're interested in computerized studies of questionable validity that nobody reads because they're wrong. To the extent that quantification is useful, I applaud it. But we have too many people in academia today who will make a statement like, 'Railroads made no difference in American history,' and then give you piles of statistics in an effort to prove their point of view. I'd like to see more common sense to go with statistics. And I'd like to see more historians communicate with the public. Too many academicians write only for each other. We should be writing, not only for our students and other scholars, but for the public at large. And we should be writing with the same degree of craftsmanship, literary perception, empathy, and imagination that supports good writing in other endeavors."

These are good times for Richard Morris. He has been married for over fifty years. His children and grandchildren are devoted to him. Friends and colleagues are generous with praise and admiration. As a colonial historian, he is very much in demand at the bicentennial celebrations that will continue through 1987. He is a patriot, proud of his country and unswervingly loyal to American institutions. Yet he remains young enough and open-minded enough to advise, "It seems to me that the Bicentennial Decade is a good time to reflect on that key word 'revolution' in celebrating the American Revolution."

"History," Morris says in closing, "is more than a quest for truth about the past. You see, societies are like people. You can't understand the society in which you live without knowing its origins any more than you can understand an adult without analyzing the child. If you don't know about the Founding Fathers; if you're ignorant of Washington and Jefferson, Hamilton and Jay; then you're just living in a country; it could be any country. And it would be a country without much of a present or future, because it would be a country without a past."

*I met Frank Macchiarola in 1964, when I was a sophomore at Colum-
bia and Frank was my dormitory counselor. Fifteen years later, I wrote
about his tenure as chancellor of the New York City school system.*

Frank Macchiarola

New York City's public-school system, the largest in the country, is
in a state of crisis. Sixty-two percent of its seventh graders cannot read at
a seventh-grade level. Almost one-third of its high-school students read
at a grade level two years or more below standard. Truancy is so wide-
spread that twenty of the city's schools show absentee rates of over 40
percent. And while there have always been some parents who chose not
to send their children to public schools, now there are more than ever—
particularly middle and upper-middle-class whites—because they just
don't think the system can do an adequate job.

At last count, the New York City Board of Education classified its one
million students as follows—black (37.9 percent); Hispanic (29.0 percent);
Oriental (2.6 percent); and other (30.5 percent). "Other" includes such
ethnic groups as Jews, Irish, Italians, and Poles; none of whom like
to think of themselves in such anonymous terms. The exodus of these
"others" from New York's schools has been a significant measure of the
problems, seen by some as "insoluble," that plague the city's educational
system.

On April 17, 1978, the New York City Board of Education set out to
resolve the crisis. Its first step was the appointment of thirty-seven-year-
old Frank Macchiarola to succeed Irving Anker as chancellor. In contrast
to Anker, who had worked in the school system for forty-three years,
Macchiarola was an outsider. A lifelong resident of Brooklyn, he had
served briefly as president of Community School Board 22 (a non-
salaried position) but that was all. With Mayor Ed Koch behind him,
Macchiarola squeaked past the board by a narrow four-to-three vote after
days of intense political maneuvering and debate.

Macchiarola took office on July 1, 1978. Almost immediately, he
asked for, received, and accepted the resignation of virtually every top aide

who served at the chancellor's pleasure. "At issue," he commented after-ward, "was the ability to work as part of a collective effort in what I hoped would be a changing environment. I wanted talented people around me who weren't too set in their ways."

Six months later, Macchiarola submitted a twenty-four-page report to the board, whose seven members bore responsibility for much of the school system's plight. Though they also held power over his own job, the new chancellor wasn't intimidated.

"Public education in New York City," Macchiarola wrote, "while bet-ter than many of its critics contend, is still in trouble. Too many of our stu-dents are being failed by the system. Our schools produce too many students who can neither read adequately, nor do basic arithmetic, nor think clearly. Too many of those who should be serving our children are only serving themselves. We have not only tolerated mediocrity, we have developed, congratulated, and promoted it."

The man who hopes to turn New York City's public-school system around personifies upward mobility in America. His father was a New York City sanitation worker; his mother, a saleswoman. Macchiarola attended local Roman Catholic elementary and high schools, St. Francis College in Brooklyn, and law school at Columbia. Subsequently, he taught as a professor at Bernard Baruch College; then served in a variety of adminis-trative posts such as assistant vice president for Academic Affairs at Columbia, deputy director of the New York City Emergency Financial Control Board, and finally, vice president for Institutional Advancement of the Graduate School of the City University of New York. Prior to his appointment as chancellor, Macchiarola had been sounded out about sev-eral positions in the Koch administration, including deputy mayor.

At $2.7 billion, New York City's annual school budget is larger than the total expenditures of any other city in the nation. Macchiarola's appointment as chancellor was a tribute to both his qualifications as an educator and his administrative and financial expertise.

A typical Macchiarola day begins with an early breakfast in the mod-est brick home in Brooklyn where he lives with his wife and three sons. By 8:30 a.m., he is at Board of Education headquarters in Brooklyn. Virtually all of his time is spent in meetings. Staff members vie for his attention on dozens of matters. A Board of Education lobbyist outlines plans to maximize federal aid from Washington. A half-dozen city and state legislators from Queens come in to complain that the proposed closing of two schools in their borough will have an adverse impact on real-estate values and increase the flight of middle-class whites to the suburbs.

Through it all, Macchiarola sits and listens. His office is large, with a cluttered desk at one end and a spacious conference table at the other. The walls are lined with photos of city schoolchildren, paintings by Macchiarola's two oldest sons, certificates, and plaques. The chancellor's style of presiding is casual. Jacket off, he leans back in his chair at the head of the conference table while listening; then leans forward to speak and gesture with a forcefulness due in part to his being, as usual, about thirty pounds overweight. His laugh, although a little hoarse, is contagious. He's a good listener, and each session is a genuine give-and-take. But he knows how to cut a discussion off when it has gone on too long. He takes few notes, committing virtually all facts and decisions to memory. He readily deciphers and absorbs everything from arcane legislative enactments to piles of statistics. He thrives on his work and loves the pace of people rushing in and out of his office. More than one colleague has likened him in terms of vitality and exuberance to the young Hubert Humphrey.

Once a week, Macchiarola meets with the Board of Education, which is charged with ratifying the policies he administers. Previous chancellors began these weekly sessions by presenting the board with alternative courses of action. Macchiarola, in effect, tells board members, "This is the problem; this is the solution as I see it. Accept my solution, or come up with something better." To date, none of his major recommendations has been rejected. This past summer, the board voiced its satisfaction with his performance by extending his contract as chancellor through June 1981.

"The board's support has been extremely gratifying," Macchiarola says. "[board president] Stephen Aiello has been very supportive. So have the mayor, [city council president] Thomas Cuite, and [city council finance committee chairman] Ed Sadowsky. Without their help, there's no way this job could be done."

However, other groups have been less supportive. Macchiarola has been attacked at various times for serving as "the mayor's hatchet man," for exacerbating teacher-administration tensions, for "moving too slowly" on minority hiring, and for "not doing enough" to turn the school system around. In response, he argues that, far from aggravating teacher-administration tensions and carrying out the mayor's bidding, he sided with the teachers earlier this year in support of a contract opposed by the mayor as "too costly." As for minority hiring, Macchiarola declares that "hiring unqualified teachers is a disservice to all our children." Yet, in the same breath, he notes, "My administration has sought out qualified minority personnel for all posts and encouraged minority enrollment in supervisory training programs." Indeed, this past year, Macchiarola rejected appointment lists submitted to him by several school districts on the grounds that minority personnel had not been adequately considered for vacant supervisory posts.

What is left, then, is the primary allegation; that Macchiarola has not done enough to turn the school system around. Some Macchiarola opponents charge that the only changes made to date have been cosmetic. A teachers' union official bitterly referred to Macchiarola as "a productivity scheme man," saying, "What he really is is the champion of those who believe that the whole problem in the city is the incompetent teacher. And if you don't support that analysis, you're made to look as though you're not for the children."

Whether such criticisms are valid or not, the basic question remains as to whether, given the problems that exist, anyone can breathe new life into the city's educational structure.

New York's public-school system is a bureaucratic nightmare. Each year, 974 separate schools vie for funds and attention, while 46,500 teachers, more than one million parents, and thousands of cafeteria workers, bus drivers, and custodians struggle to protect their own vested interests. In addition to normal educational programs, the board provides vocational education, bilingual education, and education for the handicapped. It must administer drug programs; lobby for state, local and federal aid; and negotiate contracts with a multitude of unions. As if these problems were not enough, it must also operate within financial constraints incurred as a consequence of the city's fiscal crisis. For the coming year, despite inflation, the school budget has been slashed by $100 million. And while Macchiarola would like to take advantage of the city's declining birthrate by having smaller classes with more resources, the Board of Education has been forced instead to order school closings and the consolidation of services.

"The fiscal problem is serious," Macchiarola admits, "and it could get worse before it gets better. Everyone wants to cut costs by taking so-called non-essential items out of the school budget. There's a proposal under consideration in Congress to cut federal aid to school lunch programs. That's just one example. What some people don't seem to realize is that a child is as entitled to eat as to read. We give them books, and we should give them lunch. But if present thinking continues, we'll be under a great deal of pressure to abandon that notion. The end result would be education by audit; a school system so engrossed in contracts and budgetary problems that its leaders forget that their primary mission is the education of children."

Is such a scenario inevitable?

"I don't think so," Macchiarola answers. "Obviously, we don't have as much money as we'd like. But there's no question in my mind that the public sector has been almost universally wasteful in managing its resources. There's a tradition in education that, if you spend a dollar and it doesn't work, you should spend two dollars. Not only that, you should give two dollars to the person who couldn't work with only one. I want to challenge that kind of thinking. To my mind, the solution lies in an increased effort on the part of all, especially the classroom teacher."

But will the teachers cooperate? At times, they appear to be the chancellor's staunchest adversaries. Friction between Macchiarola and United Federation of Teachers president Albert Shanker dates back several years. As deputy director of the Emergency Financial Board, Macchiarola maintained a hardline stance against teacher salary increases. At issue was a control board ruling that the incremental raises accorded teachers annually constituted a "wage increase" and were thus in violation of emergency financial legislation designed to save the city from financial ruin. Macchiarola's position was upheld in the courts. Later, as president of Community School Board 22, he forced a short-lived city residency requirement on teachers in the district. Shanker bitterly opposed Macchiarola's election as chancellor and, immediately after the selection, voiced his deep unhappiness about it.

One of Macchiarola's first acts as chancellor was to eliminate salary increases previously granted to teachers for academic credits obtained through fraudulent mail-order courses. The chancellor's order was eminently sensible, but nonetheless it was challenged by the teachers' union in an ultimately unsuccessful grievance proceeding. Next, the chancellor instructed supervisors to demand thorough documentation whenever the legitimacy of a teacher's absence due to illness was in doubt. Again the teachers' union challenged Macchiarola in an arbitration proceeding, and again it lost. This past year, as a consequence of Macchiarola's directive, teacher absences due to illness dropped by 17 percent. Then, in his landmark report to the Board of Education, Macchiarola bemoaned his teachers' "ever-increasing reliance upon the union contract as the standard of professional responsibility." He declared, "There is no escape from the fact that the job of teaching is more challenging than it ever has been. There is no escape from the fact that the job of teaching requires greater talents and abilities than many of our teachers presently possess."

Yet the city-teacher contract remains largely as it was when Macchiarola took office and is a source of increasing concern to the chancellor. "In some instances," he concedes, "we have been precluded by contract from deploying our personnel as effectively as I would like. For example, I'd love to change the contract so that teacher preparation periods could be used for additional duties rather than free time. Also, at present, it's virtually impossible to dismiss an incompetent teacher who has somehow managed to achieve tenure. The procedures for removal are extremely difficult to implement and allow for near-endless delay."

Budgeting problems, teacher inadequacies, and contract difficulties alone would pose a threat to the quality of any school system. However, many consider them secondary to what is perceived by some as an even greater threat—the type of student presently enrolled in the city's school system.

Again, Macchiarola admits, "There are problems. We've been gun-shy about confronting the issue of student behavior. Disruptive conduct has to stop. Also, in many cases, the system has failed to motivate poor learners. Quite frankly, there are schools within the system that I wouldn't send my own children to because of safety risks and the lack of an educational program suited to their needs. But my philosophical position is that all children are educable. And I have very little sympathy for white families who take their children out of New York City schools simply because they don't want their kids mixing with children from another race. That's what we're really talking about here, and it reminds me of the Boston Brahmins worrying about what the Irish would do to their school system in the early 1900s."

Macchiarola's two oldest children attend a public school that reflects the composition of the neighborhood in which they live. Their classes are 60 percent white. But an ideal racial mix, as the chancellor sees it, cannot be defined in terms of a percentage. Rather, he says, "It is a situation where everyone feels included and everyone feels welcome. Instead of worrying about ethnic percentages, what we have to do is make the teachers and administrators within the system more accountable, and see that they do the job they're supposed to do. If the system is functioning properly, it can educate any student. And the fact that no major urban school system has yet to meet this challenge is no excuse for failure."

As a first step in his program to encourage "accountability," Macchiarola denied tenure to a group of school principals and other supervisory personnel he called "below standard." In a bureaucracy steeped in civil-service ways, the move shocked some but did not achieve the desired result.

"I was hoping," Macchiarola says, "for a ripple effect; that supervisors would see what I was doing and then themselves deny tenure to their lesser teachers. Unfortunately, it hasn't happened. What we need now are realistic standards against which teachers can be judged."

On August 1, 1979, Macchiarola's denial of tenure to eighty-four supervisory personnel was upheld by the New York State Supreme Court.

"That decision," he says, "gave us an extremely important boost. The next step is to let supervisors know that, if they are lax in enforcing adequate standards when resolving teacher tenure issues, their own standing will be imperiled. For my own part, I've tried to set an example by appointing more highly motivated people to positions of power at Board of Education headquarters. There's improved administration and a new sense of purpose here. In the years to come, these men and women will enforce accountability from one level to the next throughout the system."

Macchiarola has told several associates that he will step down as chancellor when his present contract expires in July 1981. After that, his future is uncertain. On several occasions, he has been mentioned as "the mayor's candidate" to oppose Harrison Goldin in the autumn 1981 election for

New York City comptroller. Macchiarola himself scoffs at the notion, say-ing, "I'd love you to write that I have no political aspirations." Certainly his choice of jobs would appear to support that contention.

New York City school chancellors seldom go on to bigger and better things. The job is a political graveyard. Macchiarola's predecessors over the past two decades (Irving Anker, Harvey Scribner, Bernard Donovan, and Calvin Gross) all lapsed into oblivion on leaving office. The job, the *New York Times* once wrote, is "one that many educators wouldn't touch."

Still, if Macchiarola can bring enough good people into the system and institutionalize enough changes, gradual improvement could be seen. And maybe, just maybe, the Board of Education will be perceived as hav-ing turned a corner during his administration. If that happens, the voters of New York might take a long hard look at Frank Macchiarola. What they will see is a genuinely compassionate man, who is convinced that the public schools can be made workable for all who use them. For the phys-ically handicapped and the poor; for the children of bus drivers, porters, and doormen; for black militants and Spanish-speaking adolescents, as well as the sons and daughters of New York City's middle and upper-middle class. Should that perception spread, Macchiarola might find the lure of politics to be irresistible.

On the wall of the Macchiarola home, there hangs a photograph of two-year-old Frank Macchiarola Jr sitting on the lap of New York City mayor Ed Koch. In a moment of levity, the mayor inscribed the picture, "To the next mayor of New York."

Given the youth of Frank Jr, three possibilities must be considered: (1) Ed Koch plans on being in office for a very long time; (2) Frank Macchiarola Jr will be the first infant mayor of New York; or (3) when the mayor penned his inscription, he had Frank Sr in mind.

*In 1989, the plight of America's homeless was just beginning to receive
national attention.*

Robert Hayes and the National Coalition for the Homeless

"In Nazi Germany, they would have known what to do with him."
The speaker was a well-dressed woman looking down at a homeless
man asleep on the sidewalk. The implication inherent in her remark, of
course, was that this man was somehow undeserving of life. He was
unproductive, morally bankrupt, and society would be better off if he
were eliminated so no one would be forced to see or smell him again.

By contrast, there are thousands of Americans who quietly tend to
our nation's homeless. Teachers help young homeless children learn how
to speak. A nun in Brooklyn ignores her own battle against cancer to run
one of the most nurturing family shelters in the world. Rampant homelessness has elicited painfully little in the way of a response from our
national political leadership. But it has inspired countless men and women,
who start out as volunteers and become staunch advocates for practical
solutions.

Robert Hayes is one of those advocates. Born in Brooklyn and raised
on suburban Long Island, he began work in 1977 as an attorney at the
Wall Street law firm of Sullivan & Cromwell, where he specialized in
antitrust and securities law.

"Back then," Hayes recalls, "I shared the common belief that homeless
people were living on the streets by choice. Then, gradually, I began to
talk with them and learned they were there because there were no viable
alternatives. The city shelters had too few beds and were ill-run, incredibly
filthy, and dangerous. I also learned that these men and women on the
streets were human beings, and that was surprising to one as obtuse as
me."

In 1979, Hayes brought a class action against the city of New York,
obtaining a consent decree requiring it to provide clean safe shelter to

every man who sought it. Subsequent litigation expanded that right to homeless women. Then, in 1982, Hayes left Sullivan & Cromwell to found the National Coalition for the Homeless—an advocacy and direct-service organization dedicated to the principle that decent shelter and sufficient food are fundamental rights in a civilized society. Financed by corporate contributions and modest state-government funds, the coalition now has an annual budget of two million dollars, a full-time staff of twenty-eight, and active members in fifty cities across the country.

Mark Twain once observed, "Everybody talks about the weather, but nobody does anything about it." To many, that axiom could just as easily apply to America's homeless crisis. But now, finally someone is doing something about it. Hayes is forging a national movement and seeking national solutions.

Q: The common stereotype of a homeless person is of a panhandler or a mentally ill person screaming obscenities at innocent bystanders. How can you get people to overcome their revulsion to such an image?

HAYES: That's one stereotype; but like most stereotypes, it's far from accurate. In most big cities, whether your experience with homeless people is personal and direct or through television news, homelessness is equated with people who are adult and seriously mentally ill. People who act out, sometimes aggressively, sometimes quietly. People who wear coats eight sizes too big all year round, argue with invisible adversaries, and carry what appears to be garbage around in shopping bags. But you have to remember, if you're homeless trying to exist on city streets, there is an enormous premium on disguising your homelessness. If you don't look homeless, you can sit in a coffee shop for the price of a cup of coffee through a cold day. You can go into a store and use a bathroom to wash yourself up. You won't be harassed by the police. You won't be viewed with fear and suspicion by passersby. So, in fact, if you went up to our dinner program in New York at Grand Central Terminal where we feed 350 people every night, you would probably see about 10 percent of those people as recognizably homeless. Most homeless people you pass by, you can't tell they're homeless, because they're going to do everything possible to hide that for reasons of survival. Obviously, if you have some news story and you send a television crew out to get eight seconds of footage of a homeless person, they're going to look for the most obviously homeless person. So of course they're going to come back with footage of someone mentally ill acting out. But that's a misrepresentation of the true picture of homeless people today.

Q: So who are the homeless?

HAYES: Right now, at the end of the 1980s, the common denominator is that they are Americans who have lost their homes, who have been squeezed out of the housing market. Ten years ago, chronically mentally ill people were the first folks to hit the streets. Then came people who had very bad job skills and poor education. By the mid-1980s, and really ever since, the homeless have come from the ranks of families. Families headed by a single parent, usually a woman, usually with young children. Families who are not competitive in the Darwinian struggle for housing.

Q: What percentage of the homeless nationwide are children?

HAYES: Probably, about 40 percent at this point. In some parts of the country, the majority are children.

Q: Is this more of an urban problem than a rural problem?

HAYES: Some of it is an urban problem. Mass homelessness has also erupted in suburban rings around cities. And increasingly over the past several years, the problem has grown in farm states, where people are falling out of the job market. So at this point, you can find homeless folks in rural areas, suburban areas, most visibly in urban areas; but it's across the board. It has become more visible because there are more people. It's not complicated. And the frightening aspect of this is, during the 1980s, for the first time in American history, we've managed to create mass homelessness during a period of economic prosperity. Throughout United States history, until the 1980s, it took system-wide economic dislocations like the Great Depression or the Panic of 1893 to create mass homelessness.

Q: How much has the drug crisis contributed to the problem?

HAYES: It's an element, although not a fundamental element. The common denominator and the common remedy for all homeless people is that they need a place to live. Do some people become homeless because they spend all their money on drugs? Absolutely. Do some people turn to drugs because of the misery of life on the streets? Absolutely. Is it a big part of the picture right now? No. Probably 15 or 20 percent.

Q: Other than mental illness, what causes middle-class people to fall out this way?

HAYES: All kinds of events can trigger a slide that can't be stopped. Some precipitating events can be characterized as acts of moral turpitude. Very often, it's simply the intensity of competition for housing. Quitting a job out of anger, the breakup of a marriage; those kinds of precipitating events do it, too. There used to be room for mistakes in life. Now with this housing market, there seems not to be that margin for error any longer. You can blame anyone for failing to be rugged enough to win a race. But in this contest, because there plainly is insufficient affordable housing, we have preordained a system where there will be losers.

Q: Many people see this as a pretty hopeless situation. Is it?

HAYES: One of the greatest frustrations that I experience is this myth of intractability. We forget that we once knew how to do things in this country. We once knew how to build housing. We rebuilt all of Western Europe. And now we think that we just can't get housing built. We have nuns, priests, do-gooders all across the country who run wonderful supportive residences for people who are mentally ill and in need of ongoing care and housing. Mayors, governors, and secretaries of Housing and Urban Development look at these models and say, "How wonderful." Do they replicate them? No. The failure of ending homelessness is not a failure of know-how. It's a failure of political will.

Q: How much do the American people care about the problem?

HAYES: I suspect many Americans are reasonably willing, if not content, to let poor people suffer their poverty, so long as they do it invisibly. But homeless people are irritatingly visible. You can't avoid them when you see them on the streets, and increasingly they are being burned into public consciousness through good journalism. Homeless people on the evening news are becoming like Vietnam being brought into living rooms. And almost everybody—Christian, Jew, Republican, Democrat, conservative, the elderly—knows intuitively that something is wrong. For a while, we dance around. We listen to people like Ronald Reagan, who say these folks are choosing to be homeless. We believe that in some self-protective way, so that we can bear to walk past people on the streets and go into our own homes at night. But over time, lies disappear. So yes, the visibility is clearly fueling activism. And we don't appeal to the souls of politicians when we say let's get some housing legislation passed by Congress. We're sending newspaper stories reporting polls that say two out of three Americans want Washington to house homeless people. It's been a people's movement triggered by intuitive decency. The politicians have not been leaders. Yet I think now we're on the cusp of a change, where the politicians will begin rushing to the head of the popular parade that says we have to get these people decent housing.

Q: In places like New York City, there are shelters, yet many homeless people don't use them. Why not?

HAYES: When the courts ordered Mayor Koch to provide shelter for homeless people—men first, then women and children—he made the shelter system so barbaric that people were afraid of it. That's significant, because the myth that homeless people will refuse genuine offers of decent shelter is one that has a seductive, if vile, appeal. If we can walk past that woman on the street, telling ourselves, "She must want to be there; there are places she could go," we can sleep easier at night. You know, the fact is, if there were genuine offers of help, if there were real refuges for people to go to, they would not be living in train stations or on park benches. Homeless people have not suddenly lost all sense of proportion. Even mental illness is rarely characterized by an attraction to hunger or cold or physical pain. We pretend that these people are on the streets because of the brilliance of the civil libertarians who protect their right to rot on the streets. But the civil libertarians aren't that smart. And universally, there is a power of government under our Constitution to impose mental-health care, including forced hospitalization, on people who are endangered by their mental illness.

In almost every part of the country, mentally ill people don't get help and don't get hospitalization because there are no hospital beds available to them. We decided not to spend the money on providing psychiatric care, so you can be seriously mentally ill and go to the public hospital of almost any community and be told, "No beds; come back when you get a little more disturbed." People sometimes have committed horrific crimes after being turned away from psychiatric hospitals when they sought help. Many more people have literally died. Thousands of people in New York City were turned away at the door at the emergency rooms of acute-care psychiatric hospitals because there were no beds available. The problem is not an abundance of civil liberties. The problem is a scarcity of beds.

Q: Laying aside the pluses or minuses of his actions, has Ed Koch exacerbated the problem with his confrontational rhetoric?

HAYES: No. Almost everyone who panhandles increased their income after Ed Koch told New Yorkers to stop giving to them.

Q: Is that true, or is that something you're saying flippantly?

HAYES: It's impressionistically true. Can I prove it in a court of law? No. But Ed Koch is a homeless advocate's best friend. All Ed Koch does is foment confrontation. He makes problems visible, and I think his confrontational policies have helped quicken the exposure of the problems of New York's homeless. What you lose with that kind of confrontational character, of course, is the unity and competence of taking the public goodwill and converting it to bricks and mortar. So it's a mixed blessing, but there's certainly some element of blessing in some of Koch's confrontations.

Q: Why is it that, all of a sudden, housing has become unavailable?

HAYES: Two principal reasons. First, during the late 1970s, a shift in the living patterns of affluent Americans created this rush toward what's called gentrification. So many older cities, which were replete with housing affordable for people with very low incomes, were suddenly developed into communities for people we're calling—for lack of a better term—yuppies. Urban living became attractive again, and market forces caused by the increased attraction of urban living displaced some poor people. In too many instances, local governments fueled the market forces support-ing gentrification with tax dollars. So, effectively, we had governments cre-ating housing for the rich at the expense of housing for the poor. There came a point in almost every city across America where the equilibrium was broken. And government responded very slowly to that break in the equilibrium.

Reason number two for the decline in affordable housing is the rad-ical shift in federal housing policy under the regime of Ronald Reagan. Ever since World War II, there had been a non-ideological, broad-based bipartisan consensus that the private market did not work, cannot work, to create affordable housing for the poor. So since the late 1940s, there had been federal support to help fund the creation of housing for poor people through a variety of programs. Senator Robert Taft, Mr. Repub-lican in the late 1940s, was probably the chief mover of federal housing supports. Then in 1981, when Ronald Reagan took office, he claimed he was conservative, but what we saw with domestic housing policy was not conservative at all. Instead the president successfully launched a rad-ical extremist repudiation of forty years of American federal housing policy. You can't cut the heart out of federal support to house poor people and then be surprised when poor people wind up on the streets. That is the legacy of this radical shift in policy that President Reagan brought us.

Q: What's it like to be homeless?

HAYES: I can only speak derivatively. I can only speak from having, I guess now, hundreds and thousands of friends and acquaintances who are homeless. For an old woman to be homeless, it's probably the fulfillment of every nightmare. You're abandoned, forsaken, feared, pitied. And the psychic agony, I think, is in many ways worse than the physical torment. Hunger, pain, cold, heat are all there. But so too, is monotony; the awful monotony of having to put your entire energy into survival. In some areas, that means walking all day and night, collecting cans to redeem for deposit. In some cases, it means walking the Orwellian paths, day in and day out, from one soup kitchen to another, just to keep yourself fed. It means being ashamed. It means being afraid to go back and try to make contact with people who might be in a position to offer a hand. It means terror. It means being afraid every moment that you are going to be hurt. And because of the constant vigilance that's required for safety, it means psychiatric trouble; increased instability through the constant fears that you live with. Ultimately, it means physical deterioration. Sooner or later, it means death. You read in the newspapers every winter about frozen corpses. The image of the medieval death cart going through town after a cold snap is seen in the reports of death tolls after a cold snap in northern cities. But most homeless people don't die of hypothermia. Most homeless people die from being worn out. They get beaten down. A thirty-year-old man looks fifty; a fifty-year-old woman looks eighty. People die of "natural causes"—as the death certificates read—so prematurely that the fair characterization of the toll of homelessness is, in many cases, death.

Q: Do you give to panhandlers?

HAYES: Sure; to a point. Do I give to obviously inebriated men begging on the streets? No. Do I run out of money if I walk through three blocks of New York City on a summer evening? Absolutely. So Robert Hayes doesn't give dollar bills to every panhandler, because I could never afford to. Do I think most panhandlers are doing it for fun or for mischief? That's stupid. Look, you're a journalist; right? I promise you, no matter how hard you work on deadline, your labor is nothing compared to what those guys do, wiping dirty rags across windshields at the entrance to bridges and tunnels. People are not panhandling—which is an incredibly arduous humiliating task—because they have a choice. You can say we're going to outlaw panhandling; we're going to shoo people out of train stations; we're going to stop homeless people from sleeping out in public parks. But there aren't enough troops in the Western world to stop human beings from doing what they must do to survive.

Q: How do you respond to people who say that there are jobs available at minimum wage; that people could make four dollars an hour working at McDonald's, but they make more money panhandling on the streets?

HAYES: I will tell you that a quarter of homeless American adults in the late 1980s have full-time jobs and can't afford housing based on that full-time job. You have people working full-time jobs and panhandling who are still unable to break their way into the housing market. And it's been a long time since the minimum wage was adequate. If you work full-time, it pays far below what the federal government defines as the bare minimum amount of income needed for subsistence. And subsistence means food, clothing, and shelter. It doesn't mean movies. It doesn't mean drugs; it doesn't mean alcohol. It means the bare basics of human survival. So yes, we have people working forty-hour-a-week jobs who are paupers.

Q: Are there any signs that give you hope for dealing with this problem in the future?

HAYES: I'm optimistic. I don't have a lot of faith in politicians. I have yet to experience a politician who has been a leader. I mean, political leadership is almost an oxymoron to me. Yet I see the public response being decent. I see the politicians slowly picking up on the pulse of that public decency and beginning to say the right things. Koch no longer says that putting shelters up for the homeless is like spreading cancer. He says, "We've gotta help." He may not do it, but he says it. George Bush does not say what Ronald Reagan said. Reagan said people were living out on the streets because they liked it. George Bush is saying this is an appalling American tragedy; that we must end homelessness. That's progress. The rhetoric is improving dramatically. Politicians at a minimum now are feeling an obligation to make it appear as though they are doing something positive and constructive. The question now, when the rubber meets the road, is whether an appearance of acting constructively will be all we get, or will we the people demand that bricks and mortar go up and that people get a place to live? That's what will decide whether the United States becomes a third-world-like country.

Q: How much will it cost to end homelessness in America. And can you suggest some specific programs?

HAYES: There is no one response to that question. There are some parts of the country where housing assistance from Washington could come in the form of rental subsidies. In a city like Dallas, there's no housing short-age, and yet there are twenty thousand homeless people in the city. The picture now that's in my mind is the one large shelter in Dallas, run by an Episcopal priest in a warehouse. There's a concrete floor that people sleep on. They get mats; there are no beds. Yet starting in the afternoon, there's a line of men competing for concrete-floor space. And there's a second line of mothers and kids competing for the same concrete-floor space. This is in a city with a 15 percent rental vacancy rate and more than enough housing to go around; where landlords offer a free month's rent and a free VCR if a young couple will sign a lease. What's needed there is the ability to help these homeless families compete economically for the housing that exists. In cities like Philadelphia, New York, and Boston, there's a shortage of housing. We need new construction, and we need rehabilitation. We're promoting lots of measures, but the key legislation before Congress is a $2 billion bill to create a quarter of a million housing units for almost a million people. It would renovate public-housing units that are now vacant because they're unlivable. We actually have public-housing units that are vacant while people live out on the streets for lack of five thousand dollars in rehabilitation funds. We should provide funding to cities to rehabilitate and make habitable abandoned buildings that have been seized for tax foreclosures. We should provide the equivalent of vouchers to let people in other markets like the Southwest buy housing that is available but goes vacant because no one can afford it.

Look, I'm going to put this pitch for helping poor people get places to live in perspective. Okay? This year, the United States government is putting about $7 billion into assisting low-income people with their housing. Public housing, vouchers, all those programs; $7 billion. Same year; the federal government is subsidizing to the tune of $40 billion—almost six times as much—home ownership through the deductibility of the interest that homeowners pay on their mortgages. Now, there may be some abstract distinction in the Office of Management and Budget's mind about money going out of the federal treasury to help poor people, as opposed to money not coming into the federal treasury through this home ownership subsidy, but it really doesn't make a difference. I'm not saying we shouldn't help homeowners with some federal subsidies. But I am saying let's put it in perspective. If we spent that much money the next couple of years on low-income housing assistance, homelessness would be a sorry part of our history. But it would be part of our history, and not part of our present.

Q: Wouldn't a necessary first step be to do something about the state of public shelters?

HAYES: We should not have much of a shelter system in this country, so let me stop you there. Shelters, at their best, are not good places. Shelters are Band-Aids, way stations. A good shelter does two things. First, it saves people from possible death from the elements. Second, it gets human beings out of those institutions into some permanent place to live. To the extent that public shelters in the 1980s have become an alternative source of permanent low-income housing, that's wrong. Not only does it keep people living wretchedly, it breeds dependence. Over time, families spend too many years, too many months, living in emergency housing, in welfare hotels. They become institutionalized. They become unable to be independent, and the damage that a shelter causes to people over time is palpable.

  We see homeless families in the 1980s suffering from some of the same kinds of institutionalization syndromes that mental patients exhibited when they were dumped out of psychiatric hospitals a decade ago. Shelters should not be part of the ultimate solution. And the other thing—to answer a question you haven't asked—is that isn't it really bizarre how we now look at soup kitchens, bread lines, and shelters as points of civic pride? A thousand points of light. We point with pride to this great gesture. You know, a decade ago, these kinds of institutions were not common on the American landscape and were sources of humiliation and embarrassment. One of the first demonstrations we ever planned, in 1980 at the Democratic convention in New York, was to make visible a soup line because it was a disgrace to America. Ed Koch wanted all those people hidden away, so no one in America or the world could see soup kitchens in the modern age. Now we boast about them.

Q: You have a photo of John Kennedy on the wall of your office. How would he have handled this problem?

HAYES: What would Richard Nixon have done? I mean, this is not a Democratic or Republican confrontation. It's a smart, creative, and decent economy against defeatism. I was eleven years old when John Kennedy was shot, so he's just a figure in my memory. But the Kennedy spirit, the American spirit coming into the 1960s, was one of optimism, self-confidence, and the attitude that we could accomplish something. We had the same attitude in the 1940s; we could win a war. In the late 1940s, we could rebuild Western Europe. Now here we are in a period where we're replete with self-doubt. The homeless American living on our streets, more than anything, crystallizes the frustration of the American spirit. I think a John Kennedy could remind us that we are a people with great gifts, great intelligence, and the ability to accomplish something. You know, to build housing for a country's citizens is not an incredibly daunting task. The spirit of John Kennedy saying we're going to fly to the moon is the same spirit that makes me say we can build housing for our citizens. It's not that big a deal.

Q: Is there a danger that the homeless as a class will become more violent?

HAYES: Homeless people are so tired, they're beaten down and so exhausted from their quest for survival, that violence is quite rare. There's an incredible danger to homelessness, though. There's a spiritual danger. Who the hell wants to raise a child in a society that leaves weak people on the streets? What is it doing to you and to me to go home at night past prone bodies sleeping on sidewalks? What does it do to our sense of national purpose and self-confidence? How in the world do we think we can beat acid rain or create the technology to beat cancer or AIDS? We can't build housing. We can't put bricks together to create places for folks to live.

Q: What do you think will happen? Not hope, but think.

HAYES: I think we're decent. I think we're turning the situation around. I think the public is pushing the politicians. It will be slow. But I think we're at a turning point.

Q: How do you feel about people who are in favor of public housing, homeless drop-in centers, and shelters, but don't want them in their neighborhood?

HAYES: Commercial shelters and drop-in centers for homeless people are a whole different ball of wax from permanent housing. Permanent housing gives people a foothold in the community, an investment in the community. Ninety-nine times out of a hundred, folks living in permanent housing become good neighbors. Studies up to your eyeballs have demonstrated pretty definitively that property values are enhanced by the addition of such housing. It's impossible to be unsympathetic to a community that's not wild about having a thousand-bed shelter for homeless men on their block. Who wants to live next to it? Nobody should. It's bad for the homeless men who have to live in the shelter; it's bad for the community. Do we have to do it in some cases? Yes. We support drop-in centers if they're going to save people from dying on the streets. But the best things for homeless people are also the best things for communities. Small is better than large, and permanent housing is better than temporary shelter.

Q: What can private citizens do to deal with this problem?

HAYES: There are several levels of involvement. My first thought is, people should do what they're good at, what they're comfortable with doing.

When I hire someone to work in this movement, I don't make them fill a slot. I try to see what they'd be brilliant at, and then let them do it. If you live in a city where folks are scrambling to survive on the streets, buy a sandwich; buy coffee for someone. Take a step and maybe get involved by offering a friendly word that may lead to a deeper involvement in trying to help a person. That's the best thing you can do. But after you do that; after you give out a blanket, after you put a Band-Aid on the wound; you have to take the next step. People are dying, and emergency help has not been coming from Washington or state capitals or city governments, and we do have to dig in and help one another. Get mad and write to the mayor, write to your congressman. Say this is unacceptable. Find out what the legislation of the moment is. You're a civilized person, and as a civilized American you should demand that housing be considered a fundamental need that has to be fulfilled.

Q: What's the angriest you've gotten with regard to this problem?

HAYES: Probably the most abiding anger happens every time I see a kid who's homeless. Children are full of magic, and there are times when the magic overwhelms me. But given the despair and destruction that they're living through, I also know that inevitably almost all these kids are finished. Some will bounce back because of a grace that protects, but most won't. I've been doing this long enough now to see kids who have gone through early childhood homelessness, and they almost never come back.

In 1988, Robert Peter Gale and I co-authored Final Warning: The Legacy of Chernobyl. *Shortly after publication, Dr. Gale and I sat for an update.*

Dr. Robert Peter Gale

On April 26, 1986, an explosion at the Chernobyl nuclear power station in the Soviet Union sent 100 million curies of radioactive material (more than was released at Hiroshima and Nagasaki) spewing into the air. Within hours, 100,000 men, women, and children were dangerously exposed. Inexorably, the radioactive gasses and particles worked their way west. To Scandinavia, where reindeer that fed on radioactive grass were systematically slaughtered; to Poland, where iodine tablets were distributed to the population in an effort to guard against thyroid cancer; to Italy, where fresh vegetables and milk were destroyed by frightened wholesalers and farmers; and finally to the United States, where the physical effects of Chernobyl will be felt well into the next millennium. By every measure, it was the worst nuclear accident in history. As many as 50,000 people worldwide may die of cancer over the next fifty years as a direct result of Chernobyl.

Six days after the accident, Dr. Robert Peter Gale received an urgent telephone call from Soviet authorities asking for help. Within hours, he was en route to Moscow. In the months that followed, Gale journeyed to Russia six times. He mobilized a team of international medical experts to perform surgery on Soviet patients, supervised the airlift of one million dollars worth of medical equipment to Moscow, and battled the political bureaucracies of two governments. Gale was acclaimed a national hero by the Soviet media. In May 1986, he concluded an agreement with Soviet authorities that will enable him and a team of international experts to evaluate the long-term effects of Chernobyl and treat its victims well into the next century.

Robert Gale was born in New York on October 11, 1945, and grew up in Brooklyn. He attended Hobart College (a small liberal-arts school in upstate New York); then went to medical school at the State University of New York at Buffalo.

"The decision to go to medical school," he recalls, "evolved during college. In high school, I'd wanted to be a nuclear physicist. A cousin, ten years older than me and very bright, was a nuclear physicist and used to tell me wonderful stories about his work. It seemed that this was where the action was; that nuclear physics would have an enormous impact on global issues, philosophy, even mathematics. Then, in college, I turned toward the biological sciences. Physics, and particularly theoretical physics, seemed too remote. I could see the tangible impact of what I was doing in biology, and medical school became the logical direction for me."

In 1970, Gale began an internship at the UCLA Medical Center in Los Angeles where, with the exception of several sabbaticals, he continues to conduct most of his work. He's married with two daughters (Tal and Shir, ages eleven and nine, respectively) and a son (Elan, age four). His wife Tamar is Israeli by birth, but now has dual citizenship.

As a hematologist, oncologist, and immunologist, Robert Gale has devoted most of his professional life to seeking a cure for leukemia. In 1984, he became an unpaid adviser to Dr. Armand Hammer (chairman of President Reagan's Cancer Advisory Panel) and the two men established a friendship that exists to this day. It was Gale's relationship with Hammer, and Hammer's ties to the Soviet Union, that led to Gale's remarkable Chernobyl odyssey.

Q: How has your involvement with Chernobyl changed your perceptions regarding nuclear power?

GALE: Many people assumed that I would become a strong opponent of nuclear power. But the Chernobyl accident can be used to make an argument either for or against nuclear energy. This accident in the Soviet Union will have global effects and may cause thousands of cancer deaths, half of them occurring outside of the Soviet Union. You can imagine what might happen in a nuclear power plant in a less sophisticated or less stable country. On the other hand, one pays a price for all forms of energy. If we consider the current situation in the Persian Gulf with the American military presence there, one could argue that the nuclear threat inherent in defense of oil is greater than the threat from the use of nuclear energy.

Q: Do you feel that the Nuclear Regulatory Commission (NRC) is doing as much as it should to ensure the safe operation of nuclear power plants?

GALE: The public's perception of the NRC is that it is not operating in the public interest. But this might not be entirely fair. We have to strike a reasonable balance between enforcing safety standards and encouraging new and creative approaches to achieving safety. We, as a country, have lost our sense of balance in this regard. Scientists and engineers in the nuclear power industry are so focused on complying with safety regulations that there is relatively little time to develop novel approaches to harnessing atomic energy; approaches that would represent quantum changes in how we get energy from the atom. The NRC's role is primarily limited to trying to regulate safety. Regulating safety is important, but it's unlikely to succeed as a long-term strategy if reactors depend on human beings to provide the margin of safety. No regulations can reduce the risk of human failure to zero. We're making very slow if any progress in using thermonuclear fusion, developing inherently safe reactors, and improving reactor design, because most of our energies are spent complying with regulations that can never really address the fundamental issue of zero accident risk. Clearly, this objective can only be reached by technological advances, not by compliance with current regulations.

Q: Would you favor the nationalization of nuclear power?

GALE: The system we have now is compatible with American society. To have it otherwise would represent a major rethinking of our philosophy of the private sector. The advantages of a national strategy for nuclear power are that one might have a uniform reactor design and better sharing of information. But there are also disadvantages. For example, if a mistake is made, it could have colossal consequences. Also, it's unlikely that a single reactor design or a single type of reactor siting can satisfy this country's diverse energy requirements. We often actually lose ground when we nationalize things. Competition tends to produce a higher level of safety and service. What our country really needs is a careful blending of the national interest and competitive spirit.

Q: Every last person on earth is involved in the nuclear dilemma. Yet no major candidate for president has addressed the issue of nuclear power in any coherent fashion. If one of these candidates came to you and asked for your advice on this matter, what would you tell him?

GALE: In some ways, nuclear energy has become a non-issue. It would be an unusual candidate, regardless of his personal beliefs, who would risk advocating nuclear energy. Politicians are concerned with being elected. Anyone who supports nuclear energy is going to face a difficult time. This country generates 16 percent of its electricity from nuclear sources. The world energy supply is unstable. Still, our national administration changes every four or eight years, and no one wants to take a strong stand. No administrator, no utility company, and no politician. Nonetheless, there are a number of recommendations I would give to a candidate. First, we need to establish far better communication within the nuclear-power industry. Several prior accidents could have been anticipated by the analysis of data from near accidents at power stations around the country. Improved personnel selection and training is another key issue. Also, it seems unnecessary and inadvisable, given the vast size of this country, to construct nuclear power stations close to major metropolitan areas. Some solution to the nuclear waste problem must be found. But beyond these issues, every candidate must realize that there is a global responsibility for nuclear safety and the sharing of data. A nuclear accident anywhere is a nuclear accident everywhere.

The nuclear age started with the detonation of the atomic bomb in Japan. But for many Americans back then, the fact that these were *atomic* bombs was not that critical. It's hard for us to understand this more than forty years later, but it's true. Also, if you speak to Americans who lived through the war and remember the attack on Pearl Harbor, they felt that bombing Hiroshima and Nagasaki was not a wrong thing to do. It was judged to have ended the war quickly, and actually saved lives. The postwar atomic-bomb tests in the atmosphere are not well remembered and had very little impact on the public. In my opinion, Chernobyl represents the realization that these nuclear events are real; that we live in a nuclear age. Responsible candidates would bring that message home.

Q: You're one of the very few non-political Americans who has had an opportunity to see Mikhail Gorbachev up close. You met with him at some length in his office in Moscow, and you saw him briefly when he was in the United States for the summit with Ronald Reagan. If you could give our next president suggestions about how to deal with Gorbachev, what would you say?

GALE: Gorbachev is an intelligent, dynamic, well-educated, and forceful person. Many regard him as the most impressive Soviet leader since Lenin and have welcomed his ascendancy to power, since his style of politics is so different from that of his predecessors. Still, we shouldn't be deluded into thinking that Gorbachev is a closet anti-communist or a closet capitalist. His great advantage is that he realizes the current Communist economic system is not viable and that drastic reform is needed. I think we can do a lot worse than Gorbachev, and I think that taking measures designed to guarantee his downfall are ill-advised.

Q: You've written about a Russian doctor named Orlov, who went to the Chernobyl reactor complex right after the accident and stayed there for three hours, trying to help injured firefighters despite the fact that he understood the dangers involved. Orlov subsequently died from exposure to radiation. You have said numerous times that, of all the Soviet patients you had, Orlov affected you the most; partly because he was a physician about your age, and partly because he knowingly assumed the risks of radiation, giving his life to save others. Do you think that you would react the same way in a comparable situation?

GALE: I hope that I would behave in similar fashion, but I wouldn't be at all unique in this. Physicians and nurses who care for patients with AIDS or hepatitis undertake substantial risks in fulfilling their responsibilities, and I doubt that many of them would hesitate to act as Dr. Orlov did. We tend to underestimate what human beings are willing to do to help one another in times of crisis.

Let me give you an example from my own experience. A number of years ago at UCLA, I treated a young woman who developed aplastic anemia; a disease that destroys bone marrow as a consequence of hepatitis.

The average survival of a patient with the disease is about three months. Because of this, we decided to treat her with an experimental form of immunosuppressive therapy. One complication of this therapy can be paralysis, and as the paralysis spreads, the person can cease breathing. In this particular instance, a nurse and I were in the room when the young woman developed this complication. She stopped breathing and, since she had aplastic anemia and lacked platelets needed for clotting of her blood, she began bleeding from her trachea and gastrointestinal tract. I gave her mouth-to-mouth resuscitation. Obviously, this put me in direct contact with her contaminated blood. But I have to say, I didn't give it a moment's thought. Afterward, I went down to the health-personnel office, had a blood test for hepatitis, got an injection of antibodies, and went back to work. I think that's all one can do.

Q: You deal regularly with people who are sick, and often with those who are dying. What do you say to someone to help prepare him or her for death?

GALE: In this country, almost all physicians are forthright with their patients. I think it's important to discuss with them their prognosis, so they can make intelligent decisions about treatment; the risks and benefits of various interventions. However, there is a certain point at which one realizes that further interventions will probably be futile and that a patient is going to die. Very few individuals can really come to grips with the concept of dying. Yet I'm continually impressed with the integrity and courage with which the youngest of patients face death. Frequently, young children have greater appreciation of what death means than their parents, and actually have to comfort their mother or father during their final days. I would say that one of the greatest privileges of being a physician is to be part of that process; to help these people in their remaining time.

Q: Is there anything that can be said to people who are now healthy but might someday have to face an incurable illness?

GALE: In a certain regard, all of us are incurably ill. We are all going to die. About 20 percent of us, one out of five, are going to die of cancer unless major advances are made. The important thing is to come to peace with yourself when you're not dying. When you're dying, it's perhaps too late. When you face a three-year-old child dying from an incurable form of leukemia, you realize that missing a bus, missing a plane, or having your car scratched are relatively trivial events. You gain an important perspective on life.

Q: You once wrote, "I look at leukemia and I say to myself, this illness shouldn't be. No one should die from this disease. The technology is available to cure leukemia; we have the tools. What I'd like is for someone to give me a large chunk of space and money and tell me to do the job. I'd set up my own unit, take ten very good people. I know who the best players are. In ten years we'd have a cure." What would it take to set up this unit, and do you really think that in ten years we'd have a cure for leukemia?

GALE: What we would have in ten years is a focused attempt to cure leukemia beyond what has already been achieved. I believe the time is right to utilize two recent developments. One is a critical reassessment of the role the immune system plays in eradicating leukemia in patients who receive bone marrow transplants. The second is the availability of molecularly cloned growth factors that stimulate normal and leukemic cells. I'd like to see a group of investigators who are so committed to trying to cure leukemia that they would be willing to temporarily give up tenured positions at major universities; willing to, or perhaps happy to, give up competing for research dollars; and willing to put their egos aside to share as a group the risks and potential rewards. I don't mean monetary rewards. I mean the intellectual rewards of having a major impact on an important human cancer.

Q: If one of America's multimillionaires came to you and said, "I want to make a difference," realistically, how much money would you need to fund this over a ten-year period?

GALE: If we assume that the actual health-care cost, such as hospital bills, would be paid through conventional channels and address ourselves to this superstructure, I estimate the cost of such an activity might be between three and five million dollars a year. The total cost, over ten years then, would be thirty to fifty million. I'm willing to take the risk of failing to achieve this goal. I'd rather try and fail than not try at all. I'm not afraid of failure.

Q: You worked very closely with regard to Chernobyl and other matters with Dr. Armand Hammer, who has met with every Soviet leader since Lenin. He seems to play a unique role in relations between the United States and the Soviet Union. What can you tell us about that?

GALE: Communications between nations utilize diverse pathways. When relations are good, diplomatic channels suffice. On the other hand, the situation deteriorates when you have something like the Cuban missile crisis or the Soviet invasion of Afghanistan. Under these circumstances, unofficial channels such as the relationship between Hammer and Gorbachev are critical and decrease the chances of a serious mistake. I saw this illustrated best when Hammer and I met with Gorbachev in May of 1986, just after the American bombing of Libya. Most Americans felt our country's action was justified. But not unexpectedly, it was not well received by the Soviets. There had been speculation that Gorbachev and Ronald Reagan would meet in November of that year in Washington for their second summit meeting. As soon as the American attack was announced, the Soviets indicated that they were not going to proceed with Gorbachev's planned visit in November. In our meeting with Gorbachev, Hammer amazed me by spending much of our time discussing why Gorbachev ought to come to Washington; why he was likely to get a favorable reception from the American people; and why he should not assume that, because Chernobyl had been widely, and to some extent inaccurately, reported in the American press, Americans took any pleasure in this common tragedy.

Q: The same day you and Dr. Hammer met with Gorbachev, you held a press conference at the Soviet Foreign Ministry to discuss Chernobyl for the first time with the world press. In response to a question regarding the lessons of Chernobyl, you stated, "People who believe meaningful assistance is possible for the victims of nuclear war are mistaken." What would the medical effects of nuclear war, or even a single isolated bomb detonation, be?

GALE: Let's briefly consider what would happen if there were a detonation of a single small nuclear weapon over a city—let's say, Detroit; a city of about four-and-a-half million people. Depending on the height at which the bomb exploded, somewhere between a half-million and a million people would die instantaneously. An equal number would be injured, and most of them would die later. What would be the medical response to this kind of accident? First, about half the physicians would be killed and 80 percent of the hospitals would be destroyed, severely reducing the personnel and facilities able to respond.

Let's also look at two interventions needed in Chernobyl, and see how they would stack up. Our estimate is that a single megaton weapon detonation over Detroit would require about forty thousand intensive-care-unit beds for burn victims. In the state of Michigan, there are only about fifty such beds, and in the United States only about fifteen hundred. We would also require about fifteen or sixteen million units of platelets for blood transfusions to treat radiation victims. We have on hand in the entire United States on any given day about twelve thousand units. Now, that's just looking at a single nuclear weapon. The entire medical resources of the United States could not begin to cope. We only have about one-thousandth of the needed resources. If you magnify this by an all-out war between the United States and the Soviet Union, such an exchange would result in the death of more than half of our combined populations.

Q: You're best known throughout the world for your involvement in the medical aftermath of Chernobyl. But more recently, you've been involved with a radiation accident in Brazil. What happened, and how did you become involved?

GALE: The accident in Brazil, which was the largest radiation accident in the West, began last September in the city of Goiana in central Brazil. Two men came upon an abandoned radiotherapy unit that had been used to treat cancer patients. This unit contained a substantial amount of cesium, which is a highly radioactive isotope, similar to what was released by the Chernobyl accident. The unit was in a large heavy lead encasement, and the men thought they could sell it as scrap metal. They put this unit in a child's wagon and brought it home. The following day, they took it to a junk dealer, who broke it open and discovered a platinum capsule inside. Uneducated as they were, they didn't recognize the radiation danger symbol of three triangles. When they broke open the capsule at night, it emitted a bluish glow. They mistook it for some magical device and began to break it apart and distribute it to their friends and families. Some painted their bodies with it; others ingested it. The accident would not have been discovered except that the wife of the junk dealer noticed that many members of her family were losing their hair and developing skin rashes and diarrhea. She was clever enough to realize that these symptoms were probably related to this ball of cesium. She put it in a plastic bag, got on a bus, went across this town of about a million people, and brought it to a health inspector's office.

Q: How long after it was opened did she notice these symptoms?

GALE: About two weeks. It was fortunate that she didn't just throw it into the trash. As it was, about two hundred people were exposed to this radioactive source. The clerk from the health department called a representative from the nuclear agency of Brazil. They placed a Geiger counter over the cesium, and it went off the scale. Not believing it, they got a second Geiger counter, which confirmed the first. The exposed individuals were rounded up and quarantined on a football field. Then the houses where these people lived were quarantined. Over the next two weeks, about twenty individuals were flown to Rio to receive specialized medical care.

Q: What about the people on the bus who sat by this woman when she was carrying the cesium? How much were they at risk?

GALE: They obviously received radiation from the cesium source, but we can assume that they were getting on and off the bus, and that no one was exposed for a substantial period. However, the clerk who had it on his desk for several minutes received a very substantial dose of radiation.

Shortly after the accident was detected, I was contacted by Dr. Daniel Tebak of the National Cancer Institute of Brazil. I offered him my services and the resources of the Armand Hammer Center for Advanced Studies in Nuclear Energy and Health, but didn't hear from him again for another two weeks. Then he contacted me in mid-October, saying that his colleagues had encountered substantial problems in taking care of these people, and asked me to come immediately to Brazil. Quite a few individuals were extremely ill by the time I arrived, including one six-year-old girl who had ingested large amounts of cesium and become radioactive. The situation posed an extremely serious health threat, not only to the patients, but also to the physicians and nurses caring for them. It was a situation much more complex than the one we faced at Chernobyl, where the patients, although exposed to high doses of radiation, were not themselves radioactive.

The immediate outcome of the accident in Brazil was that four individuals died, including the young girl. These people had to be buried in concrete tombs to prevent them from being a risk to people visiting the cemetery. The other patients have now all recovered and are either back home or under quarantine until the radioactivity leaves their bodies. We anticipate that most of the radioactivity should be released from their bodies over the course of a year. At the end of that time, they will be able to return to living normal lives.

Q: In the Soviet Union, you were given everything you needed to do your job properly. They even allowed you to bring an Israeli biochemist, Yair Reisner, to help deal with the patients. In Brazil, were you allowed to function as freely?

GALE: One important aspect of all these nuclear radiation accidents is that they quickly leave the medical or scientific sphere and become political issues. Proponents and opponents of nuclear energy and nuclear weapons see them as an opportunity to espouse their causes. In Brazil, the patients were moved to a Navy hospital, and the military kept very tight control over the release of any information about these patients, their treatment, or their whereabouts. While I was in Brazil, I agreed to operate there without disclosing to the press any of my activities. I felt that the health care of the patients was more important than keeping the public informed, but otherwise I was generally allowed to function freely.

Q: One of the ironies to come out of your Chernobyl adventure is that you have become something of a folk hero in the Soviet Union. The Soviet government has featured you extensively on national television. There have been favorable articles written about you in the Soviet press. Outside of American political leaders and Dr. Hammer, there might not be an American who has achieved that same stature in the Soviet Union. Why do you think the Soviets have done this?

GALE: One frequently reads complex schemes and KGB plans into almost everything the Soviets do. But my belief is that it more likely represents a genuine appreciation by the Soviet people of American assistance in a crisis. Soviets have long and strong memories; for the good as well as the bad. If they like you, they really like you. And if they don't like you, they really don't like you. They are much less forgiving and forgetting than we are. I think they appreciate the fact that Americans were willing to come and help them, and that we have continued to help them in dealing with the Chernobyl accident.

Q: What does it mean to you to be accepted in the Soviet Union to the degree that you are? Do you think the Soviets see you as a symbol of the American medical establishment?

GALE: I don't think it's the American medical establishment. I think it's the American people. I think that the Soviet people, by and large, are genuinely fond of Americans. They like things American; our defense of liberty, our attempts to try anything and everything. The Chernobyl relief effort gave the Soviet people a chance to express some admiration and some warmth to Americans, which is usually difficult for them to do.

Q: In the past two years, and largely as a consequence of Chernobyl, you've become a medical celebrity. How would you like to be perceived by the world?

GALE: First and foremost, as a physician. The greatest compliment that I can receive is for a physician to refer a patient to me for a medical opinion, and for that physician to entrust me with his or her patient's care.

Tempest Storm is an icon, who has inhabited an arena that's very differ-
ent from the men and women referenced in the preceding pages.

Tempest Storm

She's seventy-nine years old now and lives in a one-bedroom apartment in East Las Vegas, the industrial part of town. Defying age, she has
managed to remain both shapely and slender. She's charming and disarm-
ing with an air of refinement and still has long fiery-red hair.

It's May 1, 2007, four days before Oscar De La Hoya and Floyd
Mayweather Jr will do battle. In another part of the city, high rollers are
descending upon the casinos in anticipation of the Big Event. Power bro-
kers are spreading their wings. There's glitz everywhere.

Trust me; the lady understands power and glitz. She was intimate with
John F. Kennedy and Elvis Presley. Check her out on the Internet. Google
her (and ogle her) at your pleasure. There was a time when she was embedded in the sexual fantasies of literally millions of men around the world.

Tempest Storm was born in rural Georgia on February 29, 1928. Her
mother and step-father were sharecroppers. She grew up picking cotton
and lived in a shack without indoor plumbing or electricity. The name
given to her at birth was Annie Blanche Banks.

Annie matured physically at an early age. When she was thirteen, five
young men (including the local sheriff's son) gang-raped her. A year later,
her stepfather wanted the same thing. "I woke up one night and he was
on top of me," she says. "That night, I told myself, 'I've got to get out of
here.' I have very few memories of my childhood. It was a horrible life,
and I've blocked out a lot of what happened to me when I was young."

Annie ran away from home at age fourteen, rented a room for a dollar
a night, and took a job waitressing for ten dollars a week plus tips. The
authorities threatened to return her to her parents, so she married a man
she barely knew (a soldier on furlough named Rural Giddens). Several
weeks later, she left Giddens and started waitressing again. At age sixteen,
she married for the second time, to a soldier named Jack Locke. That marriage lasted a year.

After the collapse of her second marriage, Annie worked in a jewelry store, a hosiery mill, and a diner. When she was nineteen, a man she waited on occasionally in the diner asked if she'd like to go to California with him. "When do we leave?" she responded. They lived together in Hollywood for two months. Then he tried to shoot her because he suspected that she was cheating on him, and she was on her own again.

Annie's dream was to break into show business, but there were problems. Her teeth were crooked; so much so that she was reluctant to smile. She had no acting experience. And at the modeling agencies, she recalls, "I was a joke, a freak [5-feet-6-inches tall, 135 pounds] with a forty-inch bosom that would never fit into their high-fashion dresses."

At age twenty-one, she took a job as a cocktail waitress at a lounge called the Paddock, which had drinking and dancing up front and bookmaking in back. A customer suggested that she audition for an opening in the chorus line at the Follies Theater in Los Angeles. She'd be one of many women onstage. She wouldn't have to take her clothes off.

Annie started dancing for forty dollars a week, but the sixty dollars a week that the strippers made was enticing. And Lillian Hunt (who produced the show) saw gold in her body. At age twenty-two, Annie took her clothes off onstage for the first time. The deal was sealed by Hunt's offer to pay to have her new recruit's teeth straightened and capped.

"This is show business," Annie told herself. "And I've always wanted to be in show business." Right before her first performance au natural (a five-minute number), Hunt instructed, "No matter what happens, keep going." Soon after, Annie took the stage name "Tempest Storm." In 1957, it became her legal moniker.

"Being in burlesque meant being pursued by men," Tempest recalls. "Famous men; rich men; guys next-door. And all of them wanted one thing. Sex."

Tempest's first "celebrity romance" began when Mickey Rooney visited her backstage after she'd been dancing for two months.

"Mickey was a big star," she wrote in her 1987 memoirs. "If he wanted to take me out, I knew what it could do for my career. Being seen with him meant bits in gossip columns, photos in magazines, perhaps breaks in other types of show business. I was learning how to handle my career, how to use the press to further my reputation and enhance my image.

There's much more to a career in burlesque than performing. I'd reached a point where I needed to be seen with name entertainers, to be talked about, to be publicized."

"Mickey took my arm and escorted me through the people backstage," Tempest remembers. "I could feel their eyes on me, and I knew they were thinking, 'There goes Rooney with another conquest.' But that's exactly what I wanted; for them, for everyone, to talk about Tempest Storm."

They went to bed together on their second date. "In his suite," Tempest later wrote, "he wasted little time. He mixed me a drink, which I really didn't want, put a record on the phonograph, and waltzed me around the room. Within a few minutes, we were in bed."

The next day, their relationship was the subject of a gossip item in the *Los Angeles Mirror*. Three weeks later, Rooney gave her a full-length mink coat ("a mink coat that said I'd hit the big time"). The liaison lasted for three months. Then Rooney went on to other women.

"He wanted something from me, but I also wanted something from him," Tempest concludes. "The world of show business can be a tough world. It's important to know how to protect yourself and your interests."

After the fling with Rooney ended, Tempest journeyed north to perform as the star attraction for six weeks at the El Ray Theater in Oakland (her first gig as a headliner). The job paid $350 a week. She dyed her brunette hair red and bought her first car (a 1951 Cadillac convertible) with the help of the manager of a local car dealership (who had seen her perform).

In 1953, she married again; this time, to a bartender named John Becker, who performed as a singer and burlesque straight man under the stage name Johnny Del Mar. Becker was physically and verbally abusive. The low point in their marriage came when Tempest attacked him with a pair of scissors ("I grabbed them and tried to stab him, but he jumped out of my reach so I threw the scissors at him"). They were divorced on Valentine's Day 1955. Thereafter, Johnny returned the favor of the scissors by trying to run Tempest's car off the freeway in Los Angeles.

Meanwhile, onstage, Tempest was developing a philosophy for her performance art. And she was becoming a star.

Burlesque in the 1950s was often upscale entertainment. It was performed in elegant theaters, not just clubs and bars.

"I wanted to be a class act," Tempest says. "I wanted to entertain, but I also wanted to be a lady about my act. Sexy, yes. Teasing, yes. Vulgar, never. And I worked hard to develop an act that set me apart from other dancers in the business. A lot of people thought it was easy work, but it wasn't. I took some ballet lessons when I started. Later, I had a choreographer and surrounded myself with high-quality musicians. I rehearsed a lot and spent a fortune on costumes. Success doesn't just happen in burlesque any more than it just happens in any other form of show business. You have to create your own style and your own way of entertaining people. You have to work at becoming a star, onstage and off. I was good copy for the gossip columnists; I had a great rapport with them; but that will carry you just so far. I was always using my imagination to develop an act that was classy and original. I never allowed my personal struggles to undermine the fantasies that people had when they came to watch me perform. The adult entertainment business today is awful. It has no class. They call lap-dancing and pole-dancing 'the new burlesque', but that's not burlesque as I knew it. Those things are just raunchy. If I was twenty years old today, I'd do something else. But for me, the key to it all was that I enjoyed performing. Onstage, I was always happy; I became a different person. When I was on-stage, in my mind, I was a little girl, all dressed up and gorgeous."

After Tempest and John Becker divorced, she returned to the celebrity dating scene. "I was single, sexy, and yearning for the good times that would make up for all those hard years back in Georgia," she wrote in her memoirs. "Nothing could have pleased the lonely daughter of a sharecropper more than to have her childhood dreams of show business and romance come true, and for me they had."

The next celebrity Tempest dated was Hugh O'Brien. ("His sensitivity was especially important to me in the difficult time after my divorce. He made me feel so special and secure.") Then Nat King Cole entered her life. ("He told me that I was the most beautiful woman he'd ever known. Our lovemaking was vibrant, warm, and wonderful. When I was with him, I felt truly connected to another human being, safe at last from the terrible loneliness of my life. Never had a woman found herself so suddenly awake and living all her romantic dreams come true.")

But two problems intruded on the relationship. First, Nat King Cole was black at a time when an interracial relationship, if it became public knowledge, could damage both parties. And second, he was married. Thus, "the good-bye of star-crossed lovers."

Also in 1955, while performing at the Casino Royale in Washington, DC, Tempest met a young senator from Massachusetts named John F. Kennedy. He attended her show two nights in a row and, the second night, she accepted an invitation to visit him at his table.

"He was charming with a wonderful sense of humor and very handsome," Tempest recalls. "The people who were with him left us alone to talk, and we made a date for the following evening, which was my night off. I knew he was married, but he told me that he and his wife were unhappy together."

Thereafter, a relationship developed. "He was a lot of fun to be with," Tempest says. "When he was elected president, I was in seventh heaven."

And then there was Elvis Presley.

"Elvis liked younger women, but he made an exception for me," she says with pride.

They met in 1957, when Elvis was twenty-two and Tempest was twenty-nine. He had entered mainstream American culture one year earlier when he appeared on *The Ed Sullivan Show* and topped the charts with "Heartbreak Hotel," "Don't Be Cruel," "Hound Dog," and "Love Me Tender."

The union of the two iconic personalities occurred in Las Vegas at The Dunes, where they were performing independently of one another. It was suggested that they pose for a publicity photo together.

"Even with his dark skin," Tempest later wrote, "Elvis blushed deeply when he saw me. I could tell he was trying not to look at my plunging neckline."

Later that day, the telephone in her room rang.

"Miss Storm," the hotel switchboard operator advised. "Mr. Elvis Presley would like to talk to you."

They met again.

"There's something we have in common," Tempest told him. "Members of the opposite sex lust after us. They don't understand that what we do onstage is an act, a performance."

Thereafter, they became intimate.

"I wanted the satisfaction of knowing that I was adored by America's hottest sex symbol," Tempest acknowledges. "And he was the most interesting younger man I ever knew."

But Elvis's manager ("Colonel" Tom Parker) didn't like their seeing each other.

"If you keep hanging around that stripper woman, those screaming teenagers are going to quit screaming," Parker told Elvis. "And when they stop screaming, they'll stop buying your records, and then where the hell are you going to be? Back in Memphis driving a goddamn truck."

"Elvis decided that the Colonel was right," Tempest recalls. "He was afraid that being linked to a stripper would ruin his career, so it ended between us."

When was the last time she saw Elvis?

"In the early 1970s," she answers. "I went to see Perry Como at the Hilton [in Las Vegas] and, after the show, I went backstage. Elvis was there and so was Pat Boone. Perry asked me, "Tempest, I used to be a barber. Is that really all your hair?" I told him, 'Perry, everything about me is real. If you don't believe me, ask Elvis.' Elvis turned and said, 'Well, it's time for me to go.' But he stayed."

"I was devastated by Elvis's disintegration," Tempest says. "I still dream about him sometimes. There's one song—"Are You Lonesome Tonight?"—every time I hear Elvis singing it, I feel like crying."

"It was hard sometimes, the way people thought about me," she admits. "I tried to do what I did with class so people would respect me. But I knew from the beginning that there was a stigma. Some people look down on burlesque dancers like we're prostitutes. I wanted Elvis to respect me for the person I was instead of thinking that I was only a stripper. But that's not the way he felt."

Still, in the world of burlesque, Tempest Storm was becoming royalty. By the late-1950s, she was making $3,500 a week. "Rich men showered me with diamonds and furs and cruises," she recalls. Michael Wilding, Vic Damone, and Sammy Davis Jr became lovers. She lived in Hollywood next-door to Marilyn Monroe. "When Marilyn sang "Happy Birthday" for the president at his birthday party [at Madison Square Garden in 1962], I thought it was terrific," she says.

In 1959, Tempest married again; this time to singer Herb Jeffries. And again, the result was disaster. "I always demanded respect in my professional life," she acknowledges. "But in my personal life, I didn't demand it often enough. The men I married always ended up treating me like dirt. Herb was lazy and jealous. He told me once, 'You're in a degenerate business.' I said, 'Excuse me. You're driving my car and sleeping in my house and living off me.'"

In 1962, Tempest filed for divorce; then learned that she was pregnant. She and Herb reconciled, and a daughter (Patty) was born. After that, Tempest went back to work. After three separations, she and Herb were divorced.

Life went on. There were more lovers and more performances. And finally, there was validation as a performing artist. On March 23, 1973, at age forty-five, Tempest Storm became the first (and to this day, only) "stripper" to perform at Carnegie Hall.

"I was a little cocky that night," she says. "Someone asked how I felt about performing at Carnegie Hall, and I told him, 'I feel like Muhammad Ali. I'm The Greatest.' But that night was important to me. I felt that the audience appreciated the art of my performance. They understood the choreography and skill and hard work that were involved. When they applauded me, they were applauding my talent."

Tempest Storm never retired from the burlesque trade. In 1999, at age seventy-one, she performed at a thirtieth anniversary celebration for the O'Farrell Theatre in San Francisco. Mayor Willie Brown issued a proclamation designating the occasion as "Tempest Storm Day." In a review of her performance, the *San Francisco Chronicle* proclaimed, "When Storm takes something off—her gown, one of several bras or multiple bottom layers—she's likely to put something else back on. She bares her breasts and almost everything else, and pulls a white boa from the wings to play peekaboo with what's left. Her skin sags a little here and there. Her movements can get a little creaky. But she hasn't lost an ounce of know-how."

In 2005, Tempest was onstage in Nashville and San Francisco. "I did about twenty minutes and got a standing ovation," she reports. "I'd still work every week if there was a place to work."

But the past few years have been hard. Tempest's world fell apart in 2001 with the death of a man she loved and was engaged to marry. Soon after, a business representative misappropriated most of her financial assets. Circumstances forced her to live in trailer for several years. Then she moved to Las Vegas.

Her apartment is small but immaculately kept. The white rug and white furniture are spotless. A photograph of Tempest with Elvis Presley and other reminders of her career line the walls. An elaborately published pictorial work entitled *The Big Book of Breasts* is prominently displayed on the coffee-table in front of her sofa.

"There's ten pages on me in there," Tempest says. "Would you like to see them?"

She also has a full binder of old photographs and news clippings that she shows to chosen guests.

"I keep myself busy," she says when the conversation turns to her life in Las Vegas. "I read a lot and go out to dinner sometimes with friends."

She seems a bit lonely. She also seems like a kind person with a good heart.

"You were born on a leap day," she's told. "February 29, 1928. That means, next year, you'll be twenty."

"In my dreams," she says with a laugh.

Tempest enjoys her status as a sexual icon in what now seems to have been an innocent age of sex. She rose to prominence before the pill changed lovers' habits; when *Playboy* was cutting edge and married couples on TV sitcoms slept in separate beds. Sexual icons limited their performances to stage and screen rather than running amok through society like Anna Nicole Smith.

That time is long gone. So are the most prominent men who marked Tempest's life. John F. Kennedy, struck down by an assassin's bullet at age forty-six. Nat King Cole, dead of cancer at forty-five. Elvis Presley, a bloated caricature of himself, dead at forty-two. But she looks back on her life with satisfaction and believes that there are still good times ahead.

On occasion, she's reflective. "Except for the men I married, I think I've made good choices," she says. "I don't blame myself for the first two marriages. I was very young then. As for the others; maybe I was punishing myself for something. Maybe I got involved with so many married men because, on some level, I told myself, 'This way, I won't be hurt.' Maybe I chose burlesque because of what happened to me when I was young. When you're onstage, the men in the audience can look but not touch. And I got unconditional love from my audience. In a lot of ways, I'm quite conventional. I wasn't a drinker. I was around all kinds of drugs but I never did them. I've led a pristine life except for my dancing and my men. That's where my wildness comes out."

"I was a wealthy woman," Tempest continues, still reflecting on the past. "That's gone now, but I can deal with it. If I have any regrets, it's that I didn't do more to pursue a career in acting. Acting was my dream. Sometimes I wish that, when I got famous, I'd been strong enough to break away from the nice clothes and fancy jewelry and glamour and risk everything to get into acting. That's what I would have done if I'd chosen my profession instead of my profession choosing me. But there are no complaints. I wanted to be a star. I worked my way to the top of the burlesque world and I stayed there. Nobody lasted in the business as long as I did. I like to think that my talent and my personality led people to respect me. I'm sure that some did and some didn't."

In her sunset years, Tempest Storm has the satisfaction of knowing that, for millions of men who never knew her, she'll be an object of desire forever.

"I've had a great ride," she says. "I didn't miss anything. Not bad for a sharecropper's daughter from Eastman, Georgia."

More on Politics

John F. Kennedy was my boyhood hero. I welcomed the opportunity to write about him at the start of the new millennium for Irish America magazine.

John F. Kennedy: An Appreciation

Young people today know John F. Kennedy primarily for being assassinated and for his presumed dalliance with Marilyn Monroe. That's a shame, because he meant something far different to an entire generation of Americans, myself included, who were young forty years ago.

When JFK was nominated for president in 1960, he was forty-three years old. He cut his hair to look older and curbed his humor to appear more serious. Ethnic and religious barriers were higher in national politics then than they are now. No Italian American or African American had ever been a member of the president's cabinet. Only one Catholic, Al Smith in 1928, had been nominated by a major party for national office. Kennedy's Irish-Catholic heritage was a formidable obstacle to election. All eight of his great-grandparents had come to the United States from Ireland, and the Kennedys were considered the epitome of a Boston Irish-Catholic family. But he shattered religious and ethnic taboos in a campaign that is now part of American political lore.

In accepting the Democratic Party's nomination for the presidency, Kennedy declared, "The New Frontier of which I speak is not a set of promises; it is a set of challenges. It sums up, not what I intend to offer the American people, but what I intend to ask of them." On the day of his inauguration, he urged each and every American to, "Ask not what your country can do for you. Ask what you can do for your country."

The Camelot Presidency followed. Kennedy was exciting and inspirational; handsome with dazzling charm, grace, and wit. His humor was spontaneous; not the canned laugh lines written by ghostwriters that we hear from politicians today. It could surface at any time and no one was immune to it. In 1961, with the Cold War at its peak, JFK met with Soviet premier Nikita Khrushchev in Vienna. At one point, he asked about a medal that was affixed to Khrushchev's jacket and learned that it was the Lenin Peace Prize. "I hope you keep it," Kennedy told him.

During his short tenure in office, JFK presided over a rebirth of American politics. The environmental movement and nuclear sanity began on his watch with passage of the Nuclear Test Ban Treaty. He was a forceful advocate for civil rights, and accelerated the space program with the goal of landing a man on the moon by 1970. He also championed the Peace Corps, which gave the United States a benign role to play overseas instead of a more aggressive presence.

But Kennedy's most important contribution to American life was the infusion of a new spirit. His words moved a nation and inspired much of what was good in the United States in the 1960s. For most politicians today, the first and last value is themselves. Politics in America is now brought to the people by television, with illusion and deceit substituted for reality. Oftentimes, candidates don't even say what they think. They say what media advisers tell them to say. Rather than act in accord with honestly held beliefs, they rely upon opinion polls to distinguish "right" from "wrong." Getting elected is the ultimate value; an end in itself, not the means to a better end.

By contrast, Kennedy was an honorable politician in that he was committed to using the power of his office to making the world a better place to live. He came from privilege, yet cared about those less fortunate than himself. Under his stewardship, there was a commitment to build a more equitable society and close the gap between rich and poor.

Kennedy was also the first American president to visit Ireland during his term of office. Viewed through the prism of history, it was a largely sentimental journey, but it meant a lot to people at the time. Over a four-day span in June 1963, JFK met with distant cousins and received honorary degrees from National University and Trinity College. He also addressed a joint assembly of the Irish Parliament in its first televised session ever.

Again and again during his days in Ireland, the president sounded nostalgic themes: "No country in the history of the world has endured the hemorrhage which this island endured over a period of a few years [during the Great Famine] for so many of her sons and daughters. . . . Ireland has never been a rich or powerful country and yet, since earliest times, its influence on the world has been rich and powerful. . . . This small island has a family of millions upon millions who are scattered all over the globe, who have been among the best and most loyal citizens of the countries that they have gone to, but have also kept a special place in their memories of this green and misty island. In a sense, all of them who visit Ireland come home."

After one speech, a Dublin native told Kennedy aide Ken O'Donnell, "All of us love your President, and that's the only thing the people of Ireland have completely agreed upon since the British passed the Conscription Bill in 1918."

At trip's end, taking his leave, Kennedy told the Irish people, "This is not the land of my birth, but it is the land for which I have the greatest affection, and I certainly will be back in the springtime."

But springtime never came for him. Less than five months later, Kennedy was assassinated in Dallas. His death traumatized the United States and, more than any event ever, showed the unifying power of television. Recurring images of the final presidential motorcade; Jacqueline Kennedy, her clothes stained with her husband's blood; the murder of Lee Harvey Oswald; the president's funeral procession being saluted by his four-year-old son. All of these images and more were instantaneously carved into the American psyche. Daniel Patrick Moynihan, then an assistant secretary of labor in the Kennedy Administration, told of a moment with newspaper columnist Mary McGrory. "Mary said to me that we'll never laugh again," Moynihan recounted. "And I said, 'Heavens, Mary; we'll laugh again. It's just that we'll never be young again.'"

In Ireland, it was said, they cried the rain down.

Kennedy's assassination was succeeded almost immediately by two more cultural touchstones. In January 1964, the Beatles arrived in America. One month later, Cassius Marcellus Clay Jr dethroned Sonny Liston to become heavyweight champion of the world. Regardless of what the calendar might have said, those months were when "the sixties" truly began. Vietnam, inner-city riots, the drug culture, and more turmoil followed.

Meanwhile, for those who lived through his magic, the memory of John F. Kennedy has a special glow.

Maureen Kenney teaches American history at an inner-city high school in New York. Now in her late-fifties, she was born and raised in a middle-class Boston Irish-Catholic family at a time when the Kennedys were a source of Irish-American pride and the political equivalent of the Notre Dame football team. Each year, she devotes a class to the Kennedy presidency. This past year, at the end of the class, one of her students asked her, "Ms. Kenney, were you in love with John Kennedy?"

For an entire generation, he was our hero.

In recent years, I've written extensively for boxing websites. Occasionally, those sites give me license to venture into the political arena. That was the case in January 2005, when I wrote about George W. Bush and an old friend.

Jack Newfield and George Bush

The second inauguration of George W. Bush seems like a good time to remember Jack Newfield, who died of cancer last month. Jack hated hypocrisy and injustice. The three public arenas of his life were journalism, politics, and boxing. Obviously, there's an abundance of the vices that he abhorred in each. But Jack fought the good fight, and the people he worked with and wrote about were well-represented at his funeral service.

Looking around the chapel, I couldn't help but think that many of the mourners seemed considerably older than they had just a week earlier. I thought about how Jack, the columnist, might have covered his own funeral. And my mind turned to our last conversation.

It was on the telephone not long after the November presidential election. "I'm weak; you talk," Jack instructed.

So I did. And the gist of what I said follows.

For many Americans, myself included, the reelection of George Bush feels like 9/11 all over again. It's like a death in the family. Our rulers have retained power by distorting the truth and twisting reality into a grotesque fantasy.

Contrary to some, we don't find George Bush charming as a person. We think he's a smug arrogant little man and we dislike him intensely. But our feelings go far beyond the personal. We're appalled and devastated by how he and his administration are changing our country.

We're horrified at what our government is doing around the world in our name. George Bush deceitfully led the United States into an ill-conceived unwinnable war in Iraq. Saddam Hussein was a malevolent dictator. But most of us are more worried about North Korea building a nuclear arsenal, the sale of nuclear weapons by remnants of the old Soviet

Army, and the sharing of nuclear technology by Pakistan. That's where the greatest nuclear peril lies.

The past was far more confused, the present is far more complex, and the future is far more contingent than people care to realize. But now we have George Bush reducing our soldiers to props by prancing around the deck of an aircraft carrier in a *Top Gun* outfit and carrying a plastic turkey into a mess hall in Baghdad on Thanksgiving Day. We have the prison abuses at Abu Gharib and 380 tons of missing explosives that are being used to cause a never-ending stream of American casualties.

There's nothing brave about middle-aged politicians who have never seen combat sending other people's children to die in battle. Yet this administration attacks the courage and patriotism of any member of the opposition party who questions the war. And the truth is, as the war goes on, our government will be unable to recruit enough soldiers to fight it. Because like Dick Cheney in the Vietnam era, when it comes to fighting in Iraq, most of the people who voted for the war have "other priorities."

What happens when tours of duty can no longer be extended and Donald Rumsfeld runs out of troops? Will George Bush seek to reinstate the military draft? If he does, the Republican Party will lose the youth vote big-time and protests on college campuses will make the Vietnam era look like a church social.

The war, of course, is being fought in the name of combatting terrorism. That leads to another question. Fifteen of the September 11 hijackers were from Saudi Arabia. None were from Iraq. The money to finance 9/11 came from Saudi Arabia, not Iraq. So why did we invade Iraq instead of Saudi Arabia? At the heart of it, of course, is oil. This administration wants access to Iraqi oil in case the flow from Saudi Arabia is interrupted. And as the war goes on, companies like Halliburton are making a nice profit.

Meanwhile, the states that suffered the most grievous losses on 9/11 (New York and New Jersey) voted overwhelmingly for John Kerry. So did our nation's two primary terrorist targets (New York City and Washington, DC). Guess which presidential candidate the people whose lives are really on the line thought would do a better job of fighting terrorism?

In terms of economic policy, this is the most reckless administration in the history of America.

The annual budget deficit was reduced to zero under Bill Clinton. When George Bush took office, the ten-year budget projection showed a surplus of six trillion dollars. The Bush Administration has given us an annual budget deficit of $450 billion. A large part of that is because of irresponsible tax cuts that are skewed in favor of the rich.

Almost 40 percent of the last tax cut went to the richest 1 percent of the American population. This administration believes in taxing the wages of working people but not income from capital gains or inherited wealth. Many of us who oppose Mr. Bush are well off financially. It would be easy for us to sit back and say, "Okay; we'll inherit more money from our parents and leave more to our children; and when the tax code is further revised, we'll accumulate even more wealth." But we don't want economic inequity to be the hallmark of our society.

At times, it seems as though the Bush administration has allowed a white-collar-crime lobby to take over America. The lawyers at most major corporations function primarily as defense counsel for senior management. Retirement funds have vanished in a wave of securities fraud.

Meanwhile, the Internal Revenue Service estimates that the federal government loses almost $300 billion dollars to tax evasion each year. Offshore accounts amount to $70 billion of that total. Yet the Bush Administration hasn't bothered to prosecute 65,000 Americans who have been identified as using offshore accounts to evade taxes. Honest taxpayers are footing the bill for this travesty, just as they pay the bill for sham tax shelters that make profits disappear on paper for tax purposes but don't affect the bottom line that corporations show to investors.

Double the budget for the IRS. Give additional funding to special units empowered to investigate tax shelters and go after off-shore tax havens. Audit all returns of taxpayers with an annual gross income in excess of one million dollars. I guarantee you that each of these steps will be cost-effective. Instead, George Bush has proposed reductions in funding for the IRS.

The Bush administration has gutted environmental safeguards in favor of corporate economic interests. In a world where lawyers change $500 an hour and CEOs are paid millions of dollars annually, it has steadfastly opposed an increase in the minimum wage, which is now $5.15 an hour.

A wage of $5.15 an hour translates into $206.00 for a forty-hour work week. That's $10,712.00 a year for loading crates onto a truck.

George Bush says that raising the minimum wage would be "bad for the economy."

Whose economy?

Now Mr. Bush wants to hand Wall Street a bonanza in the form of "privatizing" Social Security. It's true that allowing Americans to invest a portion of our Social Security accounts in the stock market will enable some of us to receive more in our "golden years." But what happens to those who invest in Enron?

Then there are the "social" issues.

Many of us don't want assault weapons in our midst and are appalled by the Bush administration's obeisance to the gun lobby.

We believe that whether or not a woman has an abortion should be decided by the woman (often in conjunction with her family and doctor); not by the government. George Bush has shown no respect for "the sanctity of human life" in his governance. We think that, on the issue of abortion, he's a phony.

We're tired of political ideologues who are so busy trying to abolish abortion, curb stem-cell research, and boost the profits of large American drug companies that they failed to secure an adequate supply of flu vaccine for the American people.

We view decent affordable health care for all Americans as a "moral" issue. The next time Dick Cheney has chest pains, let him go to the emergency room at a public health clinic and experience first-hand what this administration has wrought. Of course, in Washington, DC, unless Mr. Cheney pulls rank, he can probably get a pizza delivered to his home faster than he can get an ambulance to take him to the hospital if he has a heart attack.

The tearing down by the Bush Administration of the wall between church and state also troubles us.

After the 2004 election, there was a much-quoted statement from a woman who voted for George Bush. "I'm so happy," she said. "It feels like we've elected Jesus as president."

Guess what, lady. Jesus didn't want to be president. And more to the point: Would Jesus have invaded Iraq? Would Jesus favor tax breaks for the rich over the working middle class?

The Bush administration has done more than any other administration in history to turn religious institutions into a political lobbying force, and we resent it. More Americans now say that they believe in the Virgin Birth than in evolution. We respect the Bible, but we don't believe that the Bible should be imposed on our society as the literal word of God.

After all, the Bible countenances slavery. Leviticus, chapter 25, verse 44: "Both thy bondsmen and thy bondsmaids which thou shalt have shall be of the heathen that are about you. Of them shall ye buy bondsmen and bondsmaids."

And then there's the Biblical view of marriage. A Constitutional amendment codifying marriage on the basis of the Bible would state the following:

(1) Marriage in the United States shall consist of a union between a man and one or more women (Genesis 29:17–28, II Samuel 3:2–5).

(2) Marriage shall not impede a man's right to take concubines in addition to his wife or wives (II Samuel 5:13, I Kings 11:3, II Chronicles 11:21).

(3) A marriage shall be considered valid only if the wife is a virgin. If the wife is not a virgin, she shall be executed (Deuteronomy 22:13–21).

(4) The marriage of a believer and a non-believer is forbidden (Genesis 24:3, Numbers 25:1–9, Ezra 9:12, Nehemiah 10:30).

(5) If a married man dies without children, his brother shall marry his widow. If the brother refuses to marry the widow or deliberately does not give her children, he shall pay a fine of one shoe and be otherwise punished in a manner to be determined by law (Genesis 38:6–10, Deuteronomy 25:5–10).

(6) Divorce shall not be allowed (Deuteronomy 22:19, Mark 10:9).

George Bush talked a lot during the 2004 presidential campaign about the sanctity of marriage in the context of gay marriage. He used gay Americans as a wedge issue in the same way that Richard Nixon exploited antipathy toward black Americans in 1968. But we didn't hear much from Mr. Bush about TV reality shows where some bozo bachelor chooses a bride from sixteen contestants who are hoping to parlay their selection into a centerfold spread for an adult magazine. Maybe that's because the leader in "reality" television of this kind is Fox (a virtual house organ for the Republican Party).

Meanwhile, it should be noted that the state with the lowest divorce rate in the country is Massachusetts (5.7 divorces per 1,000 married people), which is the only state that allows for same-sex marriages.

Nothing is more appalling to those of us who oppose George Bush than the fact that millions of Americans voted for him in the belief that he somehow epitomizes good moral values.

Moral values are about more than the lavish profession of a belief in Christ. We believe that there is no sense of decency or honor in the Bush administration and that it's morally rotten to the core.

The voices of "conservatism" who are filtering our values today include a drug addict who has been divorced three times (Rush Limbaugh), a sexual predator (Bill O'Reilly), and a compulsive gambler (William Bennett a/k/a the author of *The Book of Virtues*).

Rudolph Giuliani (a hero to Republicans when it's mutually beneficial) had a much-publicized extra-marital affair with his former communications director, Cristyne Lategano. Then he embarked upon an even more public extra-marital affair with Judith Nathan before advising his wife by way of a television interview that he wanted a divorce. This is known in some circles as "thinking with your cock." And as we know from Bill Clinton's impeachment hearings, Republicans don't like it (unless of course, the cock belongs to one of their own).

Do we smell hypocrisy here? We sure do.

George Bush pledges to "leave no child behind." But millions of children are being left behind. He promises "clean air." We get dirty air. He says "clean water." We get dirty water.

So let's talk about core values.

Honesty is a core value. Without honesty, there can be no trust and the bonds that hold society together fall apart.

Rewarding hard work over accumulated wealth is a core value.

Caring for the weak, the poor, and the elderly is a core value, as is educating our children properly.

Eradicating discrimination on the basis of race, religion, and sexual orientation is a core value.

George Bush has done none of these things. Rather, his administration has been largely about serving those in power. And there's a horrible sense that, from Tom DeLay's forced Congressional redistricting in Texas to the ugly "Swift Boat Veterans for Truth" attacks on John Kerry, Mr. Bush and his cronies will do anything to maintain power.

Meanwhile, many of us are crying because we love our country. We fear that irrevocable damage is being done to our most cherished institutions and to the human community.

Jack Newfield and I were on the telephone for about twenty minutes during our last conversation. We talked about how people want to trust their leaders; how the Democrats, for the most part, have been a lousy party in opposition; and the parallels between the alienation that many of us feel today and the sense of alienation that black Americans have experienced over the decades. We talked about twists of fate and how easily the course of history is altered. If John Kennedy hadn't gone to Dallas . . . If Monica Lewinsky hadn't given Bill Clinton a blow job . . .

Then Jack strengthened a bit and started talking nuts and bolts. In recent years, the Republican juggernaut has had two distinct advantages: fundraising and campaigning in a way that frames the issues on its terms. In 2004, the Democratic Party was competitive in fundraising. Now it has to sharpen its message. 115 million voters participated in the November presidential election. Democratic senatorial candidates received more votes than their Republican counterparts. If 60,000 Ohioans had changed their choice at the top of the ballot, John Kerry would be the next president of the United States.

"So much for an overwhelming Bush mandate." Jack said.

And that's how our conversation ended, save for one final exchange.

"After the election, some friends and I didn't know whether we should sit around feeling depressed or fight back," I told him. "We've decided to do both."

"Right on," Jack exhorted.

And then he spoke the last words he ever said to me: "Keep the faith."

The results of the 2006 Congressional elections were a gratifying coda to this article.

More Important Than Boxing: 2006

I received an e-mail recently from a reader complaining about an article that I wrote twenty-one months ago. The article was entitled "Jack Newfield and George Bush" and recounted my final conversation with Jack Newfield, who died of cancer in December 2004.

The article was timed to coincide with Mr. Bush's second inauguration. In it, I wrote, "For many Americans, myself included, the reelection of George Bush feels like a death in the family. Our rulers have retained power by distorting the truth and twisting reality into a grotesque fantasy. Contrary to some, we don't find George Bush charming as a person. We think he's a smug arrogant little man and we dislike him intensely. But our feelings go far beyond the personal. We're appalled and devastated by how he and his administration are changing our country. We're horrified at what our government is doing around the world in our name."

Each year, the boxing articles that I've written the previous year are published in book form. "Jack Newfield and George Bush" was included in the most recent volume. That seemed fitting, since the three public areas of Jack's life were journalism, politics, and boxing. Indeed, after the article was posted on Secondsout.com, one of Jack's friends wrote to me, "Jack would have especially loved it that this was published on a boxing website."

The e-mail referenced in the first paragraph above was from a dissenting reader. "Dear Mr. Hauser," he wrote. "A friend gave me your new book. If I want to read about politics, I'll buy a book about politics. Take your conversation with Jack Newfield and shove it."

I assume the writer has more of an affinity for George Bush than I do. I also assume that he won't like the column that follows. But I believe that the distortion of American values by the Bush administration and its allies in Congress is more important than the result of a prizefight and should be commented upon in every forum possible. Thus, with the

November elections approaching, this seems like a good time to revisit some important issues that affect us all. Anyone who is offended by the presence of politics on a boxing website need not read on.

I believe that the administration of George Bush, acting in concert with the Republican-controlled Congress, has done more damage to the United States than any other group of politicians in our nation's history.

The invasion of Afghanistan was a necessity. We didn't take military action there on the pretense of bringing freedom to the Afghani people. We did so because the government of Afghanistan condoned, aided, and sheltered the terrorists who were responsible for 9/11.

The invasion of Iraq was a poorly chosen war of choice. It was launched on the fiction that Saddam Hussein was building weapons of mass destruction and is now justified on grounds that it is about "bringing freedom" to the Iraqi people. It is an unwinnable war. A historical equivalent would have been Franklin Roosevelt responding to the Japanese attack on Pearl Harbor by invading China. Saddam Hussein was a malevolent dictator, but neither he nor Iraq was responsible for 9/11. It is a war that has diminished our resources, led to tens of thousands of deaths, and exponentially increased hatred toward America in the Islamic world.

The "reconstruction" of Iraq has failed. Mouthing platitudes like "freedom is on the march" is not a substitute for an effective foreign policy. Iraq is in chaos, and the chaos is worsening with each passing month.

Iraqi oil production is still below pre-war levels. Baghdad has an average of slightly more than three hours of electricity per day. American and Iraqi officials acknowledge that, even as insurgents ravage the country's infrastructure, corruption within the new Iraqi government is rampant. Forty to fifty percent of all profits from the smuggling of Iraqi oil are flowing to the insurgency.

The strain on our military caused by the war in Iraq has forced military recruiters to lower standards with the result that our armed forces are now inducting soldiers who have serious drug problems and score far below what was once considered an acceptable level of intelligence for military duty. It has also led to the induction of an alarming number of recruits who belong to militant white-supremacist and neo-Nazi organizations. In April of this year, the Army acknowledged that young officers were choosing to leave the service in unprecedented numbers and that one-third of the West Point Class of 2000 opted out of the military as soon as their five-year commitment had been fulfilled.

And most significantly, a formal National Intelligence Estimate compiled with input from all sixteen spy services within the United States government determined in April 2006 that the war in Iraq has increased, not decreased, the threat of terrorism against the United States by creating a new generation of terrorists and uniting Islamic radicals in common cause around the world. National Intelligence Estimates are approved by the director of national intelligence and are the most authoritative documents produced by our intelligence community with regard to specific national security issues.

Meanwhile, it now appears from events in Haditha that some American soldiers in Iraq have engaged in the same type of slaughter of innocent civilians that Saddam Hussein and the terrorist factions we oppose have perpetrated. Last November, at least twenty-four civilians were killed without just cause by our troops in Haditha. Unfortunately, this is the logical extension of the abuses at Abu Ghraib prison and the absence of acceptable standards for the conduct of the war, particularly as those standards apply to the responsibilities of command. A nation that abhors torture is now led by an administration that promotes and utilizes torture in secret prisons around the world.

During the Persian Gulf War, General Norman Schwarzkopf evaluated Saddam Hussein's military prowess with the observation, "He is neither a strategist, nor is he schooled in the operational arts, nor is he a tactician, nor is he a general, nor is he a soldier. Other than that, he's a great military man."

The same can be said of Donald Rumsfeld, who as secretary of defense is primarily responsible for the conduct of the war. Mr. Rumsfeld's explanation for the present chaos in Iraq is that "stuff happens." He still enjoys the support of George Bush, as does Dick Cheney, who told the nation in 2003 that our troops would be greeted in Iraq as liberators. Mr. Cheney is also the military sage who assured us in May 2005 that the insurgency was "in its last throes."

The architects of the war in Iraq are reckless with other people's lives. Meanwhile, Afghanistan is devolving into chaos because we don't have enough troops there to do the job that they were sent to do. In September

2006, the United Nations Office on Drugs and Crime reported that the opium harvest in Afghanistan this year was an estimated 6,100 metric tons. That's an increase of almost 50 percent over opium production in 2005 and accounts for 92 percent of the world's total opium supply. Much of the money generated by this cultivation falls into the hands of Taliban rebels in the southern part of Afghanistan. It's now estimated that 35 percent of Afghanistan's gross domestic national product comes from the narcotics trade.

In December 2002, the Bush administration estimated that the cost of the war in Iraq would be no more than $60 billion. The invasion was launched in March 2003. To date, the bill to the American people has been in excess of $300 billion with no end to the spending or killing in sight.

Meanwhile, the war in Iraq has diverted resources that should have been used to inspect cargo entering our ports, develop an effective medical response to biological attack, and secure our nuclear power plants, chemical factories, and transportation lines against terrorism.

Let's take the operation of America's ports as an example. At present, only five percent of the containers that enter our ports are inspected. Yet, while shaping a bill on national security earlier this year, the Republican-controlled Congress removed $648 million that had been earmarked for inspecting cargo containers. The cut came at the request of the Bush administration, which said that the proposed inspection program was too costly.

Too costly? At the time of the cut, the administration was pushing to eliminate all taxes on estates left by the wealthy, which would reduce tax revenue by $355 billion over the next ten years. The federal estate tax is currently levied only on estates in excess of $2 million.

It should also be noted that, in February 2006, the Bush administration sought to transfer management of port terminals in New York, Baltimore, Miami, Newark, Philadelphia, and New Orleans to a company owned by the royal family of Dubai.

Dubai is one of three sheikdoms that comprise the United Arab Emirates. The United Arab Emirates is one of only three countries in the world that formally recognized the Taliban as the legitimate ruler of Afghanistan. Two of the 9/11 hijackers were from the United Arab

Emirates. The 9/11 Commission formed by Congress found that "the vast majority of the money funding the September 11 attacks flowed through the United Arab Emirates." The Bush administration, which is quick to invoke national security as a justification for the torture of prisoners in violation of international law and domestic eavesdropping without a warrant in violation of American law, said that national security was not at issue where the management of our ports by the royal family of Dubai was concerned.

There are many patriotic Americans who fear that the effectiveness of the Department of Homeland Security, like the financial wellbeing of Enron, is a myth. In June of this year, the DHS announced that security grants to combat terrorism in New York and Washington, DC, were being cut by forty percent while grants to cities like Omaha and Louisville were being increased. That defied common sense. Then, one month later, a report by the inspector general of the Department of Homeland Security revealed that the National Asset Data Base used by the department as a tool in apportioning funds listed 77,069 potential terrorist targets in the United States. The state with the most "targets" was Indiana. Wisconsin was number two on the list. The list included such "terrorist targets" as a petting zoo in Alabama, an Amish popcorn factory in Pennsylvania, and a "Mule Day Parade" in Tennessee. Times Square was not on the list. This is lunacy.

Indeed, the perfect metaphor for the Bush administration's "war on terror" might be Brian J. Doyle. On April 4, 2006 (while serving as deputy press secretary for the Department of Homeland Security), Doyle was arrested and charged with twenty-three counts of trying to seduce a fourteen-year-old girl over the Internet. The indictment alleged that, in pursuit of the seduction, Doyle sent hardcore pornographic movie clips, engaged in explicit sexual chat-room conversations, bragged that he worked for the Department of Homeland Security, and gave his target his government-issued cellphone number. Doyle was allowed to plead "no contest" to the charges against him, which means that, while he can be sentenced to prison, there has been no admission of guilt on his part.

A majority of Americans alive today grew up in the most privileged and secure environment in history. That security is now gone. Those of us who live in New York and Washington, DC, do so with the knowledge that our homes are primary terrorist targets that could be turned into a modern-day Pompeii should a nuclear weapon fall into the wrong hands. But the war in Iraq has rendered the United States unable for military and geopolitical reasons to halt the production of nuclear weapons by two countries that we know are in the process of producing them; Iran and North Korea.

On October 8, 2006, the government of North Korea announced that it had conducted an underground nuclear test. The blast registered a 4.3 magnitude. To put that stark reality in perspective; a single nuclear weapon contains more explosive force than all of the bombs dropped on Europe in World Wars I and II combined.

Meanwhile, in February of this year, a bipartisan statement issued by the nation's governors expressed concern that the Bush administration is stripping the National Guard of the manpower and equipment necessary to respond to terrorist attacks, natural disasters, and other disturbances. Almost one-third of the American ground forces currently in Iraq are National Guard members. More than $1.2 billion worth of National Guard equipment has been sent to Iraq without having been replaced at home.

The enormous financial cost of the war in Iraq coupled with massive tax cuts for the wealthy (more on that later) is decimating our nation's infrastructure. The Army Corps of Engineers warned that the 17th Street Levee in New Orleans was a disaster waiting to happen. But before Hurricane Katrina struck, the Bush administration and its allies in Congress cut funding requests for repairs. A June 2006 audit revealed that, in the aftermath of Hurricane Katrina, the Federal Emergency Management Agency paid more than one billion dollars in fraudulent claims and ordered a half-billion dollars worth of mobile homes that have not been used.

America's infrastructure is now characterized by crumbling bridges and inadequate water tunnels. Our national system of electric power grids is hopelessly antiquated. The issue is not if they will cease to function properly but when.

We have failed to develop an alternative energy policy. That increases our dependence upon the oil-producing countries of the Middle East. Of course, it's also good news for large oil companies. Exxon Mobil posted a

$36 billion profit in 2005; the largest one-year profit for any corporation in the history of the United States. Exxon Mobil's projected profits for 2006 are even higher.

Meanwhile, our government is presiding over the continuing deterioration of our planet's infrastructure by despoiling the environment and ignoring the very real danger of global warming.

Global warming results from the burning of coal and oil, which adds billions of tons of carbon dioxide and other "greenhouse gasses" to the atmosphere each year. It is on the verge of causing irreversible changes to the earth's climate and ecosystems. Unless we reverse course, oceans will rise to the point where, within the next century, many coastal cities will be dependent on levees for survival.

Economically, the Bush administration and its allies in Congress have serviced the wealthy in the form of massive tax cuts skewed in favor of the rich and created unprecedented budget deficits that undermine the long-term economic stability of our country.

In the last year of the Clinton administration, the United States government had a budget surplus of $236 billion. In 2004, there was a budget deficit of $412 billion. The projected deficit for 2006 is $300 billion. The national debt when George Bush took office was $5.8 trillion. It is now approaching $9 trillion. In addition to mortgaging the economic security of future generations, this debt gives foreign holders of United States Treasury obligations (such as China and Saudi Arabia) increased leverage over our economy.

The Bush administration has also been delinquent in collecting the taxes that are due under law. A February 2006 report by the Department of Commerce found that Americans failed to report more than one trillion dollars in taxable income in 2003 (a 37 percent increase in unreported income from the last year of the Clinton administration). Needless to say, union workers and others who have taxes withheld from their paychecks are the least likely to cheat.

In July 2006, the Bush administration revealed plans to cut the number of estate tax lawyers in the Internal Revenue Service from 345 to 188. The audits overseen by these attorneys are the most cost-effective audits in the entire IRS, generating more than $2,200 in delinquent taxes for each hour of legal work expended.

And not only does this administration fail to collect taxes that are due; in July 2006, the IRS acknowledged that it had sent out between $200 million and $300 million in fraudulent tax refunds in the first six months of 2006 because a new computer program designed to catch fraudulent refund claims wasn't operating properly.

According to statistics released by the Treasury Department in April 2006, 32 percent of the Bush tax cuts went to the richest 1 percent of Americans. Fifty-three percent of the Bush tax cuts went to the richest 10 percent. The four hundred taxpayers with annual earned incomes of $87 million or more now pay income, Social Security, and Medicare taxes at the same percentage of their income as people making $50,000 to $75,000 a year.

Yet in May 2006, the Republican-controlled Congress passed another tax cut for the wealthy; this one for five years at a cost of $70 billion. Eighty percent of the benefits in this new enactment will go to individuals in the top 10 percent of income recipients. One percent of the benefits will go to individuals in the bottom 60 percent.

Department of Commerce statistics reveal that, in 2005, Americans had a negative personal saving rate. In other words, the American people collectively spent all of their after-tax income and were forced to dip into savings and borrow more money to make ends meet. This phenomenon occurred previously on only two occasions; in 1932 and 1933 at the height of the Great Depression.

The federal minimum wage has been $5.15 an hour since 1997, but the Republican-controlled Congress refuses to increase it. Under federal guidelines, the "poverty line" for a family of three is $16,700. $5.15 an hour translates into $10,712 per year for a forty-hour-a-week minimum-wage job. If the minimum wage for American workers had advanced since 1990 at the same rate as the pay for the chief executive officers of major American corporations, it would now be $23.03 an hour.

This economic inequity extends to virtually every area of American life. Almost a century ago, Theodore Roosevelt warned, "The citizens of the United States must effectively control the mighty commercial forces which they themselves have called into being. There can be no effective control of corporations while their political activity remains. To put an end to it will be neither a short nor an easy task, but it can be done."

Yet more and more legislation today, from energy policy to laws governing medical care, is being written by industry lobbyists. The Department of Health and Human Services acknowledges that more than 40 million Americans have no health insurance of any kind. A staggering 30 percent of American high-school students now leave school without graduating. So much for "no child left behind."

Meanwhile, a study conducted by the Pentagon in 2005 determined that 80 percent of the Marines killed in Iraq from upper-body wounds could have survived if they'd had a form of body armor that had been available since 2003. But despite calls from military field personnel for the armor, the Pentagon declined to supply it because of the cost involved. Which is more important? Tax cuts for the wealthy or life-saving body armor for our soldiers in Iraq?

It also troubles many of us that the Bush administration and its allies in Congress have placed religion at the core of government policy. In justifying that conduct, they tell us that religion has been inbred in every society since the dawn of civilization. But so have crime and war.

The Bush administration contends global warming is "junk science" but tells us that "intelligent design" should be taught in our public schools. "Intelligent design" is theology, not science. One could, with as much validity, teach the Resurrection in anatomy class.

We're also offended by the use of religious doctrine to curb stem-cell research. Even if one regards the Bible as "the word of God" (some people do and some don't), we don't believe that right-wing clerics should have a monopoly on interpreting it. Jesus is said to have miraculously healed the sick. Isn't stem-cell research consistent with that healing?

The opposition of the Bush administration to stem-cell research is reminiscent of opposition among some elements of the Christian church to the practice of medicine a thousand years ago. The practice of medicine, it was said then, was antithetical to Christianity because it evidenced a lack of faith in God's healing power.

We find it remarkable how many people insist on taking the Bible literally when it comes to stem-cell research and teaching evolution in our public schools, but ignore the clear "word of God" when their marriage falls apart and they want a divorce.

Mark Twain once wrote, "If Christ were here now, there is one thing he would not be: a Christian." That's food for thought.

And while we're on the subject of religion, let's take a look at moral values from a slightly different perspective. Earlier this year, the Justice Department subpoenaed every search query entered on Google during a two-month period; ostensibly to help it draft an anti-online-pornography law. Similarly broad-based subpoenas might also be used to search for and prosecute those who download unlawful pornography.

Here's an idea. Let's subpoena the record of Google searches made from Clarence Thomas's home computer. Many Americans remember Justice Thomas's 1991 Supreme Court confirmation hearings and the allegation that he sexually harassed a subordinate employee at the Equal Employment Opportunity Commission with repeated references to pornographic videos and a character named "Long Dong Silver."

According to Google, more than 40 percent of all Internet users visit at least one pornographic site each month. If Clarence Thomas is one of them, perhaps he should recuse himself from cases involving pornography that make their way to the Supreme Court. And while we're at it, let's not stop with Justice Thomas. I wonder what Antonin Scalia, Karl Rove, Jerry Falwell, Rush Limbaugh, and other guardians of our moral values have been viewing online.

And then there's the whole sordid matter of Florida congressman Mark Foley and the Republican leadership in Congress. On September 29, 2006, Foley resigned from the House of Representatives when it was revealed by ABC News that he had repeatedly sent sexually explicit e-mail messages to underage male pages who worked for several of his colleagues. What makes this matter particularly troubling is that Republican House majority leader John Boehner and Thomas Reynolds (chairman of the National Republican Congressional Committee) had been advised of the matter months earlier. Reynolds says that he personally raised the issue with Speaker of the House Dennis Hastert. Hastert says that he can't recall the conversation. Either Reynolds or Hastert is lying. One doesn't forget a conversation like that. Meanwhile, through it all, Foley was allowed to retain his position as head of a Congressional caucus on children's issues. The hypocrisy of these people is breathtaking.

When it comes to governing, the Bush administration has been grossly incompetent. Perhaps that's because government programs are unlikely to succeed when they're administered by people who pay lip service to their purpose while not really believing in them. But there's one area where the Bush administration and its allies in Congress have been extremely effective. They know how to win elections.

The key to the Republicans' electoral success has been the ability to galvanize single-issue constituencies. Those who oppose gun control vote Republican to the exclusion of other considerations. It doesn't matter that they've lost their health insurance. Those who oppose abortion vote Republican. It doesn't matter if they've fallen below the poverty line. An overwhelming percentage of Evangelical Christians vote Republican regardless of whether or not they favor the war in Iraq. If you're rich and want lower taxes, vote Republican. It's irrelevant that you or a loved one might die from an illness that could be cured by stem-cell research.

But from the war in Iraq (symbolized by George Bush's *Top Gun* cameo in front of the now-famous "Mission Accomplished" banner) to disaster relief efforts in New Orleans ("You're doing a heck of a job, Brownie"), the Bush administration has been marked by arrogance and incompetence.

If a foreign power wanted to undermine the United States, it would hope that we did the following:

(1) Send our troops to fight an unwinnable war that stretches our military capacity to the breaking point and further inflames passions against us throughout the world.

(2) Stand idly by while Iran and North Korea develop nuclear weapons.

(3) Fail to enact common-sense measures to protect our ports, nuclear power plants, chemical factories, and transportation lines against terrorism.

(4) Weaken our economy through inequitable taxation, corruption, and huge budget deficits.

(5) Let our physical infrastructure crumble.

(6) Diminish our educational system through reduced funding and the teaching of religious doctrine as science.

(7) Foul our environment and fail to provide adequate health care for tens of millions of Americans.

Over the past six years, all of the above have been done by the Bush administration and it allies in Congress. There's a perfect metaphor for their conduct.

On February 11, 2006, Vice President Dick Cheney shot a companion in the chest while they were duck hunting in Texas. After the shooting, Mr. Cheney exhibited all of the qualities in a personal crisis caused by his own incompetence that the Bush administration exhibits in political ones.

First, there was secrecy. The shooting occurred at 5:50 p.m. on a Saturday. It wasn't made public until the following afternoon, when the owner of the ranch where the vice president had been hunting (Katharine Armstrong) telephoned a local newspaper. Then Mr. Cheney's proxies blamed someone else; in this case, the shooting victim for standing in the wrong place (a hunter is always responsible for when and where he shoots).

Initially, the members of Mr. Cheney's hunting party were adamant that no alcohol had been involved. Armstrong was asked and answered "No, zero, zip; no one was drinking." But four days after the shooting, Mr. Cheney sat for an interview with Brit Hume of Fox News and acknowledged that he'd had at least one beer before the incident. He also told Hume that he'd delayed making the shooting public because "this was a complicated story," and he felt that the owner of the ranch should put it out. He didn't say what was complicated about the story or why, if it was complicated, the task of making it public should fall to Armstrong.

The world is moving dangerously close to an irrevocable tipping point. We are living in a time that cries out for a leader like Franklin Roosevelt, who led the United States through the greatest depression and most horrific war that our nation has known. But instead, we have a ruling class that has brought a senseless war in Iraq upon us. It treats 9/11 as a political opportunity, not a grievous loss. It sees national security, not as an urgent imperative but as a building block to achieve other goals. Instead of offering the American people a "New Deal," it has made economic inequity a hallmark of our society. Instead of leading the scientific community, it is intent upon limiting stem-cell research and teaching our children "intelligent design."

The Bush administration and its allies in Congress have failed totally to make the world a better place or our place in it any safer. It's a matter of survival that we begin to reverse the damage that they have done. The way to start that process is by electing a Democratic majority in both houses of Congress on November 7, 2008.

The 2008 presidential election was remarkable and gratifying.

More Important Than Boxing: 2008

In 1977, I left my job as a litigator for a Wall Street law firm to write. My first book served as the basis for a feature film starring Jack Lemmon and Sissy Spacek.

Missing told the true-life story of an American named Charles Horman, who was killed by the Chilean military in the aftermath of the 1973 coup that toppled Chilean president Salvador Allende. The book and film presented evidence that Horman was executed with the foreknowledge of United States government officials because he'd stumbled upon evidence linking US military personnel to implementation of the coup. One night, I asked Charles's mother what she thought was the most important message I could convey in the book. Her answer has always stayed with me.

"Charles's death," Elizabeth Horman told me, "taught me the lesson of political responsibility. I used to think that I could till the soil on my own little plot of land and let the rest of the world care for its own problems. What our country did in Vietnam, what happened to people overseas, was no concern of mine. I was wrong. I know now that each of us is obligated to fight for what is right and take responsibility for what our government does. If we don't, sooner or later, it will affect us all."

I've quoted Elizabeth Horman here because her words are the best and most heartfelt expression I know in support of a proposition that goes to the heart of life in a democracy: The rights and privileges we enjoy as citizens are accompanied by responsibilities.

As an American who feels that his country has been tarnished and badly damaged during the past eight years, I feel a responsibility to add my thoughts to the dialogue regarding the upcoming presidential election.

In January 2005, I wrote, "Nothing is more appalling to those of us who oppose George Bush than the fact that millions of Americans voted for him in the belief that he somehow epitomizes good moral values.

Moral values are about more than the lavish profession of a belief in Christ. We believe that there is no sense of decency or honor in the Bush administration and that it's morally rotten to the core."

John McCain's choice of Sarah Palin as his running mate has galvanized "the religious right" in support of his candidacy and put the issue of moral values back in the electoral spotlight. So let's talk about moral values.

America's Founding Fathers believed it was essential that the War of Independence against England be conducted with respect for human rights. The nation they'd founded was at risk and the British were engaging in atrocities against American civilians and soldiers. But George Washington, as commander in chief of the Continental Army, deemed it essential that the revolution remain faithful to its ideals. With regard to the detention of enemy combatants, he decreed, "Treat them with humanity and let them have no reason to complain of our copying the brutal example of the British Army in their treatment of our unfortunate brethren."

During the Civil War, Abraham Lincoln forbade any form of torture and put into place the first formal code of conduct for the humane treatment of prisoners of war. Dwight Eisenhower followed that example in World War II.

The Bush administration has systematically undermined more than two centuries of American values in the conduct of war. The same people who designed and supported these excesses are in the vanguard of John McCain's presidential campaign.

John McCain's backers also take perverse pride in attacks on the environment. One of the applause lines that whipped this year's Republican National Convention into a frenzy was "Drill, baby, drill." There it was. Get some pipelines in that wilderness. Spill some oil on those beaches. We'll show those tree-huggers.

Preservation of the environment for future generations is a moral issue. The people who are telling us now that there's no need to worry about global warming are the same people who told us a month ago that the American economy was sound.

The Bush administration and John McCain have consistently opposed greater regulation of financial institutions. They told us that multi-million-dollar Christmas bonuses on Wall Street and $140,000,000 executive severance packages were good for the economy. They stood by while the price of oil rose from $25.20 a barrel on 9/11 to over $100 a barrel and saw no problem in the multi-billion dollar profits of Exxon and other oil companies.

Now the economy is in chaos. And the same people who favored letting market forces dictate the flow of the economy want the American taxpayers to spend $700 billion to bail out big financial institutions.

The situation is reminiscent of the federal bailout necessitated by the savings and loan crisis that occurred during the administration of the first President Bush. Then, as now, a Republican president molded a political climate that enabled affluent transgressors to run wild. There was economic deregulation, a systematic weakening of enforcement provisions, and underfunding of the enforcers who were supposed to monitor behavior in white-collar sectors of the economy. "Liberal" ideologies were attacked, but supposedly conservative ideologies bordering in many instances on economic plunder were encouraged.

How much is $700 billion? Roughly $2,300 for every American man, woman, and child. Or calculated differently: if someone took a stack of hundred-dollar bills and lay them end to end, $700 billion would stretch to the moon and back and more than halfway back to the moon again. It would circle the Earth at the equator almost twenty-seven times. $700 billion dollars in hundred-dollar bills would weigh 7,709 tons.

Economic equity is a moral issue. Last year, the highest-earning 1 percent of Americans received almost one-quarter of all income in the United States. The top 10 percent received almost half. No logical-thinking person suggests that all people should be paid the same salary. But there should be some semblance of fairness in the system.

With all the economic problems we face today, John McCain is still defending the tax cuts for the rich that were enacted by the Republican-controlled Congress several years ago. And keep in mind; many of the people now pleading for the government to bail out the giants of Wall Street are the same people who, last year, opposed an increase in the minimum wage, which was then $5.15 an hour. These people have few values other than the accumulation of power and the service of wealth.

Caring for the elderly and poor is a moral issue. Where do the Bush administration and John McCain stand on this issue? When the Republicans controlled Congress, they implemented changes in Medicare to preclude the federal government from using its buying power to negotiate lower prices from suppliers of medical equipment and prescription drugs. The result is that, last year, the federal government paid more than double the price that some consumers paid online and at retail pharmacies for items that range from power wheelchairs ($4,024 versus $1,452) to blood glucose strips ($36 versus $17 a box). Some suppliers of medical equipment and prescription drugs are profiting nicely from that prohibition. Meanwhile, John McCain has consistently opposed programs that would provide meaningful health insurance for tens of millions of Americans who are currently uninsured.

So much for "compassionate conservatism." Now let's get to the core "moral" issues that account for much of Sarah Palin's (and John McCain's) support. A lot of these issues revolve directly or indirectly around sex.

Last year, Deputy Secretary of State Randall L. Tobias resigned after acknowledging that he had been a customer of a Washington, DC, escort service whose owner was charged by federal prosecutors with running a prostitution operation. Tobias (who is married) had previously directed the President's Emergency Fund for AIDS Relief. In that role, he emphasized abstinence and faithfulness to one sexual partner over condom use to prevent the spread of AIDS.

Republican senator David Vitter of Louisiana has been an outspoken defender of "family values." He has repeatedly attacked same-sex marriage as posing a threat to the sanctity of marriage (which he called "the most important social institution in human history"). Six weeks after Tobias's resignation, Vitter was confronted with a similar problem when it was revealed that he too had patronized an escort service operated by the so-called D.C. Madam.

"This was a very serious sin," Vitter acknowledged. But he claimed to be off the hook, since he had "asked for and received forgiveness from God and my wife in confession and marriage counseling." The "family values senator" from Louisiana declined to discuss the matter further, saying, "Out of respect for my family, I will keep my discussion of the matter there; with God and them."

Less than a month after Vitter's confession, Senator Larry Craig (Republican of Idaho) pled guilty to a charge of disorderly conduct after being arrested for soliciting sex from a plainclothes police officer in a men's bathroom at Minneapolis–St. Paul International Airport. While in Congress, Craig has vociferously opposed gay rights, voting against expanding a federal hate-crimes law to cover offenses motivated by anti-gay bias and against a bill that would have outlawed employment discrimination based on sexual orientation.

And let's not forget Ted Haggard, president of the politically influential National Association of Evangelicals and pastor of the 14,000-member New Life Church in Colorado Springs. Haggard (one of the most powerful right-wing clergymen in America) was dismissed by the church oversight board after it was determined that he had "committed sexually immoral conduct."

More specifically, a gay escort named Michael Jones claimed to have had a three-year sexual relationship with Haggard. Initially, Haggard denied knowing Jones. Then he admitted receiving a massage from Jones in a Denver hotel room and buying methamphetamine from him, but claimed that he had never used the drugs and that they'd never had sex together. Taking Haggard at his word (which is a dubious proposition), why is a married evangelical clergyman who supports George Bush's political agenda receiving a massage from a male escort in a hotel room and buying illegal drugs from him?

Sexual misconduct isn't confined to the Republican Party. Bill Clinton, John Edwards, and Eliot Spitzer are proof of that. But the hypocrisy of the McCain-Palin campaign and their supporters on sexual issues is breathtaking.

Bristol Palin (Sarah Palin's unwed adolescent daughter) is pregnant. Television commentator Bill O'Reilly (the right-wing icon who, several years ago, paid a substantial sum to settle a sexual harassment claim lodged against him) says that Bristol's pregnancy should be off limits in the campaign and that "it's a personal matter." Of course, when Jamie Lynn Spears was pregnant, O'Reilly proclaimed, "The blame falls primarily on the parents of the girl, who obviously have little control over her."

It is hard to imagine what O'Reilly and his Republican brethren would have said and done if Chelsea Clinton had been pregnant at age sixteen. But rest assured; it would have been ugly.

Meanwhile, Bristol Palin's pregnancy shouldn't be an issue in this campaign. But Sarah Palin's crusade to ban teaching adolescents about any method of birth control other than abstinence should be.

If only Bristol had been taught about contraceptives in school. Whatever Sarah Palin taught her daughter at home, she and Mr. Palin fell short in educating Bristol in this area. There's a valid argument to be made that schools shouldn't give condoms to students. But schools should teach students what condoms do and what happens if you play sexual Russian roulette without one. In addition to getting pregnant, there are a lot of diseases that Bristol could have contracted; some of them deadly. Of course, Governor Palin is a woman whose view of educating young people is that sex education is bad but creationism should be taught as science in our public schools.

Much of the support for the McCain-Palin ticket is grounded on religious faith. But just because someone believes that Jonah was swallowed by a whale doesn't mean that he or she has good moral values.

The simple acceptance of religious dogma or experiencing a moment of religious rapture doesn't make someone a good Christian. A good Christian, like any person of faith, is defined by his or her acts.

John McCain has acknowledged being unfaithful to his first wife after she was disfigured in a car accident. Then he left her to marry an heiress.

Much of the "religious right" seems to adhere to the view, "Jesus loves you and shares your hatred of homosexuals."

These people are lecturing us about moral values?

It would be nice to see John McCain, Sarah Palin, and their followers demonstrate good moral values rather than just pontificate about them. But real empathy and compassion are unwelcome in the McCain campaign.

My guess is that, if Jesus were walking among us today, he'd be opposed to discrimination on the basis of race, religion, and sexual orientation. He might well favor stem-cell research as "pro-life." And whatever his position on those issues, I doubt that he'd be hunting caribou in Alaska with a high-powered rifle and telescopic sight. More likely, he'd be a community organizer seeking to improve the lot of the poor and downtrodden.

John McCain served this country well during the war in Vietnam. But during the past year, he has tarnished that service. The character of the campaign he has been running tells us a lot about his own character. There was a time when McCain was thought to stand for honor and principle. No more. Recent events have revealed him as the person he is, which is very different from the person he once was (or we thought him to be).

McCain could have used the 2008 presidential campaign to engender an honest dialogue about the future of America. Instead, he has allowed his political operatives to orchestrate an ugly national campaign based in significant measure on appeals to prejudice and deceit.

The choice of Sarah Palin as his running mate tells us all we need to know about John McCain's commitment to national security and the good of America. The choice was bizarre, almost frivolous. It tells us that his only "value" is winning the election and that he will put the nation at risk to achieve that goal.

Meanwhile, the conservative right has suddenly discovered that unregulated economic markets can lead to a worldwide economic disaster. Maybe that "meltdown" can be forestalled. But global warming can't be forestalled once the tipping point has passed. If terrorists acquire nuclear weapons, it will be virtually impossible to forestall their use.

Yet, on these crucial issues, McCain has no vision for the future. He simply parrots the Bush administration; the same administration that invaded Iraq to "bring freedom to the Iraqi people" and has done nothing to halt the spread of nuclear weapons to North Korea and Iran. Indeed, for all its bluster, seven years after 9/11, the Bush administration has failed to capture Osama bin Laden.

Let's be honest. If Barack Obama were white, he'd be leading by close to twenty points in the polls right now. The murky waters of bigotry are the real moral issue in this election. The question is whether or not America is ready to elect a black president; one with a strange-sounding name.

This election isn't about John McCain and Barack Obama. It's about America.

★ ★ ★

NOVEMBER 5, 2008:
A NOTE ON THE AMERICAN PRESIDENTIAL ELECTION

Anyone who reads my articles knows that I had a strong emotional investment in this year's presidential election.

I came of age in the 1960s. John F. Kennedy was my boyhood hero. I lived through the civil rights movement, the war in Vietnam, and the sexual revolution. I experienced the Beatles, Muhammad Ali, and so many other markers of that era.

At the height of "The Sixties," the presidency of George W. Bush was unimaginable. None of us could have foreseen an administration that endorsed torture, advocated teaching "creationism" in the public schools, and repudiated the notion of a "Great Society" keyed to economic and social justice.

But there was another thought that was also unimaginable in the 1960s; that four decades later, the American people would elect an African American with the strange-sounding name "Barack Obama" as president of the United States. It just didn't seem possible.

Whatever the future brings, the American people have made a statement about our collective character. I woke up this morning feeling good about being an American.

Curiosities

The first article I wrote for publication after leaving the practice of law to write was for New York *Magazine in 1977. I still remember the excitement I felt, walking to the newsstand to buy a copy the morning it went on sale. Looking back, I'm struck by how much telephone technology has changed since then.*

The Crank-Call Caper

For the past twenty-one months, I've been plagued by an anonymous telephone caller. Every night between the hours of seven and eleven, the telephone rings. As soon as I pick up the receiver and say hello, the caller hangs up. I get these calls several times a night. On weekends, I also receive them in the morning. All told, I've received over one thousand anonymous calls. That's a lot of message units.

At first, the calls did little more than pique my curiosity. But I soon became aggravated by my faceless intruder and decided to report the calls to the Annoyance Call Bureau of the New York Telephone Company.

It wasn't easy. The bureau has an unlisted telephone number. I had to leave my name and number with a business-office operator, and someone from the bureau called me back forty-eight hours later. Examination of my complaint revealed that, short of changing my number, there was nothing they could do for me. Being stubborn, I declined. Recently, though, as my caller's second anniversary neared, I took my problem back to Ma Bell.

Gus Ruesch is the manager of New York Telephone's twenty-person Annoyance Call Bureau for all of New York State below Poughkeepsie. He listened intently as I explained my situation, and then advised a cure: "Most anonymous callers are easily discouraged. Just hang up on them and they'll go away. In fact," Ruesch added, "we don't even investigate sporadic calls. It has to be an ongoing situation for us to get involved."

Fine! I have an ongoing situation, and hanging up on my caller doesn't work. What can be done?

The answer, apparently, is "not much." For ninety-five cents a month, I can get an unlisted number. But that's out of the question since I'd be perpetually convinced that the bright beautiful woman I met the other night wants to call but can't find my number.

A second defense is to live in an area that houses what the phone company calls an "electronic exchange." With an electronic exchange, New York Telephone has "an extremely good capability" for identifying the source of incoming calls. With an "electro-mechanical" exchange, that capability is "fair." In a "mechanical" exchange, it's practically nil. Needless to say, I live in one of the few remaining mechanical exchanges in the City of New York.

But hark! A third path exists. My eyes brightened as Ruesch spoke: "If a victim provides the company with a short list of suspects, we have certain devices capable of recording all numbers dialed from the suspected phones. If our tests show that your number was dialed from one of those phones at the same time you received an anonymous call, your problem is over."

"Great! All I need is a suspect. Do you have a profile of an anonymous caller?"

"You," Ruesch answered. "You . . . Me . . . Everybody."

His voice betokened resignation.

"I've seen annoyance callers ranging in age from six to eight-seven. We had a mother harassing her son because she didn't like the woman he married, and a senile old lady who called for an old boyfriend at a number which hadn't been his for twenty years. Annoyance calls are made by doctors and sanitation workers, lawyers and telephone-company employees. Some callers are people with a grudge, making calls to get even. Others are lovesick puppies. Some are rich; some are poor. One person spent $300 a month on annoyance calls before we caught him. There's no pattern."

End of profile.

In theory, annoyance calls are punishable by up to one year in prison and a fine of $1,000 for each offense. In practice, penalties are seldom meted out. The Annoyance Call Bureau received fifty thousand complaints last year. Fewer than 15 percent were investigated and a far smaller percentage of cases were solved.

"It's all very discouraging," I said. "Anonymous calls aren't your fault any more than threatening letters are the fault of the post office. Still, I wish you could do something to stop mine."

"Don't worry," Ruesch assured me. "The calls usually end on their own. Of course, you do seem to have a special case."

Terrific! My mother thinks I'm special too. Better, in this case, I should be ordinary.

"Don't feel so bad," a friend told me the other night. "Your problem is nothing compared to mine."

"What's your problem?"

"It's over now," she confided. "Several years ago, I was plagued by calls from a man who spewed forth lewd suggestions in pretty graphic detail. The calls went on for almost a year until, one afternoon, something familiar in his voice struck a responsive chord."

"Who was it?" I asked.

"My husband."

In 1977, I penned a look back at a boy's perspective on dating for
Glamour *magazine.*

My Dating History
(And You Have to Promise
Not to Laugh)

The first time I called a girl for a date, I was sixteen. Her name was
Joan Sloman (all names used herein are pseudonyms). She had short
brown hair and was cute.

Needless to say, I was nervous. Speaking with Joan about anything
more momentous than a missed homework assignment was a new experience, and the last thing I wanted was to seem like a clod. So I wrote out
my lines and her anticipated responses in advance. In draft form, my cue
sheet resembled the following:

(Telephone rings—Father or mother answers)

Me: Hello. Could I speak with Joan?

Father or mother: Just a minute.

(Pause)

Joan: Hello.

Me: Hi, Joan. This is Tom Hauser. How are you?

Joan: Fine. How are you?

Me: Okay. Did you get your homework done for Mr. Rock's class?

Joan: Yes.

Me: Me, too. It sure was hard. Would you like to go to a movie with
me this Saturday night?

I planned on ad libbing the rest. I got as far as, "This is Tom Hauser.
How are you?" Then Joan answered, "I'm sick."

My script blown, I panicked and hung up. Several days later, when I
met her in the halls at school, I mumbled something about having been
"disconnected by the operator."

The moral of the pathetic little story above is that the process of social maturation is every bit as painful for men as it is for women. For those of you who are unconvinced, here's a brief description of other notable "firsts" in my life.

FIRST EXPOSURE TO THE OPPOSITE SEX IN A SOCIAL SETTING: When I was twelve, my parents decided that I should attend dancing school on alternate Saturday nights. This interfered with watching *Have Gun, Will Travel* on television, although I usually got home in time for *Gunsmoke*. Each class started with the girls sitting on one side of the room and the boys charging toward them. One night, I outraced everyone to Cody Davenport (the prettiest girl in the room) and asked her to dance. She declined, quite loudly, on the grounds that I was "ooky." Instead of letting the matter drop, Mr. Patterson (who ran the dancing school and looked amazingly like Bert Parks) turned off the record player and made me stand in the center of the room next to Cody while he delivered a lecture on etiquette. His words, which remain etched in my mind to this day, were as follows: "Now, boys and girls; even if Tommy Hauser were ooky—and mind you, I'm not saying that he is; but even if Tommy Hauser were ooky—the polite thing for Cody to do would be to dance with him. It wouldn't kill Cody to dance one dance with someone she doesn't like."

FIRST DATE: Having been frustrated in my efforts to go to a movie with Joan, I retired from the social scene. Friday and Saturday nights were spent babysitting for my younger brother and sister. The first date I had was the high school senior prom. Ten days before the event, the school principal began calling dateless students into his office and arbitrarily assigning prom dates. Petrified at the thought of being matched with Ingrid Sokolow (braces and acne), I invited Cindy Foreman (kind of nice). We had a surprisingly pleasant time, after which I never called her again. That summer, while working as a camp counselor, I met the first girl I ever really liked who was willing to go out with me. We went to a party, a movie, and an amusement park. Just when I was falling in love, she dumped me for the baseball instructor.

FIRST COLLEGE MIXER: The first college mixer I attended was very much like the next ninety-nine college mixers I attended. The only opening line I could ever think of was, "Would you like to dance?" Since

I couldn't dance (after my experience with Cody Davenport, I had developed a mental block), I simply stood around staring at the girls, feeling uncomfortable (and, I'm sure, making them uncomfortable).

FIRST SEXUAL EXPERIENCE: I necked once during my freshman year of college. The episode occurred in a parked car behind the tennis courts at a local country club. I was so excited that I couldn't sleep at all that night. Two years later, actually losing my virginity was more traumatic. The episode occurred in the apartment of a woman I had been dating for several months, who was almost as inexperienced as I was. Laura had no more idea of what she was doing than I did. Afterward, she sat on the edge of the bed, feeling guilty, and cried.

FIRST FABULOUS PICK-UP (which meant that I had really come into my own): Having learned that I couldn't meet women at mixers, I began to look for them in classes and the university library. In my senior year of college, I stood outside a classroom building in ten-degree weather for twenty minutes in order to accidentally run into a devastatingly voluptuous redhead I had seen on campus. When she emerged, it was on the arm of a good-looking quarterback, and I abandoned my plan. One month later, while I was studying in the library, the redhead marched in, looked around, saw me, walked over, sat down directly across from me at the table I was sitting at, and smiled. With great aplomb, I pretended not to see her, buried my face in a book, grew increasingly nervous and left after ten minutes.

Fortunately, I've found that the traumas of managing one's social life decrease as one grows older. And while I don't pretend to have all the answers, I would like to pass along a few things I've learned in the fifteen years since I called Joan Sloman:

(1) The fact that someone is gorgeous is a lousy foundation on which to build a relationship. Good looks do nothing to guarantee honesty, decency, sensitivity, or intelligence. Moreover, they don't last. Cody Davenport is now fat and not at all attractive. It serves her right.

(2) There are very few valid excuses for breaking a date, and having a headache is not one of them.

(3) People who fail to return telephone calls, like people who break dates, are best avoided.

(4) One of the most painful experiences in life is breaking off a relationship with someone you love. It does not get any easier with age.

(5) Blind dates seldom work. As a general rule, the only thing worse than a blind date is a blind date on New Year's Eve.

(6) When a woman chooses not to see me again after what I thought was a wonderful night, one of three reasons usually explains her conduct: (a) she didn't like me; (b) she felt guilty about cheating on her boyfriend; or (c) we had a relationship that she didn't think would grow. Surprisingly enough, men stop seeing women for similar reasons. Just because a man fails to call for a second date doesn't mean that he's a bastard.

(7) Some women collect notches on their belts, as do some men. When a woman makes sexual advances and is rebuffed, she is capable of reacting every bit as childishly as a man in the same situation. The first time I ever said "no" to a woman, she accused me of being impotent.

(8) No one has a perfect social life. Everyone is lonely at one time or another. And though it's often unwitting, we all contribute to each other's sadness. It wasn't until recently that I began to wonder how Joan Sloman felt the night I called and then hung up on her.

In the late 1970s, I began taking martial arts lessons. My sensei *(instructor) was also the owner of a Chinese restaurant.*

Pity the Poor Restaurateur

Keath Liu owns and operates the China Gourmet restaurant on West 72nd Street in Manhattan. The business is his livelihood. Just before closing, a man and woman come in and order sesame chicken with lemon sauce. When the food is 90 percent eaten, the man calls Liu over.

"Look at this," he says, holding aloft a light brown hair. "This was in our food."

"I'm sorry," Liu answers. "Would you like something else from the kitchen?"

"I'm not hungry anymore. That hair ruined my appetite. Your kitchen must be filthy."

Liu tries to explain that all of his employees are Chinese with black hair, but the woman interrupts. "We're not paying. If you don't like it, call the police."

The police say they are too busy to come. Can't the restaurant handle its own problems?

"No problem," answers Liu, a fourth-degree black belt martial arts expert. "I'll use karate."

Four cops arrive very quickly, but are able to enforce only partial payment. "You're a Chinese Jew," the woman snaps on her way out. The woman has light brown hair.

Pity the poor restaurant owner! His patrons worry about the check. He has problems galore; many of them caused by his customers.

"What a life," moans Liu. "I pay for rent, kitchen help, insurance, and food. A white tablecloth costs thirty-five cents to launder. I sell a complete dinner for five dollars, and still I get complaints. One woman poured soy sauce all over her ice cream. She thought it was chocolate syrup. It was very funny, except I had to give her a second dessert. Another customer asked for a glass of water with ice so he could take some 'medicine.' I paid a fortune for my liquor license. I can't do business like that."

There are eight Chinese restaurants within a few blocks of China Gourmet, so Liu struggles to keep his customers happy. It's not easy. One woman went to the ladies' room to gargle and came out to report that her false teeth had fallen into the toilet. Before Liu could retrieve them, a second customer flushed the toilet, clogging the pipes and flooding the floor. A plumber had to be called to repair the damage. The first woman threatened to sue for loss of her false teeth. Liu wonders, "Why can't she gargle in the sink like everyone else?"

Customers! A restaurateur can't do business without them, but they are the bane of his existence. Customers steal ashtrays, cloth napkins, and silverware. They break dishes, glassware, and chairs. They sneak out without paying and pocket tips left by other patrons.

"You want to know about customers?" asks Michael O'Neal, part owner of the Ginger Man, a popular Manhattan restaurant. "How long can you listen? We're less than a block from Lincoln Center. That means half of our customers have concert tickets, and they all want to be served in two minutes. Purse snatchers are another headache. They come in with a coat on the arm, walk to the cigarette machine, and amble back down the aisle. If they order, it's always the cheapest thing on the menu. All we can do is watch them until they grab something. Then there are the nuts. We had a flasher come in one night with nothing on but a raincoat." O'Neal runs a hand across the back of his head. "Come to think of it, he wasn't much of a problem. I just said, 'Sir, you're not properly dressed,' and he left."

Ask any restaurant owner, and the litany of complaints continues. Kids loosen the tops on salt shakers so the salt will cascade out onto the next person's dinner. Raucous customers disturb other patrons, who then leave without eating. Indeed, after listening to the plaintive cries of one restaurateur after another, it would appear as though the only way a restaurant can survive its customers is by being a culinary version of General Motors or IBM.

Tavern on the Green stands just east of the Ginger Man on the fringe of Central Park. It has four hundred employees, accommodates eight hundred customers simultaneously, and serves 600,000 meals a year. Its operation is supervised with sleek corporate-like precision by its general manager, Bruce Axler.

"Our problems are minimal," says Axler—a man who works seventy hours a week on a regular basis. "The people who come to Tavern on the Green are celebrating. It's a big event for them, and they're on their good behavior. Once in a while, we have a professional check jumper, but what can you do? We talk to him and, if he refuses to pay, eventually we let him go. It's not worth our time to swear out a complaint and go down to criminal court. Two checks more or less make no difference to us."

Does Tavern on the Green get customer complaints?

"Not too often. A few people don't like the way a sauce is made. Their mother makes it better, or their wife uses more lemon. Someone might think the dining room is too hot or too chilly. Once, a customer was stung by a bee in the garden area. If someone has a valid complaint, we offer him a complimentary dinner. If we don't make him happy, we don't make him pay."

The bottom line is that the restaurant business is like the rest of life. The little guy has the biggest problems. Tavern on the Green is big enough to ignore customer incidents that would plague a smaller restaurant. For Keath Liu, a set of false teeth can mean the difference between profit and loss for an evening's work. That same night, Tavern on the Green might gross $50,000.

Does Liu feel oppressed?

"Not at all," he says. "In fact, sometimes the customer is right."

For example?

Liu's eyes sparkle. "I have a friend who owns a Chinese restaurant. One night, His chef mistook the dishwasher soap for monosodium glutamate. Have you ever seen soap bubbles in shrimp with lobster sauce?"

This article, written in 2005, was nostalgia driven.

V&T Pizza

Very few things in life are constant, but V&T pizza is one of them.

Vincent and Tony Curcurato were born in Manhattan and grew up on 116th Street off First Avenue. Prior to World War II, they were bakers by trade. Then they enlisted in the US Army. In 1945, they returned from the war, opened a small pizzeria on Amsterdam Avenue and 122nd Street, and named it after themselves: The V&T Restaurant.

In 1952, the V&T relocated to Amsterdam Avenue between 112th and 113th Streets. In the mid 1960s, it moved again; this time two blocks further south to its present home at 1024 Amsterdam.

My own memories of the V&T date to September 1963, when I began my freshman year of college. A small cheese pizza cost ninety cents. "Small" was six slices. The price went up in ten-cent increments for medium ($1.00) and large ($1.10).

During my years at Columbia, I ate at the V&T two or three times a week. Usually, I ordered pizza. Mushrooms and sausage were added on when budgetary considerations allowed. Frank Macchiarola (my floor counselor, who would become a lifelong friend and a nationally respected educator) shared my love of V&T pizza. "It was comfort food for a home-sick Italian kid from Brooklyn," Frank recalls.

The restaurant was also the site of numerous dates, celebrations, and other gatherings, and remains a touchstone of my college years. Ten years ago, when I created a family-run Italian restaurant for a scene in a novel I was writing, I modeled it on the V&T. Even now, I revisit for pizza every few months.

There aren't many restaurants in the Columbia neighborhood that I recognize anymore. The West End, Hungarian Pastry Shop, and Tom's are still there. So, by the way, is the huge message painted on the side of 600 West 113th Street: "The wages of sin is death, but the gift of God is eternal life through Jesus Christ our Lord." But most of the Biblical words have faded beyond legibility. The Gold Rail, Takome, College Inn, and New Moon are all gone.

As for the V&T; Vincent and Tony Curcurato sold the restaurant in 1985 to a man named Alex Gjolaj. Vincent died in the mid 1990s. Tony passed away in 2000. For Columbians of the past two decades, Gjolaj is the face of the V&T. He's there a minimum of five nights a week. On weekends, he's joined by Robert Taylor, a waiter who has been on staff for forty years.

The 2005 edition of Zagat's guide to New York City restaurants (a culinary Qur'an for New Yorkers) describes V&T pizza in no uncertain terms: "Scholars swear by the greasy saucy cheesy pizza . . . An undergrad dream."

Gjolaj estimates that half his business comes from Columbia students. Many of his other patrons are neighborhood residents. Alumni often return. Art Garfunkel, who majored in art history and earned a BA from Columbia College in 1965 remains a loyal V&T customer long after his separation from Paul Simon. "We deliver to him on East 79th Street all the time," says Gjolaj. "He gives a nice tip and pays the cab fare."

But the V&T is hardly celebrity driven. "That's our only big celebrity," Gjolaj acknowledges. "No; wait a minute. Jack Nicholson was here once about ten years ago. He was waiting for someone and the person never came. But he liked the way the pizza looked, so he went out to his limo and brought his chauffeur in to have a pizza with him."

Needless to say, I returned the V&T for this article. It was an opportunity to feel pleasantly nostalgic, enjoy a good pizza, and play food critic at the same time.

The current V&T menu is a more ambitious than it was decades ago. In addition to old standards, there are entrees like chicken *scarpariello,* veal *française,* and mussels *fra diavolo.* Naturally, prices have risen. It now costs two dollars just to put mushrooms on top of a small pizza.

As for the decor; the murals from my youth have given way to modern renditions of New York and Italian landmarks, and the blue Formica tables are covered by maroon tablecloths. The glass display case that housed salads, slices of cheesecake, and cannoli has been replaced by a large wood bar. The wine list is more elaborate than before. In fact, the simple existence of a wine list makes it more elaborate than before. Hard liquor is now served.

My dinner companion and I ordered a large pizza with mushrooms and sausage.

The pizza had a chewy crust. "The dough is handmade," Gjolaj told me later. "Not many places do that anymore."

There were gobs of cheese on top. "Whole-milk mozzarella from Wisconsin is the best," Gjolaj counseled.

And a rich tomato sauce . . . "Simple but good. We add oregano, basil, and garlic."

The mushrooms and sausage were plentiful. In truth, the pie was a trifle greasy but . . . "We don't put any oil on the pizza," Gjolag volunteered. "Whatever is there comes from the cheese. And we add a little love."

So there you are. V&T pizza is still reliable. And there aren't many pleasures one can say that about over the course of forty years.

From V&T pizza to Tiffany.

The Tiffany Box

There's a constant flurry of activity at Tiffany's flagship store on Fifth Avenue in Manhattan. Well-heeled customers mingle with the merely curious. Meticulously dressed sales personnel tend briskly to their work. Each purchase is packaged in a box and carefully tied with a white satin ribbon. The color of the box is similar to that of a robin's egg. For generations, it has been known in elegant circles as "Tiffany blue."

A word-association test keyed to a visual image of a Tiffany box is likely to elicit responses such as, "Elegance . . . luxury . . . diamonds . . . Audrey Hepburn." There's a long history behind that response.

Tiffany & Young opened for business as a stationery and fancy goods emporium at 259 Broadway in Manhattan on September 18, 1837. Its proprietors were twenty-five-year-old Charles Lewis Tiffany and John B. Young. They began their enterprise with a $1,000 advance from Tiffany's father. First day sales totaled $4.98. Sixteen years later, Tiffany took control of the company and renamed it Tiffany & Co. In 1940, the store moved to its present location at 727 Fifth Avenue.

Tiffany & Co. now sells jewelry, timepieces, sterling silverware, china, crystal, stationery, and accessories. At the start of this year [2003], there were forty-seven Tiffany stores in the United States and eighty-four overseas. Retail sales for fiscal 2002 totaled $1,706,602,000 with jewelry accounting for 80 percent of that total.

But these are cold hard numbers. It's the sight of the Tiffany blue box that zings heartstrings and evokes images of classic grandeur.

Tiffany and Co. is well aware of the marketing power inherent in its box. The company's promotional material states that, shortly after Tiffany & Young opened, "A distinctive shade of blue was chosen to symbolize the company's renowned reputation for quality and craftsmanship. The color was adopted for use on Tiffany & Co. boxes, catalogues, shopping bags, and brochures, as well as in advertising and other promotional materials."

Indeed, by the turn of the last century, the Tiffany box was so renowned that a 1906 article in the *NewYork Sun* declared, "Charles Lewis Tiffany has one thing in stock that you cannot buy of him for as much money as you may offer. He will only give it to you. And that is one of his boxes. The rule of the establishment is ironclad; never to allow a box bearing the name of the firm to be taken out of the building except with an article which has been sold by them and for which they are responsible."

Today, the Tiffany box is a status symbol unto itself. When one sees a Tiffany box, the assumption is that there's something wonderful inside and that the recipient is someone special in the eyes of the donor. The same item is perceived differently if it comes in a Tiffany box as opposed to some other wrapping. One can also be fairly certain that the gift is a luxury rather than a necessity of life.

Graphic designer Milton Glaser, who created the brilliant and omnipresent "I Love NY" logos with a heart in place of the word "love" has some thoughts on the box. "I've always been fascinated because it seems like such an unlikely color for a high-end business." says Glaser. "For a lingerie shop, perhaps. But Tiffany? One would expect deep burgundy or some combination of gold and navy blue."

"The aberrational quality appeals to me," Glaser continues. "It's bracingly different. It sticks in one's memory in a way that very few colors are able to achieve. The violation of expectation makes it strikingly effective for use of identity. And it goes against convention in that color, rather than form or lettering, is used to establish identity. Very few companies, if any, have used color so effectively. There's Kodak yellow and Coca-Cola red, but Tiffany outdoes them. Catch a flash of it and you think Tiffany."

LeRoy Neiman, America's most commercially successful contemporary artist, has catalogued "the good life" at home and abroad for years. Neiman is also captivated by the Tiffany color. "It's a distinctive blue," he observes. "Not azure, cerulean, Titian, or sky blue, but an indescribable blue. I nominate Tiffany blue to the painters color wheel."

If there's a smudge on the Tiffany box, it might be its country of origin. An innocent inquiry to Tiffany regarding where the boxes are manufactured elicited the response, "That's information we wouldn't give out." A follow-up inquiry to spokesperson Julia Kleyner met with the reply," I'm not at liberty to discuss that."

This, of course, conjures up images of eight-year-old children manu-facturing Tiffany boxes on their day off from a Nike factory in Indonesia. Hardly the Tiffany image.

Still, one successful New York career woman who has received her share of Tiffany gifts over the years acknowledges, "Whenever I see some-one with a Tiffany box, I ask myself, 'What's in it?' And if an attractive man is carrying the box, I might wonder who he is and who he's giving it to. The box suggests a lifestyle that's exciting and definitely beyond the ordinary."

Hope springs eternal.

Memo to 2000 Presidential Candidates: Read My Book

Ask the presidential candidates which book they're reading, their favorite book, or the book that most influenced them, and it's highly unlikely that you'll get an honest answer. For all I know, Al Gore is a voracious reader and the tome that turned him on to literature was *The Poky Little Puppy*. John McCain's character might have been shaped by the steadfast honor of Dr. Seuss's noble pachyderm in *Horton Hatches the Egg*. George W. Bush might have gotten a kick out of *Memoirs of a Woman of Pleasure*. But by now, all of the candidates have brainstormed with political advisors (who, in turn, have conducted extensive focus groups) to determine the most politically advantageous response to literary questions.

The Bible would seem to the most expedient answer to all literary inquiries posed in the current political season. My own choice would be *The Grapes of Wrath*, but that's 619 pages long and none of the candidates seems to have that lengthy an attention span. Meanwhile, I have a suggestion and a plea to all presidential candidates—READ MY BOOK.

I've authored quite a few books, but *Mark Twain Remembers* is my favorite. The story line is straightforward. Mark Twain is on his deathbed in 1910, reflecting back on a six-week period in his life that occurred in 1856 when he was twenty years old. It's a book that deals in eternal truths; focusing on Twain's life, slavery, and a young man coming of age. There's also a love story.

I should add that *Mark Twain Remembers* is a novel. The distinction between fact and fiction doesn't seem to matter much to writers these days. And in politics, truth is clearly secondary to whether a candidate wears Brooks Brothers or double-knit shirts. But I did want to set the record straight.

The book has gotten nice reviews. The *New York Daily News* called it "enjoyable." The *Philadelphia Inquirer* said I'd created "an unforgettable hero." Barry Farber told a national radio audience, "*Mark Twain Remembers* is one of the most remarkable books in years."

The *New York Times* didn't review the book. My publisher tells me this is because he doesn't advertise in the *New York Times Book Review*. However, to make up for that slight, *Publishers Weekly* reviewed the book twice. The first *PW* review opined that I had more audacity than wit. Then, thanks to an internal screw-up, *PW* reviewed the book a second time and declared, "A bittersweet ending perfectly caps this swift moral adventure. Succinct history lessons contextualize the tale, and the writing is so smooth it's impossible to tell which words are Twain's and which are Hauser's in this witty elegiac novel."

Anyway, it's a good book. But the business of publishing being what it is, I've run into some problems. My publisher is a small house that can't afford to pay Barnes & Noble thousands of dollars to put posters in the windows and piles of books by the cash register. There's no co-op advertising or any of the other marketing incentives that encourage today's bookstore behemoths to stock a particular title, so distribution has been poor. However, some Barnes & Noble stores do have the book in stock, and you can order a copy through Amazon.com if the website hasn't been shut down by a computer hacker.

If you get a chance to read *Mark Twain Remembers*, I'd appreciate your mentioning it during one of the televised presidential debates. That's not as good for an author as being selected by Oprah's Book Club, but it will help. Also, maybe you could get one of the pool photographers to take a picture of you reading the book. That would make me feel really good. After all, one of the nicest things about writing for a living is the realization that, on occasion, someone actually reads what I write.

This article, written in 2000, is on the serious side. Since then, things have gotten worse.

The "Standard" Book Contract: A Federal Antitrust Lawsuit Waiting to Happen

Publishing is a business. No one questions that reality. And whatever it might have been in the past, publishing is no longer the "gentlemanly" business it was once thought to be. Rather, it's about squeezing every last dollar out of every available source, and the most vulnerable source is the author.

Bestselling writers might be treated fairly by the media conglomerates that dominate publishing today. But the average author isn't. No clearer proof of that exists than the "standard" book contract. Many clauses that have been imposed on authors throughout the industry bear no relationship to any economic reality other than the best interests of the publisher. Yet these clauses flourish because virtually every major publisher insists on them and the average author has no recourse.

Kay Murray has been general counsel for the Authors Guild since 1994. "The contracts were bad enough when I got here," Murray says. "But over the past five years, they've become far more exploitative. The new technology has led to a significant decrease in cost and risk to publishers, but they simply won't share the wealth. If fact, every few months now, there's another change for the worse with all of the major publishers acting in lockstep on it."

The abuses fit into several categories.

First, there are clauses that prevent writers from being published.

In the past, when an author signed a contract with a publisher, he (or she) could safely assume that the book under contract would be published. However, as a general rule, most publishers now insist on a clause that relieves them of that obligation. More specifically, if a publisher chooses for any reason not to publish a given book, the author can keep the portion of the advance that has been previously paid but that's all. And in some instances, if the author resells the book to another publisher, even that partial advance must be repaid. In other words, the standard publishing contract today is nothing more than a one-sided option to publish.

As for traditional options, publishing contracts now often contain the following Draconian provisions: (1) The author must submit his next book in completed manuscript form to the publisher before it is considered by any other publisher; (2) The first publisher need not consider the manuscript before publication of the work currently under contract; and (3) Even if the first publisher declines to bid on the manuscript, the author must subsequently offer the publisher the chance to match any offer received at a later date from any other publisher. Thus, an author who has a book under contract to a publisher can find his career put on hold indefinitely.

In sum, just getting published is an adventure in contract law for most authors. And when authors are published, they find that their royalties have been cut precipitously by today's standard publishing contract.

For example, most publishers now require a clause to the effect that, if the publisher increases its discount to a particular book-buyer beyond a certain percentage, the author's royalty is cut in half. The logic underlying this provision is that, if a publisher has to give a giant like Barnes & Noble a break in order to sell books, then the author should shoulder part of that burden. However, the way the formula works in practice, a publisher can sometimes increase its discount to Barnes & Noble on a twenty dollar book by, say, forty cents (2 percent of list price) and cut the author's royalty in half (from $3.00 to $1.50). In other words, the publisher takes $1.50 out of the author's pocket, gives forty cents to Barnes & Noble, and keeps the remaining $1.10 for itself.

Likewise, if the publisher publishes a paperback edition of a book that it originally published in hardcover, the author might get 8 percent of list price. But if the publisher sells paperback rights in a sweetheart deal to one of its own subsidiaries, the author gets only 50 percent of the amount received from the subsidiary and the publisher gets the other half.

The handling of electronic rights is yet another form of exploitation. In this new arena, there are no warehouse costs, no printing costs, and no rational correlation between what an author is paid and the publisher's income. Premium sales and special sales are often treated in a similarly one-sided manner.

Also, it should be noted that, when it comes to royalty statements, honest accounting is not a high priority for most publishers.

Are things bad? Absolutely. And there's more.

There's nothing improper about an author being held liable if he has violated someone's rights. But most mainstream publishers now insist upon a warranty and indemnification clause that holds an author liable for damages and attorneys fees regardless of fault. In some instances, the publisher can even settle a lawsuit without the author's consent and charge the author for the cost of settlement whether or not the author has done something wrong. And on top of that, the standard publishing contract gives publishers the right to extend an author's warranty and indemnification to third parties who might not even defend against a lawsuit. Query—How would you like to be the author who's hit with a $10 million judgment from a court in Belgium?

The list goes on. The standard publishing contract is replete with clauses that strip authors of control over their books. Publishers can grant sublicenses to third parties who are empowered to cannibalize and in some cases even rewrite a manuscript, and the author has no say in the process. A publisher can sublicense a book to *Screw Magazine*; and if the author doesn't like it, tough luck. Most authors today are accorded no meaningful consultation rights with regard to book covers and dust jacket copy. Et cetera, et cetera, and so forth.

As a practical matter, publishers will negotiate on some of these issues and occasionally make changes on the margin. Small publishers and university presses are a bit more flexible than large ones. But for most authors, there is no recourse because there is no power. In Kay Murray's words, "The playing field simply isn't level. The contracts are all so bad now, it's choose your poison."

But one ray of hope does exist. As Microsoft found out recently, the antitrust laws of the United States are sometimes enforced. And while Microsoft was the target of a lawsuit that alleged monopoly abuse, the Sherman Act has a second component aimed at shared abuses of power. To wit: "Every contract, combination, or conspiracy in restraint of trade is illegal."

Quite possibly, what now passes for "standard" in the publishing industry is an illegal restraint of trade. Publishing today is characterized by powerful corporate entities acting in concert to the detriment of essentially powerless authors. And something must be done to remedy the situation because it's driving a lot of good writers out of publishing. They simply can't make a living writing books anymore.

The Antitrust Division of the United States Department of Justice should take a long hard look at the standard publishing contract.

The year after I graduated from law school, I clerked for a United States district judge named Thomas Croake. After Judge Croake's death, I paid homage to him and his sense of humor in the following article for The National Law Journal.

Thomas F. Croake:
A Law Clerk's Remembrance

Law schools don't prepare their students to practice law. Rather, in three years of Socratic dialogue, impressionable minds are taught to "think like a lawyer." Words like "remittitur" and "interpleader" are added to the vocabulary. Nuts and bolts matters such as how to draft legal documents are largely ignored. Thus, the first job a lawyer has in "the real world" is enormously important. My own first experience was ideal. After graduating from law school, it was my good fortune to clerk for Thomas F. Croake, a United States district judge who served as my mentor for the most enjoyable year of my legal career.

Judge Croake was not a scholar. Like most judicial appointments, his nomination to the federal bench was political in nature. Yet for over a decade, he dispensed justice fairly and impartially, consistent with deeply held personal beliefs. And perhaps more important from my own selfish point of view, he was a marvelous teacher. Each day was enriched by his explanation of why a certain brief should have been drafted in a given way, or how a lawyer could have improved his courtroom presentation to better serve a client.

Judge Croake died recently at age seventy-six. Since then, I've found myself reminiscing about some of the warmer, more humorous moments we spent together.

Judge Croake was Irish and fiercely proud of it. St. Patrick's Day was a holiday in chambers. Still, he was always respectful of divergent faiths. Once, I watched as he patiently engaged in a thirty-minute discussion with counsel for the Jewish Defense League on the issue of whether federal statutes or Orthodox Jewish law were the governing standard in a particular lawsuit. On another occasion, despite personal distaste for their political and religious beliefs, he ordered two Black Muslim prisoners released from solitary confinement at Green Haven State Prison. His opinion was a forerunner of later decisions by the Second Circuit Court of Appeals in the field of prisoners' rights.

Of all the anecdotes I heard in chambers, the one Judge Croake told with the greatest relish concerned Thomas Murphy—a fellow jurist who presided over the arraignment of a Black Muslim prisoner. When asked if he was represented by an attorney, the defendant answered, "Allah is my counsel." To which Judge Murphy responded, "That's very nice, but do you have local counsel?"

Like most lawyers, judges tend to establish rivalries with one another —some friendly, some not so cordial. Overall, Judge Croake was on friendly terms with his brethren. But one contemporary (I'll call him "Judge Jones") constantly rubbed him the wrong way. And the conflict was heightened when Judge Jones, who was sitting on his last case before retirement, bragged in the judges' lunchroom that every law clerk in the building had journeyed to his courtroom to look in on the trial as a respectful way of saying goodbye.

"You didn't go, did you?" Judge Croake demanded as we sat together that afternoon in Chambers.

"Judge," I admitted, "I'll be honest. I did go to Judge Jones's court-room, but it had nothing at all to do with his retirement. The truth is, word has filtered through the courthouse that Juror Number 3 is an absolutely stunning blonde, and everyone is going down to take a look."

That made Judge Croake very happy. And I should add that he himself enjoyed a pretty face. Once, when a particularly attractive woman was selected by lot from the jury pool and tentatively seated, he whispered to me, "Any lawyer who strikes that juror is in big trouble."

Judge Croake was concerned with appearances—a fact that was made very clear to his law clerks. Once, he returned from vacation and found that he was the only judge in the Southern District of New York with a law clerk who was growing a sweet potato in chambers. He actually consulted with a fellow jurist on the issue of whether a rooting sweet potato (as opposed to a philodendron or some other plant) was proper.

Of greater concern was his reaction after a four-day holiday weekend, when he returned to chambers and discovered four day's worth of moustache growing on my upper lip.

"How are you this morning, Judge?"

"Very grouchy."

But he never asked me to shave it off. I did that on my own a week later because it looked awful. And the only judicial comment on facial hair I heard that year came, not from Judge Croake, but from former United States Supreme Court justice Tom Clark. One afternoon, Clark visited David Edelstein (a former Justice Department colleague, who later became chief judge for the Southern District of New York). When Edelstein introduced Justice Clark to his law clerk (who had a full beard that was rather unkempt), Clark opined, "David, your law clerk looks just like Buffalo Bill."

Like his colleagues, Judge Croake didn't like to be reversed. He once informed me that, every time he wrote an opinion, he went to church and prayed he wouldn't be reversed "by some law professor whose elevation to the Court of Appeals proves only that hot air rises." Nonetheless, Judge Croake viewed the Second Circuit with considerable respect, and he was particularly fond of Henry Friendly.

"Henry Friendly," he once told me, "is one of the great judges of our era. Watching Henry Friendly on the bench is the legal equivalent of going surfing with the Beach Boys." And as I listened, open-mouthed, Judge Croake added, "I'll bet you didn't realize how much I knew about rock-and-roll music, did you?"

For a relatively conservative man, Judge Croake was surprisingly attuned to the sensitivities of the Vietnam Era. Once, he heard a motion from a young Westchester resident who was fighting induction into the armed forces. As was our custom, I was given the motion papers and told to write an issue memorandum. For several days, I labored over the case before going to the judge and reporting, "I've looked this over, and I can't find a way to keep him out of the Army."

"Damn it," the Judge bellowed. "I don't want you to keep him out of the Army. I want you to tell me what the law is." Then his voice softened and he added, "If nothing works on the merits, try helping him out on a procedural technicality."

Trials were a learning experience, and oftentimes fun to sit in on. My favorite moment came when a lawyer protested that he was being "unfairly strait-jacketed" by a lengthy pre-trial order. "A pre-trial order isn't a strait-jacket," Judge Croake responded. "But it isn't a kimono either."

Jurors were also a source of humor—and sometimes, inadvertently, embarrassment. One day, amidst loud noise from a nearby construction project, the Judge asked an elderly woman juror what her husband did for a living.

"He died four years ago," came the answer.

Because of the banging, Judge Croake misunderstood "died" for "retired."

"That's nice," he told her. "I hope he's enjoying himself."

Several days before I left Judge Croake to begin work on Wall Street, he sat me down for some fatherly advice. "The most important thing I can tell you," he counseled, "is don't fight personally with the men and women on the other side of the aisle. There's no reason why lawyers on opposite sides of a case can't be friends." And to prove the point, Judge Croake noted, "In my days as a state senator, on a personal level, I even got along with Republicans." Then, somewhat wistfully, he added, "Still, I enjoy irritating Republicans. I've been irritating Republicans all my life. In fact, I'm probably one of the best Republican-irritators in the business."

Judge Croake's obituary in the *New York Times* cited the requisite credentials—appointed to the federal bench by President John F. Kennedy in 1961, former vice president of the American College of Trial Lawyers, former president of the Westchester County Bar Association, and so on. But the best tribute had come years earlier from the head of litigation at a prominent Wall Street law firm, who told me, "If Tom Croake tells you that someone is a good man, then he's a good man. And if Tom Croake tells you that someone is a bastard, then he's a bastard."

I explored another corner of Irish-American heritage in this article for
Irish America *magazine.*

When Irish Eyes Are Smiling

The world has been enriched by many distinctly Irish songs. "Danny
Boy" and "MacNamara's Band" are among the diverse offerings that come
to mind. But no song is more deeply embedded in Irish hearts than
"When Irish Eyes Are Smiling."

The history of the song begins with Chauncey Olcott. Olcott's
mother, Margaret Doyle, was born in Ireland. In the 1840s, when she was
eight, her family immigrated to Canada and eventually settled in
Lockport, New York. Later, she married Mellon Whitney Olcott and the
couple moved to Buffalo where in 1860, Chauncey (christened
Chancellor John Olcott) was born. Soon after, Mellon Olcott died and
Margaret married Patrick Brennan, who was chief engineer for the
Buffalo Water Works.

Chauncy was raised in Buffalo, where he attended public school.
During the summer, he would visit his mother's family in Lockport,
where they lived in what he later described as "an Irish shanty on the
banks of the Erie Canal."

As a child, Olcott had a gift for song. Often, at the Lockport fire-
house, he was lifted onto a table and encouraged to sing Irish ballads.
Eventually, his performances became more formal. In 1879, at age nineteen, he joined the first in a series of minstrel companies that took him to
Chicago, San Francisco, London, and other locales. His good looks, Gaelic
personality, and light lyric tenor voice left him much in demand and led
to a series of leading roles in plays and light operas.

In 1886, Olcott made his New York City debut with the Lillian
Russell Opera Company as leading man in a production of *Pepita*. Thereafter, he starred in *HMS Pinafore* and *The Mikado* before returning to
London, where he made stage appearances and studied voice from 1890
through 1893. Then, back in the United States, he starred in a series of
shows with Irish themes. Among these were *Minstrel of Clare* (1896); *Sweet*

Inniscarra (1897); *A Romance of Athlone* (1899) which was highlighted by a ballad Olcott himself wrote entitled "My Wild Irish Rose"; *Garrett O'Magh* (1901); *Old Limerick Town* (1902); *Edmund Burke* (1905); *Eileen Ashore* (1906); *O'Neill of Derry* (1907); and *Barry of Ballymore* (1911). The last of these productions showcased the songs "Mother Machree" and "I Love the Name of Mary," both of which had lyrics written by Olcott with music by Ernest R. Ball.

By this time, Olcott's following among women was so great that Jean Schwartz, a popular composer-singer of the day, wrote a song entitled "Bedelia" which contained the line, "I'll Be Your Chauncey Olcott." Meanwhile, the Olcott–Ball union was becoming a fruitful one.

Ball had been born in Cleveland in 1878 and studied music at the Cleveland Conservatory. As a young man, he moved to New York. Then, in 1905, he took a verse written by an obscure state senator named James J. Walker (who later became mayor of the City of New York) and turned it into the popular song "Will You Love Me in December As You Do in May?"

Thereafter, Ball wrote songs for a Tin Pan Alley company called Witmark Music and appeared on stage as a vaudeville performer. He had a gift for writing heart-warming melodies. He and Olcott collaborated often on music and words, and it was Olcott as a performer who introduced many of Ball's most popular ballads.

"When Irish Eyes Are Smiling" marked the high point of the Olcott–Ball collaboration. Ball wrote the music and Olcott penned the lyrics with George Graff Jr The song was published in 1912 and introduced to the public with help from an Ohio socialite named Rida Johnson Young.

Young had pursued a career in theater; first as an actress and then as a writer. Starting with a play entitled *Brown of Harvard* that opened in 1906, she wrote the book and often the musical lyrics for more than twenty Broadway productions. In fact, the 2002 Broadway hit *Thoroughly Modern Millie* featured several of her songs.

One of Johnson's works was *Isle O' Dreams*, which opened at the Grand Opera House on Broadway on January 27, 1913. The play starred Olcott, and audiences were mesmerized by his rendition of its signature ballad: "When Irish Eyes Are Smiling."

Isle O' Dreams closed after thirty-two performances, but "When Irish Eyes Are Smiling" swept the nation. For several months in 1913, it was the best-selling recording in the United States. The Recording Industry Association of America cites it as one of the top-selling songs of all time. Olcott enjoyed another number-one hit in 1914, when he recorded "Too-Ra-Loo-Ra-Loo-Ral (That's an Irish Lullaby)." He also starred in *Shameen Dhu* (1913), *Terence* (1914), and *Once Upon A Time* (1918) produced by the legendary George M. Cohan. His last starring role on Broadway was in *The Voice of McConnell*, which opened on Christmas Day 1918. Seven years later, he collapsed on stage while appearing in *The Rivals*, never fully recovered, and never graced a theater production again.

Olcott died in 1932. Among the pallbearers attending his funeral at St. Patrick's Cathedral in New York were New York City mayor James J. Walker and New York governor Al Smith. Ball had died five years earlier, suffering a fatal heart attack moments after leaving the stage of a vaudeville theatre in California. Olcott was seventy-two at the time of his death. Ball was forty-nine.

Both Olcott and Ball live on in their music and on film. Ball's life was celebrated in the 1944 motion picture *When Irish Eyes Are Smiling*, co-starring Dick Haymes as the composer and June Haver as his love interest. In 1947, Warner Brothers produced *My Wild Irish Rose* based on a biography of Olcott written by his wife Margaret O'Donovan Olcott. The film starred Dennis Morgan as Olcott, Arlene Dahl as Margaret, and Andrea King as Lillian Russell.

"When Irish Eyes Are Smiling"
Music by Ernest R. Ball
Lyrics by Chauncey Olcott and George Graff Jr

Chorus: When Irish eyes are smiling,
Sure it's like a morning spring.
In the lilt of Irish laughter,
You can hear the angels sing.
When Irish hearts are happy,
All the world seems bright and gay.
And when Irish eyes are smiling,
Sure, they steal your heart away.

Verse: There's a tear in your eye,
And I'm wondering why,
For it never should be there at all.
With such power in your smile,
Sure a stone you'd beguile,
So there's never a teardrop should fall.
When your sweet lilting laughter's like some fairy song,
And your eyes twinkle bright as can be,
You should laugh all the while
And all other times smile,
And now smile a smile for me.

Chorus: When Irish eyes are smiling . . .

Verse: For your smile is a part
Of the love in your heart,
And it makes even sunshine more bright.
Like the linnet's sweet song,
Crooning all the day long,
Comes your laughter so tender and light.
For the springtime of life is the sweetest of all.
There is ne'er a real care or regret.
And while springtime is ours
Throughout all of youth's hours,
Let us smile each chance we get.

Chorus: When Irish eyes are smiling . . .

This one requires a bit more than the usual introduction.

In 1975, I did something I rarely do. I wrote a letter to my United States senator. Jacob Javits had been straddling the fence on the issue of Vietnam, and it angered me sufficiently that I wrote to him, complaining about his vote on a military appropriations bill. In due course, I got back a form response, thanking me for my support of the senator's policies. That irritated me even more, and I asked myself, "I wonder how Senator Javits would respond if he received a letter that was cute enough to be brought to his attention and unusual enough that it couldn't be answered with a form response.

Thus, "The Collected Political Letters Of Martin Bear" were born.

Using a child's handwriting, a pencil, and lined yellow paper, I sat down and wrote a rather unusual "Dear Senator Javits" letter which I signed "Martin Bear." One week later, "Martin" received a personalized response. That was enough to fuel my fire. More Martin Bear letters flowed from my pencil, and more personalized responses followed. Then I went to California on a business trip. The day I returned home, I turned on the television. And there was New York City mayor Abraham Beame reading a letter from Martin at a press conference called to discuss the city's burgeoning fiscal crisis.

At that point, I said to myself, "I've got something special here." And I sent Martin's letters, along with the responses they had elicited, to the op-ed page of the New York Times.

The Times *loved the letters. An editor called me to pave the way for publication and, during the course of our conversation, he asked about Martin. I told him Martin was my nephew. That was that. Shortly thereafter, "The Collected Political Letters Of Martin Bear" appeared on the op-ed page of "the old gray lady" and were syndicated in hundreds of newspapers around the nation. The* Times *paid Martin twenty-five dollars, which I donated to the* New York Times *"Neediest Fund."*

The letters were real. Martin was not. Several editors at the Times *were quite unhappy when I told them the truth. But they got over it, and I wrote for the paper under my own name on several occasions thereafter.*

The Collected Political Letters
of Martin Bear

Martin Bear, a nine-year-old who lives in San Francisco, spent a few months recently with a relative in New York who describes him as an "exuberant political novice." While here, Martin sent a number of letters to officeholders in Washington. Those letters and the replies he received appear below.

★ ★ ★

Dear Senator Kennedy,

I read in the newspaper that President Nixon swore all the time at the office. I think he should have his mouth washed out with soap. What do you think?

Your friend,
Martin Bear

Dear Martin,

Thank you very much for writing to me. I certainly agree that we should not use bad language, and that goes for Presidents as well as you and me!

I can tell by your letter that you must be doing very well at school. Please say "hello" to your teacher and your classmates for me, and thank you again for writing.

Sincerely,
Ted Kennedy

★ ★ ★

Dear Congresswoman Abzug,

In school today we had to write someone famous we like and ask them a question. I like you. Do you think Catfish Hunter will pitch well for the Yankees this year?

Your friend,
Martin Bear

Dear Martin,

I decided to wait until the baseball season was in full swing to answer your letter.

Catfish Hunter is one of my favorite baseball players, too. I think that, once he gets used to the Yankees, he'll improve his pitching and be an even bigger asset to the team than he is right now.

Enclosed is a book about Congress and how our laws are made. You might want to share this book with your parents and friends at school.

Thank you very much for writing to me, and I hope that you'll write again. Maybe we'll see each other at a baseball game at Shea Stadium during the August congressional recess.

Your friend,
Bella S. Abzug

★ ★ ★

Dear Senator Buckley,

In school today we had to write someone we like and someone we don't like. You're the one I don't like. I think you're stupid.

Your friend,
Martin Bear

Dear Martin,

I'm always interested in the opinions of my young constituents. Thank you for writing.

Sincerely,
James L. Buckley

★ ★ ★

Dear Senator Javits,

Could you please pass a law making April 11th a holiday. I think it should be because there are no good holidays in April except Easter. Also, April 11th is my birthday.

Your friend,
Martin Bear

Dear Martin,

Thank you for your letter asking that April 11, your birthday, be made a national holiday.

It is a very difficult thing, Martin, to create a national holiday. The only people who have been honored by our country in this manner are George Washington and Abraham Lincoln. In fact, their birthdays are celebrated together on Presidents' Day every year. Some of us have tried to create a national holiday on Martin Luther King's birthday and so far we have not been successful.

It would be nice if we could honor more Americans this way and have more days free of work and school, but I am afraid you must first prove yourself to be a great American in the tradition of Lincoln, Washington and Dr. King before this is likely to happen. I hope you do so, and that some day April 11 will be celebrated as Martin Bear Day.

Sincerely,
Jacob K. Javits

★ ★ ★

Dear Senator Humphrey,

I saw you at our temple in New York. You were late and you never stopped talking. How come you talk so much?

Your friend,
Martin Bear

P.S. Don't feel bad. The Rabbi talks too much too.

Dear Martin,

One of the nicest things about being a United States Senator is getting a letter from young people like you. It's a great satisfaction to me to know that I have so many fine young friends who wish to share their thoughts and ideas with me.

I hope you will continue to be interested in your country and your government. It will not be long before you will be old enough to vote, and our country needs interested and informed voters.

Best wishes.

Sincerely,
Hubert Humphrey

★ ★ ★

Dear Mayor Beame,

I heard that you need money. I live in New York and I like it, so here's ten cents. There's more where that came from if you need it.

Your friend,
Martin Bear

Dear Martin,

Your letter made my day.

What I tried to do for New York was understood by you, and your response is something special to me.

I know that ten cents is a lot of money to many people and that is why your contribution is of such special value. But your contribution and your letter together show the faith in our city that I have and that so many other millions also have.

I have forwarded your donation to the Finance Administrator for deposit in the New York City General Fund. Please accept my personal thanks for your interest in the future of New York.

Sincerely,
Abraham D. Beame

In 2008, I learned that the past was different from what I thought it had been.

The Case of the Missing Historical Treasure: A Columbia College Library Mystery

I visited Butler Library at Columbia University for the first time as a college freshman in September 1963. Like thousands of Columbians, I was awed by the towering columns and façade that bore the inscription: "Homer • Plato • Aristotle • Demosthenes • Cicero • Virgil." The wealth of knowledge in the building inspired me. But one particular treasure caught my eye.

The college library had a portrait of every president of the United States, matted and framed with the president's signature, affixed by brackets to the top of the bookshelves. During my years at Columbia, I walked down one side of the room and back up the other countless times, gazing at George Washington and company. Their signatures fascinated me.

Over the years, I returned to the library from time to time. Photographs of newly inaugurated presidents with signature cards were added to the collection. Then my visits to Columbia became less frequent. Thanks to the Internet, information once gleaned from the Butler stacks could be found instantly online.

Last summer, my niece and nephew wanted to see Columbia, so I took them on their first college tour. They searched for (and found) the owl in the drapery of Alma Mater. I told them about college life in the 1960s. As a final touch, I led them to the college library to see the presidential portraits.

The portraits weren't there. And the young woman on duty at the desk had no idea what I was talking about when I asked what had happened to them.

Such is life. But the memory of the portraits (and particularly, the signatures) stayed with me. So in late November, I called Anice Mills (Columbia's undergraduate services librarian) to find out where they were.

"I've been here since 1996, and I've never heard of the collection," Mills told me.

I asked if she could find out what had happened to the portraits. After all, librarians are supposed to be adept at research. Mills said she'd try. Three weeks later, I received a telephone call from Ree DeDonato (director of the Butler Library humanities-history division).

DeDonato has been at Columbia since 1994, when she was the undergraduate librarian. "I remember the portraits," she said. "They were taken down in 1996, when the Butler Library renovation began. Most of the frames were old and flimsy and started falling apart when they were detached from the top of the bookshelves. It would have cost too much to reframe everything, so we put the collection in storage."

That didn't make sense. How much could reframing cost? The signatures alone are worth tens of thousands of dollars.

"The signatures aren't real," DeDonato told me. "They're reproductions."

I felt like a six-year-old who has just learned that Santa Claus doesn't exist.

But the child in me is still alive. I wanted to see the presidential portraits one last time. So early this year, I met with DeDonato in her office on the third floor of Butler Library.

The portrait of John Tyler, matted with his signature in a fifteen-by-twenty-inch wood frame just as I remembered it, was on DeDonato's desk. I've learned a few things since I graduated from college. A quick look told me that the signature was a facsimile. It was in printer's ink, bold and black without a trace of oxidation despite the fact that Tyler hasn't signed anything since he died in 1862.

"I've asked everyone who might know," DeDonato recounted. "And there's no documentation on how the portraits came to the library. That suggests they weren't purchased or donated in a way that called for an acknowledgement. Most likely," she continued, "they were mass produced by the federal government and sent to libraries around the country, possibly as a [New Deal] WPA project. Then, as new presidents were inaugurated,

Columbia expanded the collection on its own. My grade school had similar black-and-white presidential portraits in the auditorium," she added in support of her thesis.

DeDonato reached for the portrait of John Tyler on her desk. "Let's see what we can find out," she said.

The brown paper backing crumbled as DeDonato stripped it from the frame. Next, she took a pair of pliers and removed the nails that held the corrugated cardboard backing in place. The Tyler portrait and signature (the latter on a small rectangular piece of paper) were taped to the back of the mat, which had been mounted on poster board.

The portrait and signature hadn't been archivally preserved in any way. The poster board and cardboard backing were separated by pages from a newspaper dated November 20, 1939; a good indication that the original framing had been done around that time.

Next, DeDonato performed similar surgery on the portrait of Jimmy Carter that she'd brought to her office from the storage room. The back of the signature card bore the printed legend, "Facsimile signature of Jimmy Carter, 39th President of the United States."

So much for Columbia's historical treasure.

Reconstructing history; the best guess is that the portraits of Washington through Franklin Roosevelt were sent to Columbia as a group and framed at the same time. Thereafter, as each new president took office, Columbia added a presidential signature and portrait.

Is it possible that some of the post-Roosevelt signatures are real? After all, prior to assuming the presidency of the United States, Dwight Eisenhower was president of Columbia.

"Probably not," DeDonato told me. "The Carter signature card says on the back that it's a facsimile. I doubt that any of the signatures are authentic. That's the sort of thing someone would have looked at before the portraits were put in storage."

And what will happen to the portraits in the future?

"We have no plans to re-display them," DeDonato said. "Someday, when we need the storage space, we'll probably take the portraits and signatures out of the frames, keep them with the mats, and discard everything else. The collection has no monetary value but it's interesting of its time."

Personal Notes

I went to a high school with an active reunion committee. On four occasions, I was asked to write an introductory essay for our reunion yearbook.

Reunion

Twenty-Five Years Later (1988)

Everybody defines these things differently, but still the question has to be asked. What is our twenty-fifth anniversary reunion all about?

Inevitably, certain people and events come to mind when we think about 1960–1963. John F. Kennedy's presidential campaign swung into high gear on Labor Day Weekend 1960, just before our stay at Mamaroneck High School began. Kennedy was forty-three years old then; the same age many of us are now. We trusted him through the Cuban Missile Crisis and the beginnings of Vietnam. We shared his elation when John Glenn brought us equal with the Soviets in space and felt his outrage when James Meredith was denied admission to the University of Mississippi. Then, in November 1963, just after we left MHS, Dallas happened. And if any of us needed a reminder that our days of innocence were over, there it was.

The music we listened to was our own. The Beatles and Motown were unknown. But we had Elvis, the Chiffons, Chubby Checker, Del Shannon, Bobby Vee, Little Richard, Gary U.S. Bonds, the Drifters, Frankie Avalon, Dion, Fats Domino, and the Marcels. The Yankees were always in the World Series, the Boston Celtics always won the NBA Championship, and there was no such thing as a "Super Bowl." Computers were largely science fiction. The minimum wage was a dollar an hour. The Dow Jones average was in the 500s. A first-class letter cost four cents to mail.

But all these things are external and belonged to people nationwide. Something more than 1960s nostalgia is drawing us back to Mamaroneck High School twenty-five years after our graduation and senior prom. We're older now, heavier, grayer with thinning hair. Looking back, we can appreciate what people did for us then. Things we took for granted as children seem more significant from the vantage point of later years. More than before, we realize that we grew up surrounded by privilege. We've experienced the death of grandparents, parents, and contemporaries; rejoiced at the birth of nieces, nephews, daughters, and sons. Hopefully, as a group, we're happy now. As adolescents, most of us lacked the tools to control our destiny. We were "yukky" or "cool," "out" or "in," frustrated or content, and often there seemed to be no rhyme or reason why.

So why have we come to this reunion? Partly, it's curiosity, the opportunity to reminisce, a desire to re-experience old times and see old friends. But just as important, a reunion is a chance for each of us to learn about ourselves. In order to find out more about who we are today, we have to go back to who we were long ago.

In the end then, we're here in recognition of a very simple common bond. We knew each other when we were young.

Thirty Years Later (1993)

Okay, gang ! We've got a president who's younger than we are. But as Casey Stengel once said, growing old is better than the alternative. And besides; we aren't old yet. Most of us are just reaching that high plateau where we're wise enough to understand what life is about and young enough to fully enjoy it. This reunion fits so nicely into that. After all, which one of us hasn't said at one time or another, "If I knew at age seventeen what I know now . . ." Well, here's our chance. For two days, we're seventeen again.

Looking around the room at our last reunion, I couldn't help but think that as a group we're not all that remarkable. I'm sure, every evening in the United States, there are thousands of gatherings made up of people just as nice, just as smart, and just as accomplished as we are. But there's one thing about us that's unique. We have the ability to come together and re-create our past. That's one of the reasons these reunions are special. They enable us to revisit a time in our lives when the world seemed fresh and green. How else can anyone explain the conversations of five years ago . . . "I never told anyone this, but I had an incredible crush on you in tenth grade . . . Everyone thought I got an eighty in geometry, but actually I flunked . . ."

Tonight and tomorrow, we can relive memories, good and bad; tie up loose ends. And at the same time, we can look to the future, rebuilding bonds with old friends and discovering things in common with classmates we barely knew when we were young.

So here we are, with more gray hair and more of us wearing bifocals than five years ago. Among the life challenges we face are (1) coming to terms with the fact that the Mickey Mantle baseball card we didn't keep is now worth $20,000, and (2) convincing assorted seven-year-olds that Elvis Presley was better than Billy Ray Cyrus. The next time we get together, we'll have passed "the big five oh."

Meanwhile, I can't help but think back to that line of poetry that Messrs Turner, Hanna, Geller, Joy, and Rock tried to drill into us in eleventh grade: "The Child is father of the Man." At long last, I think I understand what William Wordsworth was saying.

Thirty-Five Years Later (1998)

Twenty months ago, I had occasion to return to Mamaroneck High School under special circumstances. Muhammad Ali and I had just co-authored a book about bigotry and prejudice. As part of our effort to promote tolerance and understanding among all people, we were visiting schools throughout the country to speak with students. On the first day of our journey, we spoke at Mamaroneck.

It was a strange feeling to walk onto the stage where, thirty-three years earlier, the Class of 1963 stood to receive high-school diplomas. The auditorium looks the same as it did then. The junior high school and high school have been consolidated into one campus for grades nine through twelve, but the physical layout remains largely unchanged. What's different are the faces. Not a single teacher who taught us at MHS remains on staff. And looking at our 1963 yearbook (as I did that night), I had to smile. Our teachers, who were such authority figures back then, look far less authoritarian from the vantage point of our own adulthood. Most of them were considerably younger in 1963 than we are now.

Still, despite the absence of familiar faces, I felt very much at home returning to MHS. And reflecting on that, I realized that, more than we might have understood when we were young, the high school was our home away from home. How much time did we spend there? Six hours a day, five days a week, thirty-nine weeks a year, for years. Plus time after school for ballgames, dances, and extracurricular activities. Outside of the homes we've lived in, I doubt that many of us spent more time in any one building than we spent at MHS. And as we grow older, the high school becomes a unique physical link to our childhood. It's the one place each of us can revisit at will to re-experience that long-ago time.

T. S. Eliot once wrote, "Home is where one starts from."

Mamaroneck High School was our home.

Forty Years Later (2003)

We keep getting older; that's for sure. And a lot of the sayings we learned in high school have deeper meaning for us now. Forty years ago, we were living through the second and third of Shakespeare's seven ages from *As You Like It*:

The whining school-boy with his satchel and shining morning face,
Creeping like a snail unwillingly to school.

And then the lover, sighing like furnace
With a woeful ballad made to his mistress's eyebrow.

In 1963, we didn't really understand what George Bernard Shaw was telling us when he wrote, "Youth is wasted on the young." Now we're well into Shakespeare's soliloquy:

The sixth age shifts into the lean and slipper'd pantaloon
With spectacles on nose and pouch on side.

In other words, we're undeniably middle-aged. And the world has changed with us. Fifteen years ago, we exchanged telephone numbers at our MHS reunion. Now it's e-mail addresses. And to repeat a thought shared in our silver-anniversary yearbook, we're gathering together once again in recognition of a very simple common bond. We knew each other when we were young.

To mark the passing of some special people in my life.

Eulogies

Henry Harold Nordlinger
October 25, 1893 – March 10, 1976

The last time my grandfather was fully aware of his surroundings was this past Sunday afternoon. He said that he was not in pain and that he felt fortunate to have been surrounded by a family that had loved him all his life. Monday he could respond with his eyes but nothing more. Tuesday night, with his wife Elise at his side, he died.

I won't attempt to build in death an image of my grandfather beyond that which he was in life. He didn't envision such an undertaking when, several years ago, he asked that I speak on this occasion. And such a eulogy would be neither in keeping with his wishes nor proper. I would, however, like to share a few thoughts and memories of him.

First, let it be remembered that my grandfather was a good man. He never sought to harm anyone. He was devoid of malice. Ill will and vengeance were foreign to his character.

He was an honest man of extraordinary integrity.

He was admirably open to new ideas and curious about them.

Politically, his allegiance was to those who sought social justice.

He evinced a wide range of intellectual interests from opera and astronomy to literature and Norse mythology.

He was a brilliant man, skilled in his chosen profession of the law.

His life was a long one, encompassing Shakespeare's seven ages of man. He was a devoted son, husband, father, grandfather, in-law, and friend. He was capable of extraordinary love.

I won't pretend that my grandfather's life was free from unhappiness. But to measure the totality of his life, I would ask that each of us look back to the tale of the departed soul who came to the River Styx and was met by the mythological boatman Charon who was to ferry him across the river to the underworld. As they mounted the ferry, Charon turned to the man and offered him a chance to drink from the waters of forgetfulness. "Drink from these waters," the boatman said, "and you will forget the entire life that you have left behind."

"Do you mean," asked the traveller, "that if I drink from these waters, I will forget all my past sorrows?"

"Yes," answered the boatman, "but also your past joys."

"Do you mean," the traveller asked again, "that if I drink from these waters, I will forget all my past failures?"

"Yes," the boatman replied, "but also your achievements and your success."

"Do you mean," the traveller asked a third time, "that if I drink from these waters of forgetfulness, the memory of my enemies will fade?"

"Yes," replied the boatman, "but so too, the memory of your friends and loved ones."

My grandfather's life was a long one. In any such life, there is joy and sadness, achievement and disappointment. There were many friends and loved ones. I am sure that, as he begins his journey across the River Styx this day, he chooses to remember us.

And he can do so with pride, for he gave of himself as best he could. To his children, he gave both life and love. To his grandchildren and many others, he left a legacy of affection and warmth. With his wife of fifty-one years, he shared a union such that the two of them are inseparably entwined in our hearts, and it will be impossible for us to think at length on one without the other. It was for Elise and a few special others that a few weeks before he died, perhaps reflecting on the more difficult periods of his life, he asked that I speak the following words on this occasion:

> When in disgrace with fortune and men's eyes,
> I all alone beweep my outcast state,
> And trouble deaf heaven with my bootless cries,
> And look upon myself and curse my fate;
> Wishing me like to one more rich in hope,
> Featured like him, like him with friends possessed,
> Desiring this man's art, and that man's scope,
> With what I most enjoy contented least;
> Yet in these thoughts myself almost despising,

Haply I think on thee, and then my state,
Like to the lark at break of day arising
From sullen earth, sings hymns at heaven's gate;
For they sweet love remembered, such wealth brings
That then I scorn to change my state with kings.

We will think of my grandfather fondly and often. For as he said of his father before him:

He was wise in judgment,
Noble in bearing,
Tender in affection,
And faithful to his trust.

When the memory of this difficult past year has blurred, we will remember him in happier times; when he walked across the park to work each morning; when his mind and sense of self were intact; when he could appreciate fully the passing of the seasons and the autumn leaves. Let us remember him in this fashion, and by the words he himself read on his eightieth birthday:

My heart leaps up when I behold
A rainbow in the sky;
So was it when my life began;
So is it now I am a man;
So be it when I shall grow old,
Or let me die !
The Child is father of the Man;
And I could wish my days to be
Bound each to each by natural piety.

With that, there is little more to say, other than it would have pleased my grandfather to know that so many good people would gather here today to pay tribute to him. On behalf of those who loved him most, thank you for coming.

Elise Lehrburger Nordlinger
April 4, 1903 – December 12, 1983

Memories from early childhood are difficult to date. As years go by, specific recollections grow entangled with what we've been told. Few adults can point to a particular moment and say, "This is what I remember first." But I can.

One night, when I was three years old, I was awakened by frantic activity outside my bedroom door. My mother was visibly upset. My father was helping her put a coat over her nightgown. That's all I remember from that night. I went back to sleep. In the morning, both of my parents were gone. It was the first time I had ever woken up without my mother or father present. But I wasn't worried. Even though my parents were gone, Grandma Elise was there.

What had happened was, my mother had suffered a miscarriage. My father had taken her to the hospital and stayed with her overnight. The day that followed was remarkable because Elise, as "emergency babysitter," was obligated to prepare breakfast for me. And while legends abound regarding her list-making and organizational talents, cooking was not one of her skills.

Somewhat tentatively, she took a bowl and poured some cornflakes into it—once I showed her where the cornflakes were. Then she went to the refrigerator for milk, and I showed her how to make toast in the toaster. When the meal was ready, she handed me a jelly spoon that was too big to fit in my mouth, and I had to identify the proper silverware to use. It might have been the first, and last, time Elise made breakfast for anyone. But the important thing was, I remember feeling very secure. I knew that, regardless of where my parents were, everything would be all right because Grandma Elise was there.

Like everyone who loved my grandmother, I have a multitude of memories to look back on. Elise took me on my first trip to Washington, DC. She stood in line with me for ninety minutes in sub-freezing weather, so I could see the Mona Lisa when it was on display at the Metropolitan Museum of Art. She brought me to my first night baseball game; and it wasn't because she liked night baseball. I lived with her and my grandfather for my entire first year of law school. And two weeks ago, I enjoyed one of the nicer evenings we'd spent together in a long time. Elise took several scrapbooks out of the closet so we could look at old family photographs. As we did, her devotion to family shone through.

Elise had a sense of elegance and style in the way she ran her home. But it was also a home that radiated warmth and love.

She was an incredibly loyal friend. And the fact that she had so many good friends is a tribute to her.

Throughout her life, she was happiest when she was helping others. Whenever there was real trouble, Elise was there. When the chips were down, she was a loving, caring, supportive relative and friend. Even in her later years, she was capable of stepping in and taking charge where family matters were concerned. Recently, she told me that she had decided to assume certain planning responsibilities with regard to Ned's upcoming fiftieth birthday party. And when I suggested that Ned [her son] had already begun to plan the affair, she looked at me and declared, "A party like this should be run by The General."

I feel very sad that none of us will see Elise again. But I'm deeply grateful that she cared about us and loved us. I suspect that right now she's up in Heaven playing bridge with Harry [her husband], Richard, Polly, and Lyman [her siblings].

They belong together.

Simon J. Hauser
November 11, 1917 – January 14, 1994

This is a sad time, but not a tragic one. The tragedy occurred last April, when Dad suffered the stroke that irrevocably changed his life. Now we're here in a place he loved to bid him Godspeed on his journey to the next dimension. And while none of us knows what follows this life, most of us have a comforting faith of one sort or another in the process of what comes next.

So I'll say simply that Dad was a very sweet gentle man. He was a person of great integrity. It's to his credit that, at age seventy-five, he went to the office five days a week, maintained a full social schedule, traveled around the world, played tennis, kept the backyard looking like a biblical garden, and still had time for the people he loved. He did the best he could at everything he undertook, which is all we can ask of one another. And at the end, he taught us that there comes a time in life when it's enough to lie back and let people love you. Now that he's gone, we'll miss him at turning points in our lives, and also when the urge comes just to pick up the telephone, say hello, and share some small piece of news. But whenever we remember him, which we'll do often, his spirit will be alive again.

Dad had very definite ideas on how he wanted to live his life; and he lived it in that manner. He told us how he wanted this ceremony to be conducted; and we're carrying out his wishes. But perhaps most importantly, Dad knew that, among the thousands of people he'd come in contact with during the course of his life, there were a few relatives and cherished friends who had special meaning to him. Last April, after his stroke, I was looking through some papers in a leather box on top of his bureau, and I found a poem by James Edward Wilson. I think the best way to close this ceremony would be to read that poem as Dad's epitaph:

> I do not want a gaping crowd
> To come with lamentations loud,
> When I am dead.
>
> Nor do I want my words and ways
> Rehearsed by them with tardy praise,
> When life has fled.
>
> I only want the faithful few
> Who stood through good, and evil too;
> True friendships' test.
>
> Just those who sought to find the good,
> And then, as only true friends could,
> Understood the rest.

Alan Raphael
April 9, 1917 – April 18, 2004

Two years ago, when we gathered to celebrate Alan's eighty-fifth birthday, I recounted meeting him for the first time. Alan and my mother had started dating late in life. They were obviously smitten with one another. And I remember being very pleased because I felt that, whenever my mother was with this man I'd just met, she'd be in good hands.

I don't have to tell you all how wonderful Alan was. You knew him. He was a thoroughly gracious delightful elegant honorable man. One could easily imagine him as a star from the silver-screen era of Hollywood films. He and my mother were devoted to one another. He was a wonderful friend. I thought of him as the perfect de facto stepfather.

Four hundred years ago, Shakespeare wrote a play entitled *All's Well That Ends Well*. Alan's life ended well. His last ten years were spent in a loving relationship that brought him great joy. He died where he wanted to be with the person he wanted to be with. And I'm grateful that he was spared any deterioration of mind or prolonged physical suffering at the end.

I know that, when our sadness subsides, we'll smile whenever we think of Alan and be sustained by the good things we shared with him. I've thought about him a lot lately; and my mind keeps going back to a moment several years ago when my mother went out one morning without making her regular nine o'clock telephone call to me. It's a ritual we observe that enables me to check up on her well-being. So I called Alan. He said he'd spoken with my mother earlier in the morning and that she'd told him she was going out early.

And then Alan said to me in his reassuring voice, "I don't know where your mother is right now, but I'm sure she's fine."

I don't know where Alan is right now, but I'm sure he's fine.

Frank Macchiarola
April 7, 1941 – December 18, 2012

I met Frank Macchiarola when he was a law student in September 1964. I was a sophomore at Columbia, and he was our dormitory counselor. The floor residents were an eclectic mix, with different personalities and widely divergent interests. Every one of us knew that Frank was special.

In the decades that followed, Frank fashioned a remarkable career in public service highlighted by five years as chancellor of the New York City public school system, five years as dean of the Benjamin N. Cardoza School of Law, and twelve years as president of St. Francis College.

The core of his life was his faith and his family.

Through it all, we stayed in each other's lives. Every hour spent with Frank was "quality time." We wrote three books together; the first about educating children, the second about moral values, and the third about marriage.

My mother, who's now eighty-seven, met Frank when he came to our home for dinner in 1965. They saw each other a half dozen times over the decades. I come from a family of "secular Jews." Three years ago, my mother decided she wanted to talk with someone about the existence and nature of God. She didn't want to talk with a rabbi or other clergyman. She had lunch with Frank.

Frank and I were contemplating a fourth book—about charity—when his illness intervened. The day he told me that he had cancer, he said, "I've never had a bad day in my life. I've had days when bad things happened, but every day has been a good day."

That confirmed what I already knew; that Frank was as well-prepared emotionally and spiritually to go through the hard months that would follow as anyone I know.

Frank was my friend, my mentor, and a comforting presence in my life for forty-eight years. He devoted himself to making other people's lives better. There was an inexhaustible supply of love and goodness within him. He didn't just listen to other people talk about their problems. He'd sit with them and discuss ways to solve the problems. Then he'd roll up his sleeves and help implement the solution.

Over the years, Frank asked me on occasion to lecture at St. Francis College. Whenever I did, at the end of the lecture, I'd point to Frank and tell the students, "Study this man. Learn from his example. He's the best person I know."

I meant it.

I cried the day Frank died. I don't do that often. But I know that, when my sadness subsides, I'll smile whenever I think of him. I'm a better person because I knew him. And the most remarkable thing about Frank is that there are literally thousands of people who were touched by his spirit and feel the same way about him that I do.

He lived a glorious life and was very much loved.

A God to Hope For

This essay grew out of a conversation I had with a friend.

"Why do people believe in God?"

That was the question he asked. He wasn't referring to belief in an undefined pantheistic creator. Rather, he was curious about the belief people have in a God who is cognizant of every detail in our lives, answers prayers, and micromanages the universe.

And in truth, the question he asked was, "Why do intelligent people believe in God?" which indicated considerable skepticism on his part.

The question intrigued me. I don't pretend to know whether and in what form God exists. I'm not smart enough to answer that question. Some of the most brilliant minds in history have wrestled with it. And even when they agree on the existence of God, they disagree on God's nature and the means of proving God's existence.

Nor am I a religious scholar. There are tens of millions of people who know more about the history and rituals of the world's great religions than I do. But for the past few years, I've thought; I've read; and I've talked with people who have a firm, sometimes clearly defined, belief in God. This essay is the result of that exploration.

I freely acknowledge my limitations in the face of such a massive undertaking. One could spend a lifetime studying this subject and barely scratch the surface of possibilities. Also, my inquiry was undertaken amidst the personal and professional demands of everyday life, which often leave little time for reflection. Anyone and everyone is as qualified to write this essay as I am. I simply have chosen to write it. And I think that's fitting because I would hope that, during the course of a lifetime, everyone would at some point reflect seriously on the nature of God.

In the pages that follow, I refer to God in the male pronoun. That's because of common usage. My own belief is that whatever God exists is without gender.

No disrespect toward anyone else's religious beliefs is intended in the thoughts expressed here. I agree with Mark Twain, who once wrote, "True irreverence is disrespect for another man's God."

A God to Hope For

I
Defining God

The Greeks believed that the universe created the gods. Heaven and Earth were the first parents. The Titans were their children, and they in turn gave birth to Zeus and his brethren.

Contemporary monotheistic religions take a contrary view.

If one believes in God today, one believes almost by definition that God has always been. There was never a time before God. Time is in God, and everything came out of God.

There are many ways to define God.

God is the Creator; a being with infinite presence; a constantly emanating, overriding life force that puts things in motion and exercises power over all.

God is a reflection of our belief that a higher power is responsible for our existence.

And as Walter Lippmann, who was among the most prescient political and social commentators of the twentieth century, wrote, "God is the supreme symbol in which man expresses his destiny."

Concepts of God vary widely.

Many people, including those who embrace the Bible and Qur'an literally, believe God knows everything and directs what transpires throughout the universe. They trust in a personal God, an intimate God, a moral God; a God who looks over us, acts consciously, and hears our prayers.

Others believe in a cognizant but less involved God; one who purposefully created the universe and decreed the laws of nature, but no longer directs their operation. This is the God conceived of by Pliny the Elder, who wrote in *Natural History* two millennia ago, "It is frivolous to suppose that the great head of things pays any regard to human affairs." It is the God invoked by Isaac Newton, who believed that a law giver created the universe and made rules that would determine all future events without need of further intervention.

God, so conceived, operates only in broad strokes. He is a master watchmaker, who made the watch and perhaps repairs it from time to time. His awareness includes humanity but is not about us as individuals. He may have empowered us through His plan, but He does not direct us. It would be beneath Him to respond to mundane events on our planet. His work on Earth is in large measure our own.

"But there is a third state of religious experience," Albert Einstein wrote. Einstein rejected the concept of a "personal" or "moral" God and even a cognizant God. "I cannot conceive of a God who rewards and punishes his creatures or has a will of the type of which we are conscious in ourselves," he posited.

Rather, Einstein believed in what he called a "cosmic" God; a God synonymous with "the mystery and grandeur of the universe. . . . A God who reveals himself in the harmony of all that exists. . . . It is very difficult to explain this feeling," Einstein acknowledged; "especially since there is no anthropomorphic conception of God corresponding to it."

Einstein, in other words, accepted a pantheistic God. That is, he equated God with the forces and laws of the universe and believed that the cosmos is a single whole of interconnected parts; that this whole contains an indwelling principle and is driven by a creative life force or energy that we call God. To his mind, the world of nature was all-embracing. Indeed, Einstein went so far as to opine, "In their struggle for the ethical good, teachers of religion must give up the doctrine of a personal God and avail themselves of those forces which are capable of cultivating the Good, the True, and the Beautiful in humanity."

However, nature is unaware of the joy and suffering of individuals. Einstein's God is unknowable and unreachable. As Lippmann declared, "While this God may satisfy a metaphysical need in the thinker, He does not satisfy the passions of the believer. He is a principle with which to explain the facts, if you can understand the explanation. For the purposes of religion, He is no God at all."

Thus, much of humanity looks to a cognizant God endowed with human attributes. The God embraced by popular religions has almost always been envisioned as an adult male. In Western imagery, He resembles a strong, powerfully built, middle-aged white man with long hair and a beard. Often, He is dressed in a flowing robe and sits on a throne.

In sum, we give God the qualities we want him to have and put the concept of God within boundaries that are familiar to us. But why doesn't

God look like a sunset or rainbow? Does God even have a physical form? Certainly, the God of the Bible and Qur'an is capable of assuming such a form when He so chooses. But while man is bound to physical form, it is reasonable to assume that God is not, nor is God finite in any way that we understand. God is beyond the physical.

Following that thought, God could be a collective force; the sum total of energy from all living things; an eternal spirit; a celestial mix of chemicals.

What form does God take? God could be the soul in each of us.

Once, there were people who thought fire was God.

Defining God with specificity is an attempt to define the indefinable. Chapter 3, verse 14, of the Book of Exodus is instructive: "And God said unto Moses, I AM THAT I AM."

II
The Reasons Why People Believe In God

There are many ways to categorize humanity. One way is to divide the world into those who believe in God and those who do not.

Many people who profess to believe in God don't. That's a harsh statement. Certainly, it's difficult to look into another person's heart. But the truth is if people really thought they were communing with God each time they entered a house of worship, they would go more often. And many of those who profess to believe in an omniscient God act in a matter that negates the possibility of true belief.

"Infidelity," Thomas Paine once wrote, "does not consist in believing or disbelieving. It consists in professing to believe what one does not believe."

Some people embrace religion for social or business purposes. For others, proclamations of belief have become a scam. In that regard, the following thought is instructive:

> At present, we are witnessing a campaign for the revival of religion which is carried on with all the slickness of modern advertising techniques. Politicians of all parties, many of whom were not at all noted for piety before they began to compete for public office, make sure that they are known as dutiful churchgoers and never fail to bring God into their learned discourses.

Those words could have been written today. But they were written a half-century ago in an introduction to a book of essays by Bertrand Russell entitled *Why I Am Not a Christian.*

Is a religious revival truly underway? More people are talking publicly about God now than in the past. But there's scant evidence that these people practice what they preach. Instead, we have a plethora of televangelists, politicians with flexible consciences, and others "in the business" who pay lip service to God. "The will of God" is used to justify whatever conduct the speaker chooses. And if caught in a misdeed, miscreants often absolve themselves of responsibility with the mantra, "God has forgiven me."

Still, it's clear that millions upon millions of people have a sincere belief in God. What is the foundation for their belief?

Recent scientific studies indicate that there might be a biological predisposition to believe in God as a consequence of neurological wiring in the brain. Indeed, scientists can now chart the neural circuits that are activated during certain religious experiences. Thus, the belief in God might be as inbred in the human species as other instincts that are necessary for survival, such as fear. People believe what gets them through life. Perhaps humanity has needed a belief in God, or Gods, to keep it going through endless hardship. In Darwinian terms, we had to believe in order to survive.

Sigmund Freud taught that the popular concept of an anthropomorphic personal God is a matter of imagination. "Psychoanalysis has made us aware of the intimate connection between the father complex and the belief in God," Freud wrote. "The personal God is psychologically nothing other than a magnified father."

Many people believe in God because it's the way they were brought up. It's what they were taught by those they trusted. The belief starts at an early age when a child is sent to a religious institution the same way he or she is sent to school to learn how to read and write. Children in kindergarten aren't old enough to understand why they're there and how education can enhance their life. But it's expected of them, and they go. When a child grows up believing in something from the earliest moments of memory and cognizance, that belief becomes very strong.

A belief in God is also often inculcated as a means of control. "Religion," Seneca wrote, "is regarded by the common people as true, by the wise as false, and by the rulers are useful." Eighteen centuries later, Karl Marx concurred: "Religion als opium des volkes. . . . Religion is the opium of the people." Suffice it to say for the moment that organized religion is the most effective means of controlling minds known to humanity.

Still, for many, apart from all other considerations, a belief in God is embraced because they feel it's the most rational explanation as to how everything in the universe came to be.

Thomas Aquinas was one of the first proponents of "rational theology"—the idea that Christian beliefs can be proven by irrefutable logic in a way that brings faith and reason together. *Summa Theologiae,* written in 1273, sought to prove the existence of God by means of "natural reason to which we are all compelled to consent."

Three primary "proofs" were advanced by Aquinas:

(1) The first cause argument: Everything in the world has a cause. No matter how one explores backward in time, ultimately one comes to a First Cause and that cause is God.

(2) The natural law argument: The operation of the universe is such that a great law-giver has decreed that it be so. The law-giver is God.

(3) The argument from design: Were the cosmos and our planet constructed differently, humanity could not survive. God created this world in order that we might live in it.

Certainly, there is enough in the order of things to warrant a belief in God. Something happened, and we are here. Where did we, and everything else in the universe, come from? Looking at the order of the universe, one must conclude that there has been a force that led to it all. This, of course, leads to the question: "What came first? If God created everything, who or what created God?" One can believe that God has always been, or one can believe the same of "something else." But the theory of God as first cause and prime mover makes as much sense as any other philosophical or scientific explanation for the existence of the first infinitesimal bits of matter from which everything else came.

And perhaps most important, people believe in God because they want to.

There was a time when absolute belief was prevalent throughout western culture. God, as envisioned then, was not a synonym for the laws of nature. Rather, He was an omniscient all-powerful ruler, who commanded everything and passed judgment upon everyone in the universe.

"Nobody," Albert Einstein later posited, "will deny that the idea of
the existence of an omnipotent, just, and omnibeneficent personal God is
able to accord man solace, help, and guidance." And Einstein went further,
noting that God, so conceived, offers refuge from fear.

"With primitive man," Einstein observed, "it is above all fear that
evokes religious notions. Fear of hunger, wild beasts, sickness, and death.
Since at this stage of existence, understanding of causal connections is
usually poorly developed, the human mind creates for itself analogous
beings on whose wills and actions these fearful happenings depend. One's
object now is to secure the favor of these beings by carrying out actions
and offering sacrifices which propitiate them and make them well dis-
posed toward a mortal."

People tend to develop a belief in God when they need Him most.
They are most inclined to believe in God when death is at their door.
God offers a refuge from randomness and the assurance that all things
happen for a reason. Without God, we're on our own, and that can be a
frightening proposition. We believe; therefore, it comforts us.

For many, believing in God also gives more meaning and purpose to
life. There is a common yearning among people for justice. The existence
of God promises that ultimately justice will triumph and that there is an
order to the universe that binds together the whole of existence in a glorious manner. Moreover, if one believes in a personal God, there is always
hope; if not in this life, then in the hereafter.

"If there were no God," Voltaire wrote, "it would be necessary to
invent Him."

That, of course, is what atheists believe we have done. To committed
atheists, the concept of God is a useful fiction, a magic wand, a form of
mass delusion that induces entire societies to believe what can't possibly
be true.

Freud wrote often of the power of emotion over reason. "Religion,"
he declared, "is an attempt to get control over the sensory world in which
we are placed by means of the wish-world which we have developed
within as a result of psychological necessities. A system of doctrines and
pledges explains the riddle of our existence with enviable completeness
and assures us that a solicitous Providence is watching over us and will
make up to us in a future existence for any shortcomings in this life. The
whole thing is so patently infantile, so incongruous with reality, that it is

painful to think that the great majority of mortals will never be able to rise above this view of life."

Bertrand Russell concurred, rejecting the arguments of Thomas Aquinas and the Scholastics as based on "antiquated Aristotelian logic" and a desire for "allies in the sky." Freud and Russell both saw the belief in a personal relationship with God as a form of extreme narcissism.

The political and social power of those who believe in God has silenced many doubters. Over the ages, Plato has hardly been alone in his condemnation of atheism as "a disease of the soul." A more cogent rebuttal comes from Lippmann, who observed, "The man who says that the world is a machine has really advanced no further than to say that he is so well-satisfied with this analogy that he is through with searching any further. That is his business, as long as he does not insist that he has reached a clear and ultimate picture of the universe."

Some atheists are proud of their stance; some are indifferent. Others are men and women who feel an emptiness in their lives where they wish faith resided but, despite the best of intentions, they are convinced that God is a fiction.

Atheism, like the belief in God, is based on belief rather than on scientific proof and knowledge. Atheists may claim that it is impossible to prove the existence of God, but it is just as difficult to disprove His existence.

Therein lies the core of agnosticism.

"I have never been an atheist in the sense of denying the existence of God," wrote Charles Darwin. "The mystery of the beginning of all things is insoluble to us, and I for one must be content to remain an agnostic."

Agnosticism reflects the obstacles that skeptical people must overcome to embrace a belief in God. They consider the ultimate reality of God's existence to be unknowable. Many of them openly acknowledge, "I'd love to believe, but . . ." In some agnostics, the desire to believe is never stilled. They take comfort in the hope that it will be easier for God, if He exists, to find them than it is for them to find God.

Even among believers, there are differing degrees of awareness of and distance from God. Some people believe wholeheartedly with everything that is in them. For others, belief in God is less central to their thoughts. But there is a common denominator among all believers—faith.

It is very difficult, if not impossible, to reason one's way to a belief in God. Using reason alone, rational people can come out on either side. Faith is required.

Faith asks us to believe in and trust a power that we can only imagine. For those with faith, belief in God is the first principle upon which all other principles and beliefs are founded.

"The truth of faith cannot be confirmed by the latest physical or biological or psychological discoveries," the theologian Paul Tillich has written, "as it cannot be denied by them."

Part of faith is believing in something that doesn't make complete sense and trusting in something that can't be completely defined. Absolute faith is a conviction that cannot be shaken by contrary evidence. True believers are immune to all arguments, be they factual or logical, that contradict the notion of God as they know Him to be. Indeed, if every "i" is dotted and every "t" is crossed in one's mind, then it isn't faith.

Small things can influence faith. A child prays for something when he or she is young. The wish comes true. The child believes.

If one has faith, there is an answer to silence every doubt within.

If God is omniscient and omnipotent, why doesn't He answer all prayers?

"My son is sixteen and wants a car," a person of faith might answer. "I can afford it, but I think it's too soon to give it to him."

The players on the winning team in an athletic contest thank God for granting them victory. The losers say simply that God had other plans for them.

Wars are lost; people die horrible deaths; and it's all God's will.

Faith is like loving someone. No one can force faith upon another person. Either one believes or one doesn't. "The decision," Lippmann wrote "is rendered not by argument but by feeling. Faith is not a formula which is agreed to if the weight of evidence favors it. It is a posture of a man's whole being which predisposes him to assimilate, not merely to believe, his creed. Faith is not dependent upon intellectual assent. It is a serene and whole-hearted absorption, like that of an infant to its mother. A man cannot cheat about faith. Either he has it in the marrow of his bones or there is no conviction there to support him."

False faith is no faith at all.

Faith is a wonderful comfort. "Without faith," it has been written, "we are as stained glass windows in the dark."

By and large, people who truly believe in God are happy people. And the more one uses one's faith, the more it grows.

Even without Divine intervention, faith can motivate people to do things they might not otherwise be able to achieve on their own. It is as powerful as any force known.

The symbol and personification of faith is God.

III
The Ways in Which We Worship God

Looking back on the dawn of civilization, Albert Einstein wrote, "During the youthful period of mankind's spiritual evolution, human fantasy created Gods in man's own image, who were supposed to determine or at least influence the phenomenal world. Man sought to alter the disposition of these Gods in his own favor by means of magic and prayer."

Thousands of years later, our practices are much the same.

Religion is mankind's most travelled passageway to God. It's deeply ingrained in civilization, as are other disciplines such as agriculture, science, art, and war. There is no known society, extant or extinct, in which religion has not played a role.

Religion is characterized by beliefs and rites.

The one universal belief among religions is that a higher power governs the universe and intervenes in our world. Often, the tenets of religion are based on the wisdom of great thinkers. Generally, their thoughts are reduced to a series of commands, promises, punishments, and rewards that common men and women can understand.

Religious rites are designed to ensure everything from bountiful harvests to eternal life, and have ranged from high beauty to the slaughter of innocents as human sacrifices to God. These rituals bind adherents and serve as a vehicle for teaching and practicing particular religious faiths. Without them, it is likely that a given set of religious beliefs will atrophy and disappear.

By and large, religions have a structure. They are characterized by organization, hierarchy, doctrine, and rituals. Religion is taught. Many of its trappings are external. Some people have a clear concept of what they want when they embrace a religion. Others don't. Most people who adhere to the teachings of a particular religion embrace the religion that is practiced by the society around them.

The oldest of the world's monotheistic religions is Judaism. Judaism introduced a new concept; the belief that there is one God, who is the Creator of all things; that God is possessed of ethical attributes; and that it is the responsibility of each individual to conform to the ethical demands of God.

Early Jews considered themselves a "chosen people" in that they had been designated by God to teach the truth of His existence to the rest of humanity.

The most widely practiced religion in the world today is Christianity, the many denominations of which have approximately two billion adherents comprising one-third of the Earth's population.

Christianity is based on the teachings of Jesus, who was born in Bethlehem circa 4 BC, ministered to the poor and dispossessed, and proclaimed a Kingdom of God that would be open to all who repented of their sins and loved both God and their neighbor. After his crucifixion in 30 AD, Jesus's followers reported his resurrection, and a new faith based on his teachings was spread by the Apostles in their missionary travels.

Christianity is founded on the belief that God made mankind to know Him, love Him, serve Him in this world, and be happy with Him forever in the world to come. Jesus was the Son of God, sent by his Father to live on Earth as mankind lives, suffer as mankind suffers, and die in order that all who believe in Him and transform their lives accordingly shall have eternal life and rise gloriously to Heaven. It is fundamental to Christianity that one know God through his son; that, as stated in the First Epistle of Paul to Timothy, "There is one God and one mediator between God and man, Christ Jesus."

Christ's victory over death lit the flame of the Christian faith. As the German philosopher Ernst Bloch wrote, "It wasn't the morality of the Sermon on the Mount which enabled Christianity to conquer Roman paganism, but the belief that Jesus had been raised from the dead. Christianity was in competition for eternal life, not morality."

For three centuries, believers in Christianity were persecuted as fiercely as any people on Earth. In a single decade, between 303 and 312 AD, an estimated half-million Christians were executed by the Roman

Empire. Since the population of the world at that time was approximately 250 million people, that's equivalent to 12 million deaths today. Then, in 313, emperor Constantine decreed that Christianity would be tolerated throughout the empire. In 325, he convened the Council of Nicaea, which adopted the Nicene Creed: Christ is true God from God; through him all things are made; He was made flesh, suffered, and rose again for our salvation.

By the end of the fourth century, Christianity was the official religion of the Roman Empire. A faith born in opposition to power had been joined with the power of the state.

Although early Christianity was divided in some respects, the overwhelming majority of those who called themselves Christians embraced the Catholic Church. Like the Roman Empire, the Catholic Church was divided into provinces and dioceses. An archbishop presided over each province, while dioceses were headed by a bishop. In major cities, the presiding bishop was called a patriarch.

As the Roman Empire disintegrated, the eastern and western wings of the Catholic Church separated over disputes regarding doctrine and authority. "Orthodox" traditions continued in the east, while the western wing flourished with Rome as its center.

For centuries, the Roman Catholic Church dominated Western Europe. Heads of state ruled as Christians with their authority presumed to have been bestowed upon them by God. Coronations were religious services. As Lippmann wrote, "The Catholic Church by its splendor and power and universality during the Middle Ages made easily credible the conception of God the Ruler. It was a government exercising jurisdiction over the known world, powerful enough to depose princes. At its head was the Pope, who could prove by the evidence of scripture that he was the successor to Peter and was the Vice-Regent of God. To ask whether this grandiose claim was true is to miss the point. It was believed to be true in the Middle Ages. And because it was believed, the Church flourished. When men said that God ruled the world, they had evidence as convincing as we have when we say that the President is head of the United States government. They were convinced, because they came into daily contact with God's appointees administering God's laws."

One thousand years after Constantine embraced the Christian faith, every aspect of western culture was touched by it.

The power and prestige of the church reached its zenith at the end of the medieval period. Meanwhile, however, the seeds for dissension were being sown. Power corrupts. Within the Catholic church, the sale of ecclesiastical offices, clerical concubinage, and other abuses had become common.

In 1377, the English theologian and reformer John Wycliffe was accused of heresy by Pope Gregory XI for criticizing the worldliness of the church. During the next three decades, two and then three claimants sought recognition as pope. In 1415, Jan Hus was excommunicated and executed for protesting the sale of indulgences and other papal excesses. The flashpoint for revolt followed.

On October 30, 1517, on the eve of All Saints Day, Martin Luther posted his seminal "Ninety-Five Theses" on the door of the Castle Church in Wittenberg, Germany. Luther challenged the right of the pope to divert funds from Germany to build a basilica in Rome. He decreed that the treasury of the church was the Gospel, not its sprawling financial empire, and that the papacy should be a purely spiritual institution. But Luther's most radical proclamation was that faith alone could bring salvation; that "good works" and indulgences purchased from the church could not.

Luther was excommunicated from the Catholic Church and, with the assistance of northern German princes, began the formation of new Protestant churches in Germany. Thus began the Reformation. Soon, other reform movements were springing up across Europe.

In 1534, King Henry VIII challenged the power of the pope over churches in England and established the Church of England, which was responsible to the crown. In 1536, John Calvin, a French scholar, published a treatise entitled *Institutes of the Christian Religion*, which served as the foundation of the Presbyterian Church. Luther had undermined the claim of the Holy See that it was the exclusive representative of God on Earth. And ultimately, the seeds of that denial flowered into a realignment of religious authority and political power.

Meanwhile, the youngest of the world's universal monotheistic religions, Islam, was establishing its primacy in the Middle East.

Islam is based on the teachings of Muhammad, who is revered by Muslims as the last prophet, chosen by God to deliver His final message to all mankind.

Muhammad was born in Mecca in the year 570. One night, at age forty, he is said to have been visited by the archangel Gabriel, who came to him in a vision and ordered him to "recite." Thereafter, Muhammad received a series of revelations that continued until his death, and he became convinced that he was God's vessel for social and religious reform.

In 622, threatened by the entrenched powers of Mecca who were outraged at his teachings, Muhammad fled to the city of Yathrib. That journey of 220 miles is known as the Hegira and marks year one on the Muslim calendar. Eight years later, Muhammad returned to Mecca in conquest. By the time of his death in 632, he was recognized both as a prophet and a secular ruler in the Arab world.

The word of God, as it is believed to have been given to Muhammad, is preserved in the Qur'an, which is the summation and culmination of all God's teachings. Much of the Qur'an parallels the Bible, and all of its words are held holy by Muslims. Its most important doctrines are monotheism and the concept of the Last Judgment.

In the century after Muhammad's death, Islam swept eastward from Arabia into India. It established a foothold in Spain, and was poised to move further into western Europe until 733 when the advance of Muslim armies was halted in France at the Battle of Tours. Those armies remained in Spain until 1492.

Meanwhile, in 1095, Pope Urban II called upon the Christian armies of Europe to retake holy sites in Palestine. The first such Crusade led to the capture of Jerusalem and Bethlehem, which were then lost, regained, and lost again in future Crusades. At the start of the thirteenth century, The Fourth Crusade led to the capture of Constantinople, which had once been the capitol of the Eastern Roman Empire. But in 1453, Ottoman Turks of the Islamic faith reconquered Constantinople and began a military push into Europe from the east. That effort continued until the defeat of Muslim armies near Vienna more than two centuries later.

More than any other universal religion, Islam, with one billion adherents today, represents a total system of living and encompasses every aspect of life. Religion, politics, social structures, and economics are intertwined. God is the absolute and sole master of all people and the universe. He sees everyone in all places at all times, and His teachings must be obeyed.

No universal religion has come into being since Islam fourteen centuries ago. Still, history tells us that, over time, some religions become extinct while others flourish and grow. The Gods of Greece and Rome are no longer honored except as literary characters. A new religion that sweeps the world could come into being tomorrow.

Nor are all of the world's great religions monotheistic. Hinduism is practiced by 800 million people; most of them in India. There are 350 million Buddhists, situated primarily in Central and Southeast Asia. Roughly 500 million people practice various other religions; some of them monotheistic and others not.

In sum, there are many ways of searching for God's design. Yet too many of us glorify our own religious beliefs while deriding others as superstitious, fanciful, heathen, or idolatrous.

Christian fundamentalists tell us that four billion non-Christians are going to hell. Muslim fundamentalists respond that five billion non-Muslims will burn for eternity. We're appropriately horrified by the Aztec ritual of slaughtering young virgins and presenting them to the Gods. Yet we revere the heritage of Abraham's willingness to sacrifice his son. The crucifixion of Jesus is seen by many as the central saving event for mankind. But two thousand years later, Jews are condemned for their role in fulfilling God's plan and serving as actors in a drama that is considered by Christians to have been essential to salvation.

All armies in battle invoke the name of God. At the height of the Civil War, Abraham Lincoln wrote, "We on our side are praying to Him to give us victory because we believe we are right. But those on the other side pray to Him and look for victory believing they are right. What must He think of us?"

What, indeed, must God think of the way that humanity worships Him? All the great religions of the world are at odds over significant teachings. Any structured set of beliefs created or interpreted by man is fallible. If there is a cognizant God, it's hard to believe that He constructed a universe in which the vast majority of people who ever lived will be denied entry into heaven. Yet that's precisely what most religious fundamentalists tell us.

This is the "closed fist" that Elie Wiesel protests against when he writes, "Catholic integralism matches that of the Protestants, which matches that of the Muslims, which matches that of the Jews. It repels me in all its forms. Whoever declares that he knows the path leading to God better than others causes me to turn away."

Twenty-five centuries ago, the Chinese philosopher Lao Tze wrote, "The broad-minded see the truth in different religions. The narrow-minded see only their differences."

If there is one God, why does religion do so much to separate and divide? And more to the point, if God is in all of us and created all of us and watches over all of us, do we really need religious institutions to mediate between us and God?

The Archbishop of Canterbury William Temple once opined, "It is a great mistake to suppose that God is only, or even chiefly, concerned with religion." Further in that vein, it should also be noted that organized religion today has, in many respects, become a very cold business. It's more about institutions than the relationship between God and humanity, and seems in some instances even to have become an impediment to people finding God.

Too often, religious leaders and religious hierarchies appear more concerned with authority and control than spirituality and good works. The great churches, mosques, and temples of the new millennium operate at times like secular institutions, whose leaders practice politics with a cross, crescent, or star.

It's possible, of course, to hold a belief in God and not accept the teachings of any religion, just as those who don't believe that God answers prayers, sometimes pray as an expression of feeling or a moment of self-reflection. This kind of spirituality is often without doctrine. It's not based on a God conceived in man's image. But it is no less valid than other forms of religion.

In sum, no one religious faith has a monopoly on truth or communication with God. And if there is no one true religion, then it can also be said that no religion is false. All religions are deserving of respect when they serve to bring out the best in humanity.

IV
God and Science

Science is based upon proof of facts. Religion is based upon faith. Their interaction is often contentious, and the schism between them far more pronounced than a simple divide between those who believe in the Bible as fact and those who believe in Darwin.

Science is agnostic. It seeks to explain the workings of the universe with absolute moral neutrality. Religion reflects the search for a world the way humanity wants it to be.

Thus, Ignatius Loyola wrote, "The sacrifice most welcomed by God is the sacrifice of our intellect." And Albert Einstein, after pondering the transitory nature of religion and politics, closed with the thought, "An equation is for eternity."

Any evaluation of the conflict between science and religion is best begun by looking at the Bible and other sacred texts. These books embody the doctrines of faith and are the spiritual inheritance for much of humanity.

No book has been more widely read and more disparately interpreted than the Bible. The Old Testament God of Law and New Testament God of Love are central to Western thought. Moses and Jesus are heroes of civilization, who have been endowed with their stature over thousands of years. "This great book," Abraham Lincoln wrote, "is the best gift God has given to man. But for it, we could not know right from wrong."

To many, the Bible is not simply a book of wisdom. It's the uncorrupted word of God. Although written by mortals, it is perceived as having Divine authority in the same manner than fundamentalist Muslims regard the Qur'an.

Are the world's sacred texts revelations from God or the product of man's imagination? Do they contain truths certified by the highest power in the universe or are they comprised largely of fairy tales and folk history?

One way to explore that question is to examine the historical foundation of the Bible.

The Old Testament begins with the Book of Genesis, which is divided into two parts. Chapters 1 through 11 deal with primeval history. In the beginning, there is the Creation. Then come Adam and Eve, Cain and Abel, Noah and the Flood, and the Tower of Babel. These chapters are followed by the saga of Abraham, Isaac, Jacob, and Joseph, which starts with God entering into a covenant with Abraham and ends with the twelve tribes of Israel settling in Egypt (chapters 12–50).

Genesis is followed by Exodus, Leviticus, Numbers, and Deuteronomy. Taken together, these writings comprise the Five Books of Moses and culminate with the children of Israel poised to enter the Promised Land. The remainder of the Old Testament recounts the conquest of Canaan, the rule of judges, and the formation and destruction of various kingdoms.

The New Testament recounts the story of the birth, life, death, and resurrection of Jesus Christ.

Best estimates are that the Old Testament was codified between the tenth and third centuries BC as oral tales were fashioned into the written Hebrew Bible. The New Testament is founded upon the Gospel narratives of Matthew, Mark, Luke, and John, which were first written in colloquial Greek roughly four decades after the death of Jesus.

Because the Bible provides an underpinning for so much of Western culture, its accuracy and authoritativeness are of significant import. Regarding the Old Testament, it's a matter of historical record that, three to four thousand years ago, several generations of Hebrews experienced what they believed were revelations from God. Thereafter, memories intertwined with faith, and historical fact comingled with poetry to create Scripture.

The Biblical recitation of the history of Israel after the reign of King Solomon is, in many respects, corroborated by contemporaneous Egyptian and Assyrian writings. Also, some personages found in the latter part of the Old Testament, such as Nebuchadnezzar and Jeremiah, appear to have existed. But most scholars regard Abraham, Isaac, and Jacob as fictitious. And there is no archeological evidence whatsoever of a Hebrew sojourn in Egypt.

The Ten Commandments are a cornerstone of Western thought. They go to the heart of the relationship between man and God and the relationship between man and his fellow man. Yet no record of Hebrew enslavement, the life of Moses, or a mass exodus exists in Egyptian chronicles. Archeologists have yet to unearth a single relic from the forty years that Moses and his followers are said to have wandered in the Sinai Peninsula. A massive exodus leading to the destruction of Pharaoh's army would have sent shockwaves through the region, yet there is no indication of such a happening other than in Biblical narrative.

There is also considerable controversy over the difference between "the historical Jesus" and "the risen Christ of faith." Jesus may well be the single most influential figure in history. But there is limited evidence other than the Bible to support the often-told story of his life. The only contemporaneous non-Biblical text is a short passage written by Falvius Josephus, a first-century Jewish historian, who described Jesus as a wise man, a doer of startling deeds, and a teacher, who was crucified and thereafter attracted a posthumous following known as Christians. Contemporary Roman chroniclers were silent about Jesus.

That leaves scholars with four Gospels written by believers. But whether the goal of the authors was to preserve an accurate record of Jesus's life or convey fragments of history transformed by faith is subject to debate. There are many factual discrepancies among their reports. Matthew says that the resurrected Christ first appeared to Mary Magdalene. Luke says it was to Peter. Matthew says that, after his resurrection, Jesus came to the apostles in Galilee. Luke says that it was near Jerusalem.

Why are these issues important?

Walter Lippman states the obvious: "The historic influence of Christianity on the mass of men has depended upon their belief. The veracity of the story of the virgin birth, the life, the ministry, the death, and the resurrection of Jesus Christ is fundamental to the Christian Church. For while all the ideal values may remain if you impugn the historic record set forth in the Gospels, these ideal values, once deprived of their root in historic fact, are not certified to the common man as inherent in the very nature of things."

Certainly, it's possible to revere Jesus as a great moral teacher even if not Divine. But Jesus himself is portrayed in the Bible as stating that he is the Son of God. Thus, it's difficult to separate the teachings of Jesus from teachings about Jesus. Author and academician C. S. Lewis said as much when he opined, "A man who was merely a man and said the sort of things Jesus said wouldn't be a great moral teacher. He'd either be a lunatic or something worse."

In sum, over the years, religious teachings have been vigorously tested. And over the past four centuries, science has been a particularly harsh inquisitor. Once, thunder and lightning were believed to be caused when an angry Zeus hurled thunderbolts. Volcanoes were thought to erupt because horrific creatures imprisoned in mountains were struggling to get free. But starting with the Enlightenment in seventeenth-century Europe, the authority of science began to expand, displacing religion as the primary explanation for the nature of things.

For centuries, the cosmos was regarded as proof of God's glory and the exalted place of man in His order. Earth was the center of the universe. The other planets and stars, except for the sun, were considered of minor importance. Angels were thought to dance throughout this sacred geography.

There had been some sophisticated observation of the heavens over the millennia. By 1400 BC, the Chinese had determined that a solar year lasted 365 days. In the second century AD, Ptolemy mapped the motion of celestial bodies, albeit in flawed fashion. And while Europe was mired in the Dark Ages, Islamic scholars made great strides in algebra, geometry, and optics. But the prevailing view of the world at the start of the sixteenth century was described by Martin Luther, who decreed, "Theology should be empress; natural philosophy [science] and the other arts merely her servants."

Then, in 1543, Nicolaus Copernicus published *De Revolutionibus*, positing that Earth orbited around the sun and was not the center of the universe. In 1609, Johann Kepler published the first two of three mathematical statements accurately describing the elliptical revolution of known planets around the sun. That same year, Galileo constructed the first modern astronomical telescope, which he used to confirm Copernican theory.

What followed was the spectacle of theologians waging war on the laws of nature. The first society devoted primarily to science had been founded in Naples in 1560, but was closed almost immediately by ecclesiastical authorities. In 1633, Galileo himself was put on trial, censured, ordered to recant, and sentenced to house arrest for teaching Copernican theories in defiance of papal orders.

Galileo died in 1642. That same year, Isaac Newton was born. Forty-five years later, Newton published *Philosophiae Naturalis Principia Mathematica*, which set forth three laws of motion and explained how universal gravitation impacts upon both falling bodies on Earth and the motion of planets, stars, and comets.

Newton changed humanity's understanding of the physical world. He offered a largely mechanical view of a universe that operates upon mathematical rules that are predictable and constant. Yet he left room for God in his plan, stating that God had designed and sustained the cosmos. "No sciences are better attested," Newton wrote, "than the religion of the Bible."

However, the religion of the Bible was to be further tested by science. In 1859, Charles Darwin presented the world with *The Origin of Species*. Twelve years later, he published *The Descent of Man*. These books enunciated a theory of evolution completely at odds with the Biblical view that the world was created by design and that humans are a Divine creation. Instead, Darwin posited that mankind and apes have a common ancestor and, rather than the world being made in a certain way so that various species can live in it, living creatures mutate and adapt to their environment in order to survive.

The Catholic Church now accepts evolution as fact. "It has been proven true," Pope John Paul II has said. But many religious fundamentalists, particularly Protestant fundamentalists in the United States, continue to reject Darwin's theories in favor of a doctrine known as "creationism."

Creationism is based on the belief that every word in the Bible must be taken as absolute truth. Thus, the heavens and earth and everything in them were created over a six-day span as time is measured today. Eve was created out of Adam's rib. And adhering to the genealogies set forth in Genesis, "the beginning" occurred slightly more than six thousand years ago.

In truth, the evidence in support of evolution is overwhelming. As for creationism, one problem with interpreting the Bible literally is that there are millions of species of animal life. It's highly unlikely that there would have been room for two of each on Noah's ark. But creationists have an answer for everything. Hear their voices:

"You have to understand, it was a really big ark. . . . God put false clues in the ground to test our faith. He created the Grand Canyon in a way that made it appear to have been carved out of the land millions of years ago. He fashioned the bones of dinosaurs that never actually lived and gave properties to various artifacts that would allow them to be dated by carbon-testing as any age He chose. . . . God in his wisdom constructed everything as though it had a past, but that past is only six thousand years old."

As science has advanced over the past five hundred years, the role of religion in explaining the way the world works has dwindled. The one area where religion has remained supreme concerns matters relating to the beginning and end of life. But now, that too is changing.

Twenty-four hundred years ago, Hippocrates posited that the workings of the body are dictated by natural laws rather than the supernatural. There have been four revolutions in medicine since then. The first occurred with the advent of sanitation systems; the second, with the discovery of anesthesia; the third, with the development of vaccines and antibiotics. Now genetic engineering is on the verge of altering the rules of life itself.

Thus, the divide between religion and science is once again in danger of widening. But the conflict is not between God and science. It's between a particular view of religion and a particular approach to science. Thus, some thoughts on reconciliation are appropriate.

Science deals with the empirical universe; that which is capable of being verified or disproved by observation and experiment. In scientific inquiry, hypotheses are stated and tested to determine their validity. It's the most reliable method of knowledge at our command.

Unfortunately, we live in a world that is characterized in many quarters by the refusal to accept what should be universally accepted scientific conclusions. Christianity, to be sure, is based in part upon a belief in occurrences that run counter to science. These events—"miracles"—are said to occur outside the laws of nature by special act of God. The Virgin Birth, the Resurrection, and various acts performed by Jesus to prove his Divinity all fall within this domain.

However, there comes a time when strict adherence to religious doctrine is nothing more than the promulgation of ignorance. And today's creationists, unlike their predecessors, don't have the excuse of an unenlightened society around them to justify their lack of knowledge.

People have an obligation to study and understand the world with the tools that have been given to them. Deafness to science is a risk that our small planet can no longer afford. Our climate is changing. Oceans are rising. Nuclear annihilation is at our door. The definers of God once told us that the Earth was flat and that the sun orbited around it. How can any one religious leader or single group of clerics now claim Divine knowledge of the truth?

Having said that, though, it should be noted with equal vigor that there are limitations to science. The world is too vast and too complex to be fully explained by what we know of science at the present time. And the great values of life—indeed, the very purpose of life—are beyond the reach of scientific experimentation.

Thus, the role of religion is best embraced when it serves to guide humanity in a spiritual way toward the values of truth, justice, and love. Viewed in this context, religion and science don't conflict. To the contrary, they complement one another, and an understanding of both is necessary for true wisdom to be acquired. As Einstein wrote, "Science without religion is lame. Religion without science is blind."

The twentieth century witnessed extraordinary advances in science, but no creative artists on a par with Michelangelo, Shakespeare, or Beethoven. Some segments of society became more aware of human rights, but others implemented mass murder on an unprecedented scale. For all its knowledge of the empirical world, science was unable to improve upon human nature or the moral fiber of our times. From a spiritual point of view, scientists whittled away at the number of causes that were once unknown or ascribed to God, but that's all.

Thus, in reconciling science and religion, one would do well to turn to Paul Tillich. "Faith cannot guarantee factual truth," Tillich wrote. "But faith can and must interpret the meaning of facts from the point of view of man's ultimate concern. In doing so, it transfers historical truth into the dimension of the truth of faith."

"The truth of faith," Tillich continues, "cannot be made dependent on the historical truth of the stories and legends in which faith has expressed itself. Faith can say that the Old Testament law which is given as the law of Moses has unconditional validity for those who are grasped by it, no matter how much or how little can be traced to a historical figure of that name. Faith can say that the reality which is manifest in the New Testament picture of Jesus as the Christ has saving power for those who are grasped by it, no matter how much or how little can be traced to the historical figure who is called Jesus of Nazareth. Faith can ascertain its own foundation; the Mosaic law, Jesus as the Christ, Mohammed the Prophet, or Buddha the Illuminated."

"If this is understood," Tillich concludes, "the conflicts between faith and science appear in a quite different light. The conflict is actually not between faith and science, but between a faith and a science each of which is not aware of its own valid dimension. Only if the symbols of

God in Heaven and demons below the earth are taken as descriptions of places populated by divine or demonic beings can modern astronomy conflict with Christian faith. On the other hand, if representatives of modern physics reduce the whole of reality to the mechanical movement of the smallest particles of matter, denying the real quality of life and mind, they express a faith and a monstrous symbol; namely, a universe in which everything including their own scientific passion is swallowed by a meaningless mechanism."

The mysteries of creation will never be fully understood through science or faith or a blending of the two. Whether one reads the Bible, Qur'an, and other holy books as historical fact or as truth in a larger sense, it's unlikely that the existence of God will ever be empirically proven or disproven. Thus, in our own imperfect way, we would do well to let science unearth facts, and then act upon these facts in accord with well-considered religious, ethical, and moral codes.

V
Good and Evil

Justice does not rule the world. There are many good people in it. On occasion, a leader like Buddha, Jesus, Gandhi, or Nelson Mandela appears to remind us of what we can be. And all of us come in contact with extraordinarily decent loving people in our personal lives. But the reality of life is that tragedy and evil lurk just beneath the surface. Natural disasters and accidents are common. Disease and hunger are constant companions. The human mind is capable of conjuring up extraordinary evil.

Earth is where Mozart created wondrous music and Michelangelo painted the ceiling of the Sistine Chapel. But it's also a place where hate, violence, war, and prejudice flourish. A single individual can end another person's life and wreak havoc on the lives of the victim's loved ones. A small group of plotters can cause incalculable harm and, in today's nuclear world, make apocalyptic visions real. Collective acts of monstrous evil such as slavery and the Holocaust provide us with pictures of hell.

"The God of the Bible and Qur'an," social commentator Arthur Krystal writes, "is also the God of cancer, multiple sclerosis, puss, phlegm, chancre sores, paralysis, crib death, child molestation, poverty, famine, pestilence, war, race hatred, floods, earthquakes, rape, mutilation, death marches, Zyklon B, and suicide. He's got the whole world in his hands, and they're covered with blood."

Thus, the question: How does one explain the existence of tragedy and evil in a world governed by an omnipotent and loving God? Does God not care? Is God preoccupied with other matters in other parts of the cosmos? If God consciously created evil, is He not God as we think of Him? If evil is caused by forces beyond God's ability to control, is He not omnipotent?

"Nothing," Walter Lippmann wrote, "puts a greater strain upon the faith of the common man than the existence of utterly irrational suffering in the universe. The problem which tormented Job still troubles every devout and thoughtful man who beholds the injustices of nature. The greatest of all perplexities in theology has been to reconcile the infinite goodness of God with his omnipotence. Tacitly or otherwise, either His infinite power or His infinite love is denied."

Still, fervent believers are undeterred. "God gave man great freedom," they say, "and part of that freedom is the freedom to do evil.... The devil comes with the world because God chose to create it that way.... Each person can wipe evil from his or her own thoughts, but evil will never be eradicated from the world unless God wills it.... God lets nature take its course. So if someone contracts cancer and dies, God is simply letting nature have its way.... God allowed the Holocaust to happen to create a climate for the establishment of the modern state of Israel.... Whatever happens, whatever goes wrong, God will make things right in the end; if not in this world, then in the next one."

Yet, for others, tragedy and evil rebut the notion of an infallible personal God who micromanages the universe.

Commenting on the death of his son in a traffic accident, the political activist Reverend William Sloane Coffin said, "Do you think it was the will of God that Alex never fixed that lousy windshield wiper; that he was driving too fast in a storm; that he probably had a couple of beers too many? Do you think it was God's will that there were no streetlights on that road and no guardrail separating that right-angle turn from Boston Harbor? God doesn't go around this world with his finger on triggers, his fist on knives, his hands on steering wheels." To believe that He does, Coffin concluded, would be to think of God as a "cosmic sadist."

Bertrand Russell noted the spectacle of tragedy and evil and opined,

"Is there not something a trifle absurd in human beings holding a mirror before themselves and thinking that what they behold is so excellent as to prove that a Cosmic Purpose must have been aiming at it all along? Would not a world of nightingales and larks and deer be better than our human world of cruelty and injustice and war. There is something a little odd about the valuations of those who think that an omnipotent, omniscient, and benevolent Deity, after preparing the ground for many millions of years, would consider himself adequately rewarded by the final emergence of Hitler, Stalin, and the H-bomb."

Thus, the questions from skeptics mount . . . Why the assumption that God is good? . . . Is it possible that God is imperfect and makes mistakes? . . . Why would God demand that His Son be nailed to a cross? . . . And these questions are compounded when "the will of God" is invoked in an attempt to justify the commission of evil.

Over the millennia, religion has fostered acts of extraordinary generosity and caring. But much of the evil in the world has religious roots, and some of history's greatest crimes have been perpetrated in the name of God.

Religion has been used to support doctrines that range from the divine right of kings to ritual murder. For centuries, Leviticus, chapter 25, verse 44, was relied upon as God's endorsement of slavery: "Both thy bondsmen and thy bondmaids which thou shalt have shall be of the heathen that are about you. Of them shall ye buy bondsmen and bondsmaids."

Too often, the cross and crescent have been wielded as swords. In time of war, opposing armies virtually always believe that God is firmly on their side. The terrorists who destroyed the World Trade Center on September 11, 2001, genuinely thought that they were carrying out the will of God. Consider their final written instructions:

Purify your heart and cleanse it of all earthly matters. The time of judgment has arrived. Hence, we need to utilize those few hours that are left to you to ask God for forgiveness. If God supports you, no one will be able to defeat you. You should feel complete tranquility, because the time between you and your marriage in heaven is very short. Afterward begins the happy life and eternal bliss in the company of the prophets, the companions, the martyrs, and the good people.

When you enter the plane, continue to pray: "Oh God, open all doors for me. Oh God, who answers prayers and answers those who ask you, I am asking you for your help. I am asking you to lighten my way. God, I trust in you. I lay myself in your hands. I ask with the light of your faith that has lit the whole world and lightened all darkness on this earth to guide me. There is no God, but God. There is no God who is the God of the highest throne but God, the God of all earth and skies. We are of God, and to God we return."

When the plane takes off, remember God as He said in His book: "Oh Lord, pour your patience upon us and make our feet steadfast, and give us victory over the infidels." Prepare to carry out His role in a way that would satisfy God. Know that you will be entering the happiest life, everlasting life. The gardens of paradise are waiting for you in all their beauty, and the women of paradise are waiting, calling out, "Come hither, friend of God." Remember that this is a battle for the sake of God.

Tens of millions of people believe that the nineteen terrorists who followed these instructions are martyrs who will reside in Heaven for eternity. However, judged by a different view of reality, they conform to Elie Wiesel's description of "madmen of faith."

What motivates people to do evil in response to what they believe are sacred commands?

"The fanatic is a zealot," Wiesel writes. "Blinded by passion, he turns divine beauty into human ugliness. Like God, he strives to make every man in his own image, but smaller. He wants everyone to resemble him, yet remain humble and humiliated, bowed before his throne. Convinced that he is the sole possessor of the meaning of life, he gags or kills the other in order not to be challenged in his quest."

But it would be a mistake to think that this sort of religious fanaticism takes hold only in alien cultures. It took a thousand years to convince the leaders of Western civilization that there is no such thing as a witch. In Salem, Massachusetts, in 1692, eighteen women and one man were executed for witchcraft.

Think about that! Reflect on it for a moment. The judicial process in one of the cradles of American democracy was the vehicle by which nineteen people were tried, convicted, and burned at the stake—actually burned to death—because they were thought to be witches.

There's a difference in scale, but Salem is similar in many respects to Osama bin Laden decreeing that the United States is the Great Satan and must be destroyed. We now look at Salem from the vantage point of the twenty-first century and see evil in the trials and executions. But our fore-fathers believed they were eradicating evil in furtherance of the Biblical command, "Thou shalt not suffer a witch to live." They thought that those burned were possessed of the devil and that it was the obligation of good Christians to kill them in order to purge the world of the devil.

Thus, the question of how evil survives in a world ruled by God is further complicated by the issue of who defines good and evil. If morality is considered absolute by virtue of Divine command, we must deal with a body of clerical "experts" who take it upon themselves to interpret the word of God for us. However, the reality of today is that most people no longer believe they are being constantly watched and judged by God.

"Once," Walter Lippmann wrote, "men believed that they would be judged at the throne of God. They believed that He saw not only their deeds but their motives; that there was no hole deep enough into which a man could crawl to hide himself from the sight of God. The moral problem for each man, therefore, was to make his will conform to the will of God. There were differences of opinion as to how this could be done. There were differing conceptions of the nature of God and of what He most desired. But there was no difference of opinion on the main point that it was imperative to obey Him. This was the major premise upon which all human choices hinged."

Now, however, we live in an age of moral freedom. The sources of authority for morality today include, not just religion, but family, secular law, and other environmental influences.

"Individuals," author and academician Alan Wolfe writes, "are expected to determine for themselves what it means to live a good and virtuous life. We decide what is right and wrong, not by bending our wills to authority, but by considering who we are, what others require, and what consequences follow from acting one way rather than another."

In other words, in today's world, many people consider themselves accountable first and foremost to their own conscience. But where does that leave God?

Sigmund Freud gave one answer. "The world is not a nursery," he wrote. "The ethical commands to which religion seeks to lend its weight require some other foundation, since human society cannot do without them and it is dangerous to link obedience to them with religious belief." Then Freud went further, declaring, "If one attempts to assign to religion its place in man's evolution, it seems to be parallel to the neurosis which the civilized individual must pass through on his way from childhood to maturity."

Thus, the question: Is there an ethical system that exists above and beyond the one that humanity has created for itself? That's an important issue because, as stated by Lippmann, "Ethical codes cannot lay claim to unhesitating obedience when they are based upon the opinions of a majority or on the notions of wise men or on estimates of what is socially useful. For they are then felt to be the outcome of human and fallible decisions. They were not given by God to Moses on Sinai. They are not commandments of God speaking through his Infallible Church. And they are not a necessary part of the government of the universe."

In other words, a system of moral values is absolute only if it is founded upon a moral concept of God. But regardless of one's religious beliefs, one can be forgiven for concluding that morality is fragile. The doctrine of original sin teaches that each of us is predisposed to do wrong by virtue of inheriting Adam's sin at birth. And at the other end of the spectrum, Darwin's theory of natural selection posits a process unfettered by morality.

Moreover, morality deals with ethics and logic, which are functions of memory. And memory can be overridden by the portion of our brain that deals with biology and emotion. When that happens, people are capable of giving in to their worst instincts and sinking beneath the level of animals. Animals instinctively care for their young. Some humans throw them in trash cans.

Yet one would be hard-pressed to deny that a collective moral force of some sort exists on our planet. For example, each of us knows that it's wrong to kill another person in anger. And more important, each of us is possessed of an individual identity.

We live in an age where much of the known universe is explicable in terms of physics and chemistry, and science seeks to define the activity of the human mind in terms similar to the rest of the body. But there remains the human soul.

There is nothing collective about the human soul.

"It is only to the individual," Einstein wrote, "that a soul is given." And even today, the existence of the soul is beyond the realm of science to explore.

In sum, good and evil are not simply in the air. They reside within individuals. And no matter how much good or evil is present in a particular society, there will always be individuals who run against the grain. There were "righteous Gentiles" in Nazi Germany. Lot lived in Sodom.

One test of a religion is how much love and hate the practice of that religion engenders among its adherents. But good and evil, like love and hate, are the result of individuals making individual choices one person at a time.

VI
Afterlife

Most of us have frozen at the thought of death; perhaps at that moment when we first realized with clarity that we won't always be here.

"You are going to die," Arthur Krystal writes. "Maybe not today; maybe not tomorrow. But one day, your time will come. Perhaps you have made your peace with mortality, or believe in a life after death, or anticipate a pleasant bonding experience with the universe. But for most of us, death is a pretty scary proposition."

Our lives, Thomas Carlyle posited, are "a little gleam of time between two eternities." But death seems different from the dark void that existed before we were born. We fear death and the idea that we'll be reduced to nothing except memories that ultimately fade from the thoughts of others. We distance ourselves from death. Few of us have actually been present when someone died. And we hope that the universe is constructed in a way that allows for the continuation of our existence in some meaningful way.

Some religions, such as Christianity and Islam, invert life and death so that death becomes a passageway to continued existence. It is central to Christian belief that Jesus rose from the dead three days after his crucifixion and, forty days later, ascended to heaven to sit at the right hand of God. By so submitting to death, Jesus destroyed its power and made eternal life available to everyone who embraces him. "For God so loved the world," reads John, chapter 3, verse 16, "that he gave his only begotten Son, that whosoever believeth in Him should not perish but have everlasting life."

Many people believe that the Resurrection, like other portions of the Bible, should be read metaphorically; that Jesus did not literally rise from the dead. But the risen Christ is central to Christian faith. The first letter of Paul to the Corinthians unequivocally states: "If Christ be not risen, then our preaching is in vain and so is your faith." Corinthians I, chapter 15, verse 14.

In sum, as noted by religious scholar Frank Mead, "Either the resurrection is a vast watershed in history or it is nothing. It cannot be tested for truth. It does not compel belief; it resists it. But once accepted as fact, it tells more about the universe, about history, and about man's state and fate than all the mountains of other facts in the human accumulation."

And as written by the Irish bishop John Dunne, "The Resurrection is an enormous answer to the problem of death. The idea is that the Christian goes with Christ through death to everlasting life. Death becomes an event, like birth, that is lived through."

Thus, to true believers, eternal salvation is far more important than temporal life and death. And the Kingdom of Heaven is as real a place as Rome or Mecca. But the promise of eternal life, should it be false, is a promise for which no religion can be held accountable. And there's a significant body of thought to the effect that humanity has created the grandiose fantasy of an afterlife simply to deal with its fear of death.

Thus, Bertrand Russell wrote, "I believe that, when I die, I shall rot and nothing of my ego shall survive. I am not young, and I love life. But I should scorn to shiver with terror at the thought of annihilation. Happiness is none the less true happiness because it must come to an end, nor do thought and love lose their value because they are not everlasting."

And to Russell's thoughts, Albert Einstein added, "An individual who shall survive his physical death is beyond my comprehension, nor do I wish it otherwise. Such notions are for the fears or absurd egoism of feeble souls. Each of us is here for a brief sojourn; for what purpose we know not. The mystery of the eternity of life and the inkling of the marvelous structure of reality together with the endeavor to comprehend a tiny portion of the reason that manifests itself in nature are enough for me."

No one can prove that an afterlife doesn't exist. Many of us derive comfort from thoughts such as those expressed by William Jennings Bryan, who posited, "If the invisible germ of life in a grain of wheat can pass unimpaired through three thousand resurrections, I shall not doubt that my soul has power to clothe itself with a new body suited to its new existence when this earthly frame has crumbled to dust."

But concepts of an afterlife vary. Thus, the question: If there is an afterlife, what form does it take?

For many, to be emotionally satisfying, the idea of an afterlife requires envisioning a continuum of life on Earth. Each of us must survive with our individual identity intact; our memories must come with us; and we should be reunited with loved ones. This is consistent with traditional Christian thought, which holds that both the body and soul have eternal life.

Some believe in an afterlife, but hold that there will be no remembrance of our life on this planet. As we came out of the womb, that is how we will approach Him.

Others think that the soul defines the essence of a person, and there will be no physical form for any of us hereafter. These people reflect on times when they've felt moments of great joy, caring, and love. They tell themselves that we're more than bodies. Indeed, our bodies limit us and are just earthly suits, clothes for the spirit. Form means nothing to those who believe that intelligent spirits are as real as the physical.

"Life," Mark Twain wrote, "does not consist mainly or even largely of facts and happenings. It consists mainly of the storm of thoughts that is forever blowing through one's head. What a wee part of a person's life are his acts and words. All day long, every day, the mill of his brain is grinding. And his thoughts, not those other things, are his history."

In some religions, the soul doesn't even maintain the identity of its previous holder after death. Rather, it animates a new being or merges with other forces.

One can also question whether the afterlife, if there is one, is eternal. Traditionally, we think of it as such. But just because we conceive of something in a certain way doesn't mean that it's so. Even if an afterlife exists, perhaps it's just another stage on our road to personal oblivion. Scientists tell us that the universe is forever expanding and will degenerate into virtual nothingness in tens of billions of years. A God who chose to create dimensions within the universe could also choose to destroy them.

And last, one might ask, given the supposition of an afterlife, whether character and religion matter.

For many people, a belief in God and an afterlife comes from the need to make moral sense of their lives. "We know there is great injustice," Bertrand Russell wrote. "Often the good suffer; often the wicked prosper; and one hardly knows which of these is the more annoying. If you are going to have justice in the universe, you have to suppose a future life to redress the balance of life here on earth."

Thus, many people believe in heaven and hell with God passing Final Judgment upon each of us. Heaven is paradise in the presence of The Almighty, while hell is a fiery grave where the skins of inhabitants are roasted through and replaced as the burning continues for eternity. There's simplicity and a degree of equity in these concepts, but no proof other than heartfelt belief that an afterlife, if one exists, will so be divided.

As we get older and face mortality, each of us is more inclined to hope for and believe in an afterlife. Certainly, there are dimensions of energy, time, and space that are completely beyond the capacity of scientists today to understand. Each of us can ponder life as we know it versus the possibility of life that needs a completely different environment for sustenance.

Moreover, as Blaise Pascal expounded, "What reason have atheists for saying that we cannot rise again? Which is the more difficult: to be born, or to rise again? That what has never been should be, or that what has been should be again? Is it more difficult to come into being than to return to it?"

Martin Luther voiced a similar thought, declaring, "Our Lord has written the promise of the Resurrection, not in books alone but in every leaf in springtime."

Ironically, even if there is an afterlife, it wouldn't prove the existence of God to those who are skeptical. The skeptics would simply note discrepancies between the afterlife they found and the afterlife described in the world's great religious texts and then set about explaining the afterlife within the framework of the scientific knowledge at their command.

Here, though, a personal thought should be advanced. If there is an afterlife and character matters, I believe that each person's fate will be determined, not by religious affiliation and not by specific spiritual beliefs, but by how each person acts in the face of his or her beliefs and in the context of a larger moral framework.

If God is just, He sees us the way we are—as one. He doesn't recognize the existence of different nations, different skin colors, or different forms of organized worship. No one will get into heaven on a group plan. People who live a virtuous life should have no fear of the hereafter, whether or not they adhere to a particular view of God. And beyond that, it should be noted that, if one's motivation for performing good deeds is a desire to go to heaven, then that's being cost effective, not good. The motivation and reward for living a virtuous life should be the joy of being good.

Robert Ingersoll, the nineteenth-century humanist, once asked, "Is there a God?" Then he answered, "I do not know. Is man immortal? I do not know. I do know that neither hope nor fear, belief nor denial, can change the fact. It is as it is, and it will be as it must be. We wait and hope."

If our maker is God, we'll go to meet God. If our maker is the cold hard principles of atoms and subparticles, we will simply disintegrate to that form. All of us in moments of truth hope that something good will follow.

VII
A God to Hope For

Over the course of the past century, man's scientific understanding of the universe has evolved in ways that are difficult for most of us to comprehend.

Einstein determined that time and space are warped; that they are relative; and that, contrary to what was once believed, neither is absolute. Then quantum mechanics opened a world of sub-atomic physics in which particles jump from one point to another without traversing the space in between. This means that, rather than providing a passive background against which events unfold, both time and space are active participants in the life of the universe.

It's now generally believed by scientists that time, space, energy, and the universe as we know it began with a cataclysmic "bang" fifteen billion years ago, and that the entire universe was born of a mass smaller than a single atom. In the first second after creation, all energy took the form of electromagnetic radiation. Then quarks joined as protons and neutrons, which in turn joined in various combinations to form the nuclei of all atoms. One billion years later, the first stars began to coalesce. Our sun came into being nine billion years after that. Earth was created 4.5 billion years ago.

For almost a billion years, Earth's surface was a fiery molten mass beneath huge vapor clouds. Then heavy rains came and oceans were created. Life in the form of the grouping of chemicals began after that, most likely near volcanic vents on the ocean floor. Two billion years ago, green plants began to convert sunlight and chemicals into more complex creations. Collapsing the Earth's history into a twenty-four-hour span, Neanderthal Man emerged less than two seconds ago. The Great Pyramids of Egypt were built in the past one-tenth of a second.

Our galaxy—the Milky Way—is considered small in terms of the cosmos. It stretches one hundred thousand light years across and has one hundred billion stars. The universe contains tens of billions of galaxies. Astrophysicists are now mapping the position of galaxies seven billion light-years away and charting supernovae that exploded eleven billion years ago. Numbers like these are virtually beyond the scope of human imagination. *Miracles that are believed to have occurred on Earth and are derided by skeptics are trivial when compared with the reality of the cosmos.*

Much of this, of course, is just theory. Some cosmologists suggest that the "big bang" was a rebirth of sorts—a transformation from another universe with a different form of time and space—and that the universe is endlessly reproducing itself. However, contemporary scientific wisdom is less sanguine. Recent observations from the Hubble Telescope seem to confirm that the contents of the universe are expanding, and will continue to expand, at a faster and faster pace. This means that there will be no future contraction followed by another "big bang." Rather, tens of billions of years from now, each galaxy will be alone, and ultimately all matter will decay into lifeless forms of radiation.

One can accept or not accept the above recitation. But even if one embraces the idea that a great explosion created the cosmos out of a primordial void, there is still the issue of where the first mass came from. And

there remains the question of whether the cosmos were created by accident or by design. Was the universe brought into existence and put in
motion entirely by chance or is its creation and our appearance in it part
of a master plan?

The "big bang" theory does not foreclose the possibility of a purpose-
ful Creator. And the most fundamental argument in support of God's
existence remains Thomas Aquinas's statement of "First Cause"—Everything in the world has a cause. No matter how one explores backward in
time, ultimately one comes to a First Cause and that cause is God.

The alternative to the idea of God as First Cause is the concept of
nature as a morally neutral creative force. Earth is viewed as just another
planet; our sun is just another star; and Homo sapiens is just another part
of the ecosystem like any other form of life. "Nature was not constructed
as our eventual abode," academician Stephen Jay Gould writes. "It didn't
know we were coming and doesn't give a damn about us."

In other words, nature is indifferent to our values. According to this
line of reasoning, stars explode all the time. If our entire solar system dis-
appeared tomorrow, it would cause no more of a cosmic blip than the dis-
appearance of a solar system in the Andromeda galaxy.

All we know with certainty is that something started it all. The universe came from somewhere. And the source of that is the source of
everything. This is where the interaction of religion and science can only
theoretically occur.

Meanwhile, mankind keeps trying to learn and understand. But while
our knowledge of science has grown exponentially over the past millennium, our knowledge of God has been largely stagnant. Even the most
vocal religionists claim little knowledge of God other than his interaction
with our planet. And to think that the ultimate creative force in the universe is preoccupied with what we do on Earth is extremely narcissistic.
Also, in recent centuries, the dialogue has been skewed. Those who
believe most fiercely and vocally have tended to believe in the God of the
Bible and the Qur'an to the exclusion of beliefs in a different kind of
God. But if God exists, He is what He chooses to be. He isn't bound by
our definition of Him.

Our ability to understand God is limited by our comprehension of
the forces around us. We're much too small in our understanding of what
God can be. We reduce God in our minds for our own purposes. God is

not a cosmic errand boy who bestows favors upon us when we ask for them. Whatever God is, wherever God is, God is an entity of incomprehensible form and intelligence. God exists, not in human terms, but in dimensions of time, energy, and space that are beyond our ability to fathom.

Speaking of God in precise literal terms deprives God of His majesty. Where does God reside? What does God look like? Questions like these are inapplicable to God. The God we pray to is a surrogate deity substituted for a far greater creative force. Direct knowledge of this force is impossible. Albert Einstein equated the quest for an understanding of God with the search for "knowledge of the existence of something we cannot penetrate." Elie Wiesel has written, "Where God is concerned, all is mystery. He is, and that must be enough for us."

It may even be that the universe itself is God. That at the "big bang" (the beginning of time as we know it), God transformed Himself into everything that is; that the voice of God is the sound of falling rain, music, and the laughter of children; that sunsets, roses, and every living creature reflect the face of God; that Nature is God's soul, the Spirit of God.

Does the universe have a moral core that each of us will in some way be held accountable to; or is there nothing in play but morally neutral physical forces? When there was nothing but darkness, did good and evil exist? In the age of dinosaurs before human thought, was there right and wrong? Or do right and wrong only exist if there are moral choices to be made and beings with the capacity to make them?

No knows with certainty the answer to these questions. Rather, the vastness of the universe reminds us of how much we can't possibly know. There are potential dimensions of spirituality and being that we can't even begin to understand. Certainly, though, it's not unreasonable to suggest that Earth is a place where our Creator does special work. And while the size of the cosmos is intimidating, this same size is also comforting.

There is an awesome creative force somewhere. Something created massive planets made out of cold hard rock and the fiery furnaces of molten ore that we call stars. Something created black holes. And something created life—green leaves, lilacs, amoebae evolving into dinosaurs and eagles and tigers . . . and mankind. The fact that we're here is so stunning that anything is possible.

If the universe has a moral core, whatever else follows will follow. For skeptics and for believers, this is a God to hope for.

The End of the Year

This was the first of several holiday articles that I wrote for the New York Sun.

The Origins of Santa Claus

Santa Claus is the contemporary embodiment of Nicholas of Myra, a fourth-century bishop who is revered by the Roman Catholic Church as a saint.

According to legend, when Nicholas was an infant, his mother nursed him twice a week and he fasted on the other five days. He is said to have rescued drowning sailors by halting a storm at sea and saved the life of a prisoner by seizing the executioner's sword.

Nicholas was also reportedly quite rich, adored children, and delighted in giving gifts to the deserving poor. The most famous tale regarding his wealth concerns three sisters whose father, unable to give them a dowry, resolved to cast them into a life of prostitution. One morning, the sisters awoke and found three bags of gold that Nicholas had thrown through their window during the night. Thereafter, the sisters were married.

Many religious scholars believe that St. Nicholas never existed. Regardless, his birthday (thought to be December 6) was celebrated throughout the Middle Ages and Renaissance by giving presents to children as the saint himself had done. Meanwhile, the Dutch came to venerate him as the patron saint of sailors, known as "Sinter Klaas."

When the New World was settled, the Dutch brought Sinter Klaas with them. In 1804, the New York Historical Society was founded with St. Nicholas as its patron saint, and its members engaged in the practice of gift giving at Christmas. In 1812, Washington Irving penned a revised version of *A History of New York* and described Nicholas as riding in a wagon over trees.

But most portraits of the original Saint Nicholas portray him as severe-looking and gaunt; dressed in gray, not red. The Santa Claus we know today is a jollier presence and largely the creation of three men.

The first eyewitness sighting of the contemporary St. Nicholas has been long credited to a professor of divinity named Clement Clark

Moore. Some revisionist scholars attribute memorialization of the sighting
to Henry Livingston Jr, a poet who lived at the same time as Moore.

What is not in dispute is that, on December 23, 1822, Moore read his
children a poem as a Christmas treat. The following year, "An Account of
a Visit From Saint Nicholas" was published in *The Troy Sentinel*, and a new
vision of the saint began to spread:

> His eyes how they twinkled; his dimples how merry;
> His cheeks were like roses, his nose like a cherry;
> His droll little mouth was drawn up like a bow,
> And the beard on his chin was as white as the snow.
> He had a broad face, and a little round belly
> That shook when he laughed, like a bowl full of jelly.
> He was chubby and plump; a right jolly old elf;
> And I laughed when I saw him in spite of myself.

But Moore's Santa was little and dressed in fur, not red. Then, four
decades later, the American political cartoonist Thomas Nast turned his
attention to St. Nicholas. Beginning with an 1862 illustration for the
cover of *Harper's Weekly*, Nast drew Santa for the rest of the century.
However, his creation—albeit kindly, warmhearted, and rotund—was
elflike.

Finally, in 1931, American capitalism had its say. Coca-Cola commis-
sioned a rendition of Santa Claus from an artist named Haddon
Sundblom. Sundblom delivered a large modern-day Santa dressed in red.
Coke plastered millions of copies of the image across the country in a
massive promotional campaign. Previous visions of Santa were all but
eradicated.

That's the Santa Claus most of us know today—a commercial version
of a political cartoonist's vision based on a poem that might have been
written by a doctor of divinity.

But the question remains: "Does Santa Claus really exist?"

The *New York Sun* is an authority on the subject. In 1897, an eight-
year-old named Virginia O'Hanlon, who lived on the Upper West Side of
Manhattan, wrote a letter to the newspaper that read: "Dear Editor—I am
eight years old. Some of my little friends say there is no Santa Claus. Papa

says, 'If you see it in *The Sun*, it's so.' Please tell me the truth, is there a Santa Claus?"

In response, Francis P. Church, an editor at *The Sun*, penned the now-legendary, "Yes, Virginia, There is a Santa Claus." Church's missive appeared in *The Sun* as an editorial and was reprinted every Christmas thereafter until 1949, when the paper (temporarily) ceased publication.

So to repeat Virginia O'Hanlon's question: "Is there a Santa Claus?"

Of course, there is. Someone has to put all those presents underneath the tree for children to open on Christmas morning.

For several years after leaving the practice of law, I wrote a column on legal issues for McCall's magazine. On occasion, I wrote articles for the magazine that were more fun.

Christmas Carols

Joseph Mohr, a twenty-six-year-old assistant pastor in the Austrian village of Oberndorf, had a problem. It was the day before Christmas 1818, and a mouse had chewed its way through the organ bellows at St. Nikola's Church. That meant Mohr's congregation would be without musical accompaniment for Christmas mass. Hoping to ease the blow, Mohr wrote words for a new song and gave them to Franz Gruber, the church organist, who set them to music for the guitar. That night, the church choir performed the new carol for the first time. In a matter of hours, and largely by chance, Joseph Mohr and Franz Gruber had written "Silent Night"—perhaps the best-known Christmas song of all time.

Many Christmas carols have church origins. Others have come out of secular settings. But whatever their source, these carols transcend differences of people and place. Some of us enjoy Beethoven but don't like Aaron Copland. Others appreciate Frank Sinatra but abhor the Rolling Stones. Virtually everyone loves the songs of Christmas. They are the music of our youth, reminding us of family and a time when life seemed simple and particularly joyful. Each year, we feel a comforting sense of community when we join with others to sing the familiar unchanging melodies.

Many of our Christmas carols come from anonymous sources. Regarding "Deck the Halls," we know only that it originated in Wales in the 1500s, and that Mozart later borrowed the melody for a violin-and-piano sonata. Another traditional English song, "God Rest Ye, Merry Gentlemen," achieved particular literary fame. According to Charles Dickens's *A Christmas Carol*, a caroler came to Ebenezer Scrooge's door on Christmas Eve, put his mouth to the keyhole and began to sing:

God bless you merry gentlemen!
May nothing you dismay!

"At the first sound," recounted Dickens, "Scrooge seized a ruler with such energy of action, that the singer fled in terror."

Words and music to "The First Noel" were printed in the 1800s, but the song is believed to have originated as a shepherd's tune centuries earlier, possibly in France. Legend has it that, during the Christmas season when shepherds sang in the fields and mountains, angels would accompany them from on high by singing the chorus to "The First Noel."   ·

But while some carols are anonymous in origin, the beginnings of others are well known. In 1865, Phillips Brooks, the thirty-year-old rector of Holy Trinity Church in Philadelphia, took a trip to the Holy Land during the Christmas season. Three years later, still inspired by what he'd seen, he wrote the words to "Little Town of Bethlehem" and gave them to his church organist, Lewis Redner, who set the words to music.

Another equally popular Christmas carol was the work of two men born a century apart. Charles Wesley (a co-founder of Methodism) wrote the words to four thousand hymns. "Hark! The Herald Angels Sing," published in 1739, was among them. A century later, Felix Mendelssohn composed an oratorio celebrating the four hundredth anniversary of Johann Gutenberg's invention of the movable-type printing press. In 1855, eight years after Mendelssohn's death, Wesley's words were joined with the second choral movement from Mendelssohn's work to give "Hark! The Herald Angels Sing" its present form.

"Joy to the World" is another product of different eras. The words are based on the Old Testament's Psalm 98 and were written by an English theologian named Isaac Watts in 1719. The music was composed a century later.

"Adeste Fideles" is the most popular Christmas carol sung in a single tongue worldwide. The music was written by John Reading in the 1600s. John Francis Wade composed the words in the eighteenth century in Latin. Since then, "Adeste Fideles" has been translated into more than 120 languages, including English ("Oh Come, All Ye Faithful"), but the Latin verses are still commonly sung.

Unlike its European counterpart, American Christmas music is not particularly religious. "Jingle Bells," written by James Pierpont of Boston in 1857, is a seasonal song that doesn't even mention Christmas. Twentieth-century songs such as "Santa Claus Is Coming to Town," "Frosty the Snowman," "Winter Wonderland," and "I Saw Mommy Kissing Santa Claus" are equally secular.

"Rudolph the Red-Nosed Reindeer" is uniquely American in origin. In 1939, Robert May created the character of Rudolph as part of a promotional campaign for Montgomery-Ward stores. Rudolph's story was published in book form in 1947 and, two years later, John Marks (Robert May's brother-in-law) wrote the song. Soon, Gene Autry—America's "singing cowboy"—had a hit record with it, and Rudolph became the first new successful Christmas character since Santa Claus.

However, Rudolph's record sales pale in comparison to those of America's preeminent Christmas song. "White Christmas" was written by Irving Berlin in 1940 and featured in the 1942 movie *Holiday Inn*. Bing Crosby's version of the song has sold 30 million copies. By the end of 1987, 176,253,407 recordings of "White Christmas" had been sold in the United States and Canada alone; more than any other copyrighted song in the history of the world.

Despite the popularity of Christmas carols, the best-known song of the holiday season is "Auld Lang Syne."

Auld Lang Syne

New Year's Eve is impossible to ignore. People who avoid parties and resist turning on the television to watch the ball descending in Times Square still find themselves reflecting on the state of their lives. Despite the revelry, the night is often a bittersweet reminder of unfulfilled dreams and growing older.

There's also a school of thought that New Year's Eve is improperly named since virtually everything about it bespeaks of the year soon to be gone. "Old Year's End" might be more appropriate. Indeed, one can argue that all of January should be classified as part of the old year. After all, January is designed for tying up loose ends. Wallets thin out as purchasers pay old Christmas bills. Candidates elected to office are inaugurated. The National Football League play-offs cap the previous year's season.

Future generations might opt to begin the new year in early March, when the first crocuses bloom. Still, there's one particularly nice thing about New Year's Eve. Everyone gets to sing the world anthem: "Auld Lang Syne."

"Auld Lang Syne" is the traditional song for English-speaking people the world over for bidding farewell to the old year. No song in any language is better known. It derives from Scottish folk music that was reworked by Robert Burns, who put the words through several drafts before settling on the final verses.

Fragments of what became Burns's lyrics have been found in three sources: (1) an anonymous sixteenth-century ballad entitled "Auld Kyndnes Foryett"; (2) a poem by Sir Robert Ayton published in *Choice Collection of Scots Poems* in 1711; and (3) lyrics by Allen Ramsay published in 1720 in *Scots Songs.*

The lineage of these fragments is murky. However, it's undisputed that, on December 17, 1788, Burns sent a letter to a Mrs. Dunlop in which he declared, "There is an old song and tune which has often thrilled through my soul. I am an enthusiast in old Scotch songs. I shall give you the verses on the other sheet. Light be the turf on the breast of the heaven-inspired poet who composed this glorious fragment. There is more of the fire of native genius in it than in half a dozen of modern English Bacchanalians."

The accompanying lyrics that Burns sent to Dunlop were his first version of "Auld Lang Syne." He then sent revised lyrics to the music publisher James Johnson, who had previously published much of his work. In so doing, Burns acknowledged that the verses were a hybrid of folk lyrics and his own.

Soon after that, Burns sent yet another version of "Auld Lang Syne" to George Thompson (the publisher of *Scottish Airs*). This submission was accompanied by a letter declaring, "One song [revision] more, and I have done "Auld Lang Syne." The air [melody] is but mediocre; but the following song—the old song of the olden times and which has never been in print, nor even in manuscript until I took it down from an old man's singing—is enough to recommend any air."

James Johnson declined to publish "Auld Lang Syne" because it had been submitted by Burns with the same melody that had appeared with the previously published Ramsay lyrics. That led Burns to send a second letter to George Thompson in which he declared, "The song you saw [is not] worth your attention. The words of "Auld Lang Syne" are good, but the music is an old air." In the same letter to Thompson, Burns referenced "a common Scots country dance." Thompson matched that dance with Burns's lyrics and published "Auld Lang Syne" in *Scottish Airs*. This is the "Auld Lang Syne" that the world now knows.

Burns never claimed authorship of "Auld Lang Syne," but the final version is largely his work. Also, it's worth noting that, despite its universal appeal, most people don't know the words to "Auld Lang Syne." And many who do aren't sure what they mean. After all, who or what is Auld Lang Syne? Some fellow with a long white beard who looks like Father Time?

Not at all. And so, with a tip of the hat to eighteenth-century Scottish dialect, I bequeath the following New Year's message to you all:

Auld[1] Lang[2] Syne[3]

Should auld acquaintance be forgot,
And never brought to mind?
Should auld acquaintance be forgot,
And days o' auld lang syne?

(CHORUS)   For auld lang syne, my dear,
For auld lang syne,
We'll tak a cup o' kindness yet,
For auld lang syne.

And surely ye'll be[4] your pint-stowp[5],
And surely I'll be mine,
And we'll tak a cup o' kindness yet,
For auld lang syne.

CHORUS

We twa[6] hae[7] run about the braes[8]
And put[9] the gowans[10] fine;
But we've wandered mony[11] a weary foot,
Sin[12] auld lang syne.

CHORUS

We twa hae paidlet[13] i' the burn[14]
Frae[15] morning sun till dine[16];
But seas between us braid[17] has roar'd,
Sin auld lang syne.

CHORUS

And there's a hand my trusty feire[18]
And gie's[19] a hand o' thine;
And we'll tak a right gude willie waught[20]
For auld lang syne,

CHORUS

Footnotes

1. old
2. long
3. ago
4. pay for
5. narrow drinking vessel
6. two
7. have
8. hills
9. picked
10. wild daisies
11. many
12. since
13. waded
14. stream
15. from
16. noon
17. broad
18. friend
19. give us
20. ale